A History of South and
Central Africa

D1077371

A History of South and Central Africa

DEREK WILSON

CAMBRIDGE
UNIVERSITY PRESS

PUBLISHED BY THE PRESS SYNDICATE OF THE UNIVERSITY OF CAMBRIDGE
The Pitt Building, Trumpington Street, Cambridge, United Kingdom

CAMBRIDGE UNIVERSITY PRESS
The Edinburgh Building, Cambridge CB2 2RU, UK   www.cup.cam.ac.uk
40 West 20th Street, New York, NY 10011–4211, USA   www.cup.org
10 Stamford Road, Oakleigh, Melbourne 3166, Australia
Ruiz de Alarcón 13, 28014 Madrid, Spain

First published 1975
13th printing 1999

Printed in the United Kingdom at the University Press, Cambridge

ISBN 0 521 20559 X paperback

Contents

V

Maps

vi

Acknowledgments

Illustrations in this volume are reproduced by kind permission of the following:

Weidenfeld & Nicolson Archives, pp. 2, 19; Musée Royal de l'Afrique Centrale, pp. 3, 127, 193, 261, 279, 280, 285; British Museum, pp. 8, 12, 14; National Archives of Rhodesia, pp. 24, 29, 33, 35, 42, 162, 163, 178, 233; Bodleian Library, pp. 32, 43, 71, 166, 257; Cambridge University Library, pp. 47, 57, 117, 129, 132, 133, 170, 253; Africana Museum Johannesburg, pp. 52, 77, 80, 89, 99, 102, 110, 140, 144, 146, 156, 202, 221; Zambia Information Services, pp. 66, 241, 291, 293, 300, 301, 302, 311; J. C. N. Humphreys Collection, p. 83; Congregational Council for World Mission, p. 101; W. H. Coetzer, p. 103; African Tribal Art Ltd, p. 182; Horniman Museum, London, p. 198; National Army Museum, p. 206; Anglo-American Corporation, p. 213; Portuguese National Office, pp. 231, 250; Roan Consolidated Mines Ltd, p. 237; Consolidated Diamond Mines, p. 264; Imperial War Museum, p. 273; Associated Press Ltd, pp. 283, 286, 287, 323; Paul Popper Ltd, pp. 288, 324, 332, 333, 334; Malawi High Commission, p. 295; Central Office of Information, p. 314; Portuguese Information Services, p. 318.

Preface

This is a history of Africa south of the Congo Forest from about the year A.D. 1000 to the era of the establishment of independent modern states. In planning and writing this book I have had in the forefront of my mind the needs of secondary school students preparing for School Certificate and similar examinations in various parts of the continent and particularly of those studying for Paper 2 of the E.A.C.E. in East Africa where I had the pleasure of teaching for many years. Indeed, most of this book was written in Nairobi and if I am to dedicate it to anyone it must be to the young men of Kenya who taught me as much as ever I taught them during my stay in their exciting country.

Most textbooks on African history are too much dominated by modern political boundaries which, of course, have no ethnic or geographical validity. I have long felt that such limitations do a profound disservice to students of Southern Africa. Bantu, San and Khoikhoi migrations, long-distance trade routes, the Mfecane dispersal, the journeys of white adventurers – these and other important events make a nonsense of categories such as 'South' and 'Central' Africa. On the other hand, students preparing for public examinations are forced to take note of these artificial divisions. In this book I have tried to 'have my cake and eat it' – treating the whole of Southern Africa as a unit and yet following, fairly closely, in the chapter headings the subject divisions favoured by examiners. For example this book covers those parts of the E.A.C.E. syllabus referred to as 'The History of Central Africa' and 'The History of South Africa'.

In the past there has been little detailed but readable information available for students on the earlier history of Central Africa. This is because this vast area has only in recent years been subjected to close examination by archaeologists and historians. Their findings have largely been available only in scholarly books and unpublished papers and theses. In *A History of South and Central Africa* I have tried to present, in a simple form, much of the work of contemporary researchers and to give as complete a picture as possible of the early history of Central Africa.

Acknowledgements for quotations are made in the text, and for illustrations, below, but I would like to thank here colleagues in Kenya who allowed me to use material from papers delivered at meetings of the Historical Association of Kenya and the authors of papers presented at the Workshop on the Teaching of Central and East African History in Lusaka in August 1970.

PART I

ORIGINS OF AFRICAN SOCIETIES 1000–1800

1. Iron Age states

(1) The Luba and Lunda Empires

By A.D. 1000 there were a large number of Iron Age settlements in the area south of the Congo forest and between Lake Tanganyika and the Kasai River. They were occupied by small communities each of which probably acknowledged the leadership of a chief. They moved quite frequently, sometimes conflicting with other communities, and in course of time some of them covered great distances.

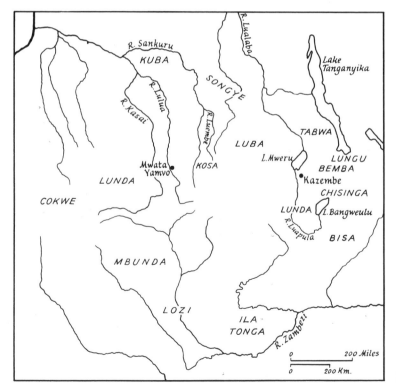

Luba Empire

It is only from about 1500 that we can detect among this shifting pattern of Bantu movement events of greater political significance. Sometime in the fourteenth century a new group of people, the Songye, led by a chief called Kongolo came from the north, and entered the region between the Luembe and Lualaba rivers. They found the area occupied by a number of small chiefdoms of the Kalanga people. Kongolo managed to assert his authority over the Kalanga thus setting up what is usually called the first Luba Empire, with its capital at Mwibele near Lake Boya. The Kongolo dynasty ruled for several decades before being overthrown by fresh invaders.

Around the beginning of the sixteenth century there was considerable political turmoil in this area of Central Africa as population increased and bands of warriors led by chiefs roamed the country seeking new places to settle. One such Kunda group invaded the Songye Empire, overthrew the Kongolo dynasty and established a new dynasty, being careful to take over the ritual and political institutions of the old dynasty.

Luba expansion took place in two ways: through small migrations of chieftains' clans, and by conquest. The system of succession to the throne and appointment of chiefs led many disappointed con-

African iron workers as pictured by an early European traveller

2

Luba craftsmanship. A statuette of Kata Mbula, chief of the Kuba.

testants to seek new lands to the south-east. These leaders established their control over other peoples either by conquest or because of their superior political and ritual skills. Thus the Luba system of government spread over a considerable area of what is now central and eastern Zambia (see the map at the beginning of this chapter).*

Very few of these states maintained any allegiance to the Luba Empire. It was as a result of a definite policy of territorial expansion

---

* It should be noted that some historians consider that the establishment of the second Luba Empire occurred as much as eighty years earlier than the date suggested here, which reflects the opinion of most scholars at the present time.

in the eighteenth century that that state grew to its greatest extent. Mwine Kadilo became king in about 1700. It was he who began, through warfare, to extend the boundaries of his empire. Chieftaincies east of the Lualaba, and the Songye rulers to the south were either incorporated into the Luba Empire or forced to pay tribute. Territorial aggrandisement continued under Mwine Kadilo's successors: Kekenya, Ilunga Sungu and Kumwimba Ngombe. By the end of the century the Luba Empire extended from Lakes Mweru and Tanganyika in the east to the Sankuru River and beyond in the west. Southward expansion had brought it control over most of Katanga. It is difficult to assess the precise limits of the Empire because allegiance weakened with distance from the centre and beyond the boundaries of the Empire there existed, as we have seen, many 'Lubaised' societies whose political and religious traditions were very similar to those of the Luba.

By 1800 the Luba Empire had already begun to disintegrate, though it was to remain a powerful factor in Central African politics until the colonial era. There were two basic weaknesses which contributed to this collapse. One was the degree of power retained by the chiefs. As patrilineal descendants of Kongolo and Kalala Ilunga and possessors of *bulopwe* they felt themselves to have political and religious authority which entitled them to a certain degree of autonomy in local affairs. The other weakness was a lack of precise laws governing royal succession. This paved the way for quarrels between brothers and half-brothers. Towards the end of the eighteenth century succession disputes, civil wars and the breakdown of central authority had become prominent features of Luba life.

The Lunda Empire

The other great Central African empire of this period was the Lunda Empire. The story of the foundation of this empire only exists in the form of myth. The tale runs as follows: The Lunda originated in the northern part of the region, around the middle reaches of the River Kasai, from where they expanded southwards and westwards. The first king known by name is Mwaakw, who presumably reigned sometime in the fifteenth century. His successor, Nkond, had two sons, Kinguri-kya-Bangela and Chinyama Kakenge. These young men, being cruel and ambitious, tried to kill and overthrow their father in order to seize power for themselves. The king was only saved by his daughter, Rweej. So moved was he by the behaviour of his children that he named Rweej as his successor. These events occurred at the same time as the

4

Kunda conquest of the Songye–Luba Empire and the story now goes that a son of Kalala Ilunga, the new Luba king, entered Lunda territory and married Rweej. This was Kibinda Ilunga, who became king on the death of his father-in-law. Rweej provided Kibinda Ilunga with no children, and it was from his marriage with Kamunga Lwaza that the royal line of Lunda sprang. After a few generations the Lunda kings took the title Mwata Yamvo. Their capital of Musumba on the Lulua River was sometimes also known as Mwata Yamvo. Kinguri and Chinyama tried to overthrow the usurper but when they failed they migrated westwards and southwards respectively and founded new kingdoms (we shall trace their history later).

The story of Rweej and her wicked brothers seems to have been invented to explain how the Lunda succession became matrilineal and to ascribe legitimacy to the dynasty founded by Kibinda Ilunga. Lunda territory was obviously invaded by Kunda warriors at about the same time as or a little later than the first Luba Empire. Probably Kalala Ilunga's son, Kibinda Ilunga, realising that he would not inherit his father's new kingdom, travelled further west to find a kingdom for himself. Probably he waited some years before making this move for he took many Luba traditions with him. These, combined with existing Lunda customs, resulted in a politically advanced and stable society.

The Lunda Empire did not suffer from the weakness of having semi-independent chiefs all of whom could claim descent from the

Lunda expansion.

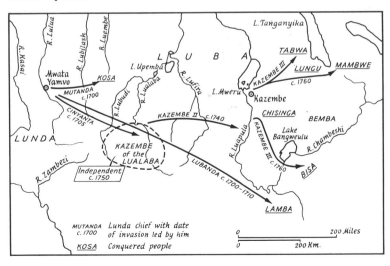

200 Miles

200 Km.

MUTANDA c. 1700 Lunda chief with date of invasion led by him
KOSA Conquered people

5

founders of the state. Descent was matrilineal and the succession was not governed by such strict laws as controlled the Luba succession. The Mwata Yamvo appointed chiefs and in newly conquered areas local chiefs were given Lunda titles. As in the Luba Empire, chiefs sometimes migrated to set up kingdoms elsewhere. But they always maintained close ties with the central Lunda state, preserving the political and religious customs of their homeland and also maintaining allegiance to the Mwata Yamvo. For these reasons the Lunda Empire grew into the largest and most unified state in Central Africa during the eighteenth century.

Apart from these migrations there was deliberate imperial expansion on the part of succeeding Lunda rulers. The work was begun by Luseeng and Naweej in the sixteenth century and by 1600 the whole area around the upper and middle reaches of the Lulua and Kasai Rivers owed allegiance to the Mwata Yamvo. Steadily, successive rulers consolidated their power while Lunda chiefs migrated east, south and west with their supporters to establish states which retained a close alliance with Mwato Yamvo.

It was during the seventeenth century that the Portuguese occupation of the west coast began to have an effect further inland. Guns, ammunition and new vegetables, such as maize and cassava, reached Musumba along the trade routes. Better food probably resulted in a growth of population, which spurred on Lunda migration and expansion. New weapons made empire-building easier. Under Muteba, who became Mwata Yamvo in about 1690, a new surge of territorial aggrandisement began. He invaded Kaniok, to the northeast. He sent warriors to push the boundaries of the empire as far as the River Zambezi to the south.

The most spectacular series of conquests were those which carried the Mwata Yamvo's authority right across the Congo basin to Katanga and beyond and established the powerful kingdom of the East Lunda, otherwise known as Kazembe. This began shortly after the accession of Muteba. He sent one of his chiefs, Mutanda, to attack the Kosa people to the east. The Kosa submitted and their leader, Cinyanta, became a firm ally. Meanwhile Lubanda, an ironworker, had left Musumba and set himself up as a chief along the upper reaches of the River Lualaba. The story goes that this smith had been responsible for starting a fire in the capital and that he had fled to avoid punishment. But Muteba determined that Lubanda should not escape and sent his ally, Cinyanta, to deal with him. Lubanda fled further, to the bank of the Luapula. Cinyanta, instead of pursuing him, led his army against other chiefs in the region until he had reduced all the land west of the Lualaba to allegiance to the Mwata Yamvo.

When Cinyata died (c.1710) his son, Nganda Bilanda, continued the work of conquest. Muteba gave him the title of Kazembe and entrusted to him the consolidation of his father's gains and the further expansion of the empire. Having subdued the Lualaba region to his satisfaction he left one of his chiefs behind as 'Kazembe of the Lualaba' and crossed the river in search of fresh victories.

Before he could achieve very much Kazembe died and there followed a period of chaos as rival chiefs fought for the succession. At length the new Mwata Yamvo, Mukanza, appointed a man called Kaniembo as Kazembe II. Furthermore, realising how difficult it was to exercise firm control from the capital over Kazembe II's territory the Emperor made Kazembe II virtually his equal, with considerable powers and freedom in the east. Kazembe immediately began to build up the East Lunda state into one which should rival Mwata Yamvo in size. He extended his control as far as the Luapula and established his capital south of Lake Mweru. However, while he was occupied in the east his son, Mukerji, seized power as 'Kazembe of the Lualaba' and declared himself independent of both his father and the Emperor.

Kazembe II died in about 1760 and was succeeded by Lukwesa (Kazembe III). The new king carried Lunda conquests still further east onto the plateau to the south of Lake Tanganyika. He invaded the Tabwa, the Lungu and the Mambwe. Further south still he carried out raids on the Bisa and the Chisinga. Only the powerful Bemba succeeded in halting the Lunda advance, but not before the kingdom of Kazembe (which had come to be known by the title of the ruler) had become the largest and strongest centralised state in Central Africa.

The Cokwe

The Cokwe, who now occupy large areas of Congo and Angola, trace their descent from Chinyama Kakenge, the Lunda prince who left home after an unsuccessful attempt to overthrow Kibinda Illunga. The Cokwe settled around the headwaters of the Kasai and Kwango Rivers. They were considered by the Mwato Yamvos to owe tribute to the Lunda rulers but they lived so far away from Musumba that their allegiance to their parent state can seldom have been enforced. They were farmers but this was not their main occupation. They lived the semi-nomadic life of hunters and traders. They were also skilled ironworkers. Because of their various skills they were welcomed by neighbouring people through whose lands they passed.

This, in fact, gave them the opportunity to increase their power and territory. Small Cokwe groups would settle in an area, living 7 peacefully with the local people. Their numbers would gradually increase. Because of their special skills and knowledge their popularity with their hosts also increased. Then, when an opportunity presented itself, they would lead a rebellion against the local ruler and set up a new ruling dynasty. In this way Cokwe power had begun to increase before 1800.

The Lozi

The Lozi are also believed to be derived from the Lunda people. They came as conquerors into the fertile plains of the upper Zambezi region probably in the seventeenth century, and established their rule over the earlier inhabitants of the region. Soon after they arrived they split into various groups, led by members of the royal clan who wished to set up independent chiefdoms. It took several decades for the central Lozi government to bring all these groups under control.

A Lozi statue in wood.

Another problem for the government was the immigrant groups which continued to enter the Empire from the north and west. One such group which proved very useful to the ruling régime was the Mbunda, who reached the Zambezi valley in the late eighteenth century. They introduced new crops to the region – cassava, millet and a type of yam. They also brought new weapons – bows and arrows and a superior kind of battle axe. With the aid of the Mbunda the Lozi were able to establish their power quite firmly and to strengthen their frontiers against raiders such as the Luvale and Nkoya.

The rule of the Lozi was efficient, though in some respects harsh. They organised the agriculture of the Zambezi flood plain to the best advantage. They regulated trade within the empire and with neighbouring states. They raided for cattle, especially among the Ila and the Tonga. They organised public works such as the building of fish dams. Under their guidance the empire enjoyed, either from home produce or trade, an abundance of grain, meat, fish, salt, iron implements, basketwork, pottery, woodwork and barkcloth. But all this could only be achieved by very firm control. Subject peoples did not enjoy the same privileges and freedoms as the true Lozi. They paid tribute and other taxes. They had to work on government projects. The Lozi raided for and used slaves. But for organisation and efficiency the Lozi Empire was one of the more advanced states in Central Africa.

Major areas of power c. 1800.

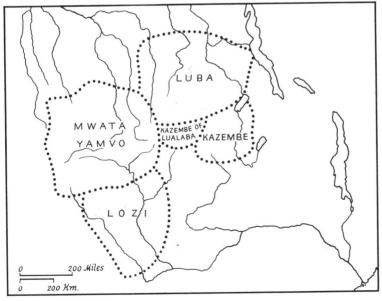

9

2. Iron Age states
(2) West Coast states

Kongo

The history of the kingdom of Kongo can be traced back to about the thirteenth century. At that time the plateau land to the south of the lower Congo River was occupied by Ambundu and Ambwela peoples. Then a conqueror called Were, who was the son of one of the chiefs of Burgo, north of the river, appeared. Within a few years he and his followers had made themselves masters of what came to be the Kongo kingdom. Were, who took the title Mani Kongo, allied

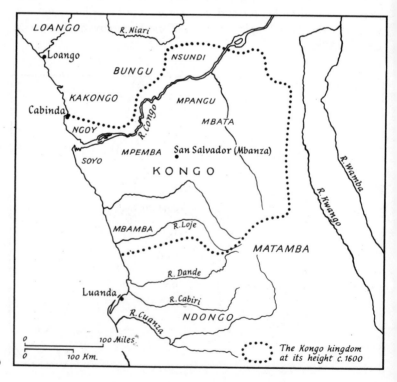

himself with the ruling families of the conquered peoples and took over many of their traditions, beliefs and political concepts.

The first rulers of Kongo extended their rule over a wide area. The degree of conquest experienced by various peoples depended on a number of factors: their military strength, their political stability and their distance from the Kongo capital. Thus the kingdom of Mbata was incorporated in the empire but its kings continued to rule, though as governors under the control of the Mani Kongo. More distant states such as Ndongo and Matamba were occasionally forced to pay tribute to the Mani Kongo but were not effectively controlled from the capital, Mbanza. By the end of the fourteenth century the kingdom extended from the River Loje in the south to the River Congo in the north (it even included a stretch of land beyond the Congo in the region of Luozi). From the coast the Mani Kongo's authority reached inland almost as far as the River Kwango.

Portuguese exploration

In 1483 a Portuguese expedition led by Diego Cão reached the mouth of the Congo. Cão left four of his men ashore to make contact with the Mani Kongo while he travelled on to explore the coast further south. Since the four Portuguese had not returned when Cão called back the Portuguese leader seized four Kongo citizens and carried them off with him as hostages. They were taken to the court of the Portuguese king, John II. As they learned to speak the white men's language they told the king of the power and wealth of their own monarch. John II realised the importance of the Mani Kongo and his kingdom. He treated his African guests well and made every effort to impress them with the wealth of Portugal, the power of its king, and the Christian faith. After a year at John II's court the four Kongolese were returned to their homeland. The expedition was, once more, led by Diego Cão.

By the time that Cão reached Mbanza in 1485 the Mani Kongo, Nzinga Nkuwu, had realised by what he learned from his Portuguese visitors that close relations with the Europeans would be an advantage. He asked Cão to arrange for Christian missionaries, builders, farmers and tools to be sent from Portugal, and sent some of his own leading men back with Cão to learn European skills. Contact between the two countries remained on a friendly basis. In 1491 a party of Portuguese missionaries and skilled workers arrived in Kongo. Within a very short space of time Nzinga and a number of his people had been baptised as Christians. The Mani Kongo relied more and more on European advisers.

Between 1494 and 1506 there was very little direct contact between Lisbon and Mbanza. The Portuguese king was too absorbed in problems at home and overseas to spare much thought for Kongo. For Portugal the most exciting development of these years was the successful voyage of Vasco da Gama round Africa to India (1497–9). This laid the foundation for Portugal of a rich trading empire in the East and made her West African interests seem comparatively unimportant. The regular trading voyages to India which soon began did not hug the western coast but stood out into the Atlantic until

The lid of a carved ivory casket in the form of a Portuguese ship.

making a landfall at the Cape of Good Hope. There was therefore no need for regular Portuguese visits to the Congo mouth and no trading post was established there.

Nzinga, who had taken the name John at his baptism, was disappointed at this lack of support from his Christian 'brother monarch'. He also found the restrictions imposed by his new religion tiresome and before long he reverted to paganism. He now found himself on bad terms with the Christian missionaries. He made their work difficult for them and when they succeeded in converting his heir, Afonso, he exiled the young man and some of the missionaries to the province of Sundi.

Now there were disputes between Christian and non-Christian groups at court. When Nzinga died in 1506 the electors ignored his chosen heir, Afonso, and supported a younger brother, Mpanzu a Kitima, who led the pagan faction. Afonso marched towards the capital, met up with an army led by his brother, and, though his own force was smaller, won a great victory. This was seen by the Christians – and others – as a sign of the superiority of the white man's god. Afonso now became a zealous Christian and pro-European. He asked for more missionaries from Portugal and for soldiers to help him spread Christianity to all parts of his kingdom.

At the end of the fifteenth century the Portuguese colonised the island of São Tomé. The island attracted settlers of the worst type – adventurers, ex-criminals, greedy and unscrupulous men. Within a few years São Tomé had developed two main economic activities: there were large sugar plantations, and the island became the leading slave trade depot for the Lower Guinea coast and the Congo region. The new ruler of São Tomé, the *donatario*, wanted to maintain as much independence as possible from Lisbon in order to exploit the trade of the nearby parts of Africa to the full. The merchants wanted a good supply of slaves both for the São Tomé plantation and for export. The *donatario* did all in his power to upset relations between Mbanza and Lisbon and to make sure that it was his agents and not the king of Portugal's who went to Kongo.

By 1512 São Tomé had gained almost complete control of trade between Kongo and Europe. Merchants and their agents were trading and raiding for slaves. Afonso was horrified. He sent letters to the king of Portugal but they were usually intercepted in São Tomé and the messengers delayed, sent back or taken into slavery.

The behaviour of the missionaries and official agents sent from Lisbon came as a shock to Afonso. Some complained about conditions in the capital and demanded to be allowed to return home. Almost all of them treated the Africans with contempt. Afonso's 13 great plans for evangelising missions throughout the country came to nothing when the priests who did remain preferred to set up home with their mistresses in Mbanza or take an active part in the slave trade.

In 1512 King Emmanuel issued a *regimento*, a document promising support for Afonso and setting out a code to govern relations between African and European in Kongo. He also sent Simão da Silva as ambassador and adviser to the court of the Mani Kongo. But da Silva died shortly after his arrival and, in any case, lacked the power to control the Portuguese merchants and adventurers, who were stirring more and more of the Kongolese to defiance of their king. Several district chiefs were involved in slave raiding. Frequent expeditions set off from the coast led by Portuguese adventurers or their African or half-caste agents (known as *pombeiros*) and between 4,000 and 5,000 slaves were being shipped annually to São Tomé.

When Afonso died (sometime between 1541 and 1545) his kingdom was hopelessly divided. His chosen heir, Pedro, was soon overthrown by a cousin, Diogo, who had the support of many Portuguese and African slave traders. Diogo attempted to limit the activities of the slave traders, but he too was plagued by African and foreign factions each urging different policies on him. In 1548 a Jesuit mission arrived in Mbanza. Thousands of converts were baptised and a number of churches was built. After one of them, the church of São Salvador, . the capital was renamed. But within four years most of the Portuguese Jesuits had left and relations between Kongo and Portugal were all but broken off.

One result was that the São Tomé traders turned their attention more to Ndongo in the south. Diogo regarded Ndongo as a vassal state which had no right to make private arrangements with the Europeans. Urged on by one of the Portuguese factions, he declared war on Ndongo. The results were a disastrous defeat for the Kongo and the final establishment of Ndongo independence (1556). Other misfortunes were still to come. When Diogo died in 1561 the nation was plunged into a bloody civil war. Scarcely had Kongo recovered from that when it was invaded by the Jaga.

The Jaga

The Jaga were migrants from the east and may have been related to the Lunda or Luba. They almost certainly moved westwards as a result of the invasions and disturbances in Central Africa referred to in the last chapter.

By the mid-sixteenth century the Jaga, under the leadership of their ruler, Kulemba, had reached the area between the upper

Dutch ambassadors with Mani Kongo Alvaro II. Dutch interest in Kongo and Angola was of brief duration but Alvaro saw them as valuable allies against the Portuguese.

Kwango and Kwanza Rivers. Here they encountered a people known as the Imbangala. These were none other than the followers of Kinguri kwa Bangela who had left Lunda in recent decades (see p. 5). Some sort of agreement seems to have been made between the two leaders and possibly their followers raided together for a time. Within a few years, however, the two groups went their separate ways; the Imbangala to attack Ndongo (see below, p. 20) and the Jaga to devastate Kongo.

They looted and killed throughout the south-eastern parts of the kingdom, defeated any army put into the field by the Governor of Mbata, and in 1568 attacked São Salvador. The Mani Kongo, Alvare I, and his people fled. Alvare turned for help to the Portuguese. It was 1571 before the Governor of São Tomé, Francisco de Gouveia, arrived with 600 men. Together the Kongolese and Portuguese forces drove the Jaga southwards out of the country in 1572.

Decline of the Kongo kingdom

The royal authority had suffered a severe blow as a result of the Jaga invasion. The various regions threw off the control of the Mani Kongo and his position became little more than honorary. It seemed that he could not maintain his authority without Portuguese power and the Portuguese were no longer prepared to come to his aid.

Portuguese traders and royal agents turned their attention further south, to Angola. In 1576 a fortified post was built at Luanda and thereafter there was little European activity in Kongo. Having entrenched themselves in Angola the Portuguese made a few attempts to conquer Kongo by force. An invasion in 1590 was driven off by the combined armies of Kongo and Ndongo and a great victory won at Ngoleme-Akitambo. In 1617 and 1623 fresh military expeditions were mounted but pressure was relaxed after the Mani Kongo had appealed to the Pope and the king of Spain. In 1665 yet another invasion took place as Portuguese soldiers and adventurers poured into Kongo in search of (non-existent) gold, silver and copper. They found nothing and destroyed much, killing the Mani Kongo and many of his leading men in various battles.

By 1700 the kingdom of Kongo had ceased to exist. It had split into small chieftaincies. São Salvador was a deserted city, its walls and buildings in ruins. Slave raiding, kidnapping, and petty warfare were rife.

Ndongo

Ndongo was founded in about 1500 as a tributary state of Kongo, and it was certainly regarded as such by successive Mani Kongo until 1556 when Ndongo established its independence. It was clear to the ruler (the Ngola) that he could not preserve his new-found freedom without the continued aid of the Europeans. He asked the Portuguese for missionaries and advisers. By this time the power of the Ngola was formidable: he controlled all the land bounded by the Cuanza, Lukala and Dande Rivers. When the requested Portuguese mission arrived at the capital, Kabasa, in 1560, its leaders found a new, confident Ngola on the throne who dismissed most of the Europeans and kept four as virtual hostages.

Unfortunately, Ngola Ndambi's confidence was misplaced. His position was far from secure. Malcontents within Ndongo and powerful neighbours without threatened the stability of the state. In 1565 he was forced to release his hostages and seek Portuguese military aid. One of the freed hostages, Paulo Dias De Novais, returned in 1575 at the head of a military expedition to overrun the country and administer it on behalf of the king of Portugal.

War for the control of Angola

The conquest of Ndongo took the Portuguese over a hundred years to accomplish and many more decades after that were needed to secure the frontiers of the new colony of Angola (named, like other African states after the title of its king). The first phase of the conquest lasted from the re-arrival of Dias in 1575 to the establishment of a shaky peace in 1622. Dias had the responsibility of establishing permanent white settlement in the area granted to him as *donatario*.* He took his task seriously. Within months he had begun the building of a permanent mainland settlement at Luanda and in 1578 he despatched other colonists to establish a similar base at Benguela Velha.

In 1579 Dias began the move inland towards the fabled silver mines of Cambambe. The Ngola retaliated by murdering Portuguese merchants at Kabasa and launching an attack on Luanda. Though the Portuguese suffered many setbacks Dias and his successors pushed on relentlessly with a policy of penetration and expansion. By 1583 a fort had been built a hundred miles up the Cuanza at Masangano. The Ngola was so alarmed by the advance of the white men that he managed to arrange an alliance between Ndongo, Kongo, Matamba and groups of the marauding Jaga. In 1589 their combined forces inflicted a heavy defeat on the Portuguese.

In 1603 the acting Portuguese governor, Manuel Cerveira Pereira, reached Cambambe and realised that the supposed mineral wealth of the area did not exist. The only Europeans who did like Angola were the slave traders whose numbers and activities grew as Portuguese armies forced their way further inland. Urged on by these traders the Portuguese leaders committed themselves to further conquest.

The European and African forces were well matched until 1614. In that year the Jaga were induced to make an alliance with the invaders. The result was devastating. The power of Ndongo crumbled. The Jaga raided and looted everywhere. Slave traders depopulated whole villages. Even the Portuguese leaders were frightened by the situation and were pleased to discuss peace terms with Ndongo representatives. Peace was eventually signed at Luanda in 1622.

The person who negotiated with the Portuguese on behalf of the Ngola was his sister Anna Nzinga. This remarkable woman was to dominate the next phase of Angola's history from 1623 to 1663.

---

* A *donatario* was a gift of land from the crown, a common practice in European feudal societies and one which was extended to the colonial sphere as Europeans began to settle other lands. Dias was granted a large area of land in the south of what is now Angola and the right to administer an even larger area. The grant of a *donatario* carried conditions. In this case Dias had to settle at least 100 peasant families, explore the coastline to the south, establish Christian missionary work, build fortresses, and ensure '... that the kingdom of Angola be subjected and captured'.

Queen Nzinga

Having obtained very favourable terms under the treaty, Nzinga returned to her brother's island fortress on the Cuanza. There the following year the Ngola died, under circumstances which suggest that he was poisoned, and Nzinga became queen. One of her first acts was to fling a challenge at the European conquerors who were ignoring the 1622 treaty; either they kept the terms of the treaty or she would renew the war.

Nzinga spent the next few years forging alliances with Jaga groups and other neighbouring rulers. She offered refuge to all who were fleeing from Portuguese oppression. She incited rebellion among Portuguese vassal chiefs. Later, when the Dutch appeared in Central Africa as commercial and colonial rivals of the Portuguese, she gained their support also.

Between 1626 and 1628 the Portuguese twice forced Nzinga to flee from her island stronghold, but twice the Portuguese, frightened by the prospect of Dutch attack from the sea, retreated without being able to capture the queen. They did, however, 'depose' her as ruler of Ndongo and set up a puppet king, Philip I, at Punga a Ndongo. But Nzinga made an alliance with the Imbangala of Kasanje and with his aid conquered a new kingdom for herself – Matamba (1630).

Queen Nzinga negotiating with the Portuguese. When she was refused a chair by the haughty white men the queen used one of her servants rather than appear inferior.

Now followed another period of consolidation and alliance-making with peoples in the region of the Lukala and Cambo Rivers. The ruler of Kasanje, preferring to remain independent so that, when the conflict was over, he could establish friendly relations with the victors, broke off the alliance with Queen Nzinga. But her party grew larger and stronger until in 1639 the Portuguese government in Lisbon, realising that she was not to be easily overthrown and fearful of Dutch intervention, ordered peace terms to be discussed.

This peace lasted no longer than that of 1622. By early 1641 the Portuguese had marched a large army eastwards once more. But now the Dutch menace became a reality. For years they had been inciting the Kongolese and the Dembos to rebel. In August 1641 they themselves invaded Luanda from the sea and captured the town. Dutch troops made their way inland while African leaders threw caution aside and joined forces with Nzinga. Portugal's army suffered defeat after defeat. By 1648 there was little left to them but the fortress of Masangano and the surrounding land. When all seemed lost the Portuguese king sent to Brazil for an army to relieve his West African colony. In August 1648 this army arrived, under the leadership of General Salvador de Sa y Correa and within a few months the situation was reversed. The Dutch at Luanda surrendered without a struggle and soon there was not a Dutch soldier left in Angola. Without their European allies Queen Nzinga's forces were unable to continue the siege of Masangano. De Sa turned defeat into victory and carried out savage reprisals on the rebels. The Kasanje hastened to make friends with the Portuguese. Soon Nzinga had few friends left.

Still she refused to give in to the Portuguese. In 1650 she began bargaining with the conquerors. The treaty making went on for six years. At the end of this period Nzinga was forced to recognise Philip I as Ngola, and Ndongo became a vassal state of Portugal, but Nzinga remained queen of Matamba and fully independent. She remained so for the rest of her life. Though she became a Christian and allowed European missionaries to work in her territory she never accepted Portuguese authority. She died in 1663, one of the most colourful and influential rulers of Central Africa.

1648 marked the end of effective African resistance to the Portuguese in western Central Africa. Ndongo remained firmly in the grasp of its white conquerors apart from an attempted rebellion in 1670–1. From there the Portuguese were able to extend their authority along the valley of the Cuanza, northwards to the River Dande and eastwards as far as the borders of Matamba and Kasanje. The colony was administered from Luanda, the capital, and other important towns were Benguela and Masangano.

The Jaga and the Imbangala

Throughout the history of Kongo and Angola groups of Jaga and Imbangala have appeared from time to time as invaders, allies or enemies. We must now try to trace the movements of the major Imbangala and Jaga groups during the years before 1800.

During the last quarter of the sixteenth century the Imbangala, under the leadership of Kinguri kwa Bangela, were moving westwards along the upper Kwanza. At a place called Bola Kasash they settled for a while and here it was that Kinguri was killed either in battle against the Ndongo or as a result of intrigue and treachery. The next important leader was Kasanje ka Imba. He led his people further west in the hope of linking up with the Portuguese, whose marvellous weapons and possessions he had heard of and perhaps even seen. He found his way blocked by the Ndongo and had to defeat them and the Mbundu of the coast before he could meet the European leaders. Kasanje formed an alliance with the Portuguese which he and his successors maintained with a few intervals until 1800 and after. It was to prove greatly to the advantage of his people as the Europeans made themselves more powerful in the land.

Kasanje's Imbangala turned eastwards once more, fighting with the Portuguese against the Ndongo and their allies. At last they settled at Ambaca but were forced by famine to move on once more. Reaching the plains between the Lui and Kwango Rivers they drove out the Pende people and finally settled to a new kind of life in this new land. During their wanderings the Imbangala had mingled with groups of Jaga and learned much from their methods of warfare. The new state took the name of its great leader, Kasanje. The alliance with Portugal often stirred up the hostility of neighbouring states, particularly Matemba, but Kasanje benefited greatly from it. The capital, Cassange, became the main slave market of the interior and attracted European and African traders from a wide area. The importance of Kasanje as a slave trading state preserved it from attempts at Portuguese domination until well into the nineteenth century. During their travels the Imbangala had split into several marauding groups and it is important to remember that the Kasanje were just one (though probably the most important) of these groups which settled in what is now Angola.

Similarly there were many Jaga bands wandering in west Central Africa in the sixteenth and seventeenth centuries. After the invasion of Kongo in 1568–71 Jaga groups turned southwards and ravaged over a wide region. It may have been the development of trade with 20 the coast which encouraged many of the Jaga to settle. During the

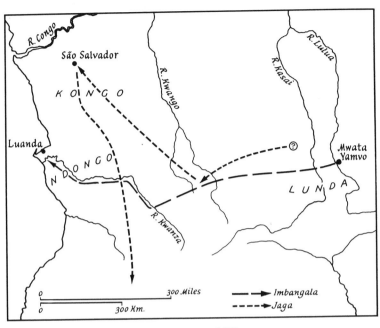

Imbangala and Jaga invasions of Kongo and Ndongo.

first half of the eighteenth century a number of Jaga kingdoms were established on the plateau lands of southern Angola. The original inhabitants were conquered and new states established which had a detailed and complex political organisation. They remained militarily powerful – too powerful to be challenged by the Portuguese. From the beginning trade played an important part in their economy. The most important kingdoms were: Bihé, Kiyaka, Kakonda, Mbailundu, Ndulu, Ngalani and Wambu. Together they are known as the Ovimbundu, and the Ovimbundu have been called 'the greatest traders of Bantu Africa'. We shall be examining their trading activities in a later chapter. It is enough to note that by 1800 Bailundu and Bihé had become important inland trading centres, that long-distance trade routes were well established, and that the Ovimbundu kingdoms dominated tens of thousands of square miles of western Central Africa.

3. Iron Age states
(3) Eastern Central Africa

Early Iron Age inhabitants

Around A.D. 1000 the area to the north of the middle Zambezi was occupied by small, scattered Iron Age communities. Some were Bantu farmers, others were wandering pastoralists. Because archaeologists have done a great deal of valuable work in Zambia we have a considerable amount of information about these early communities. Experts divide the Iron Age communities into a number of different cultures, marked by different kinds of pottery, varying skilfulness as iron-workers and different living habits. But, despite their differences, the settled Iron Age agricultural communities appeared to have many things in common. They lived in villages for as long as fifteen or twenty years at a time, until the soil would no longer produce good crops. Then they moved to a place where the soil was fresh. It would probably be a hundred years or more before their descendants returned to the original village. Many sites have been excavated which show evidence of periodic occupation.

The people lived by a mixture of agriculture, pastoralism and hunting. They grew cereals, kept short-horned, humped cattle and other livestock, stalked the plains game and gathered food from wild plants. They were skilled in the use of snares and traps and attacked the larger game including even elephants – with iron-tipped spears and arrows. Their dwellings were very simple shelters of sticks and grass, though some communities built more solid, round pole-and-thatch houses. Each group of houses would be surrounded by a thorn fence to protect the domestic animals. These farmers naturally took for themselves the best land. As their number increased the earlier inhabitants – the Bushmen – were forced out.

Some of these early Iron Age communities not only knew how to extract and work iron; they were also manufacturers of copper and gold objects. There were outcrops of ore-bearing rock in Zambia from which the metals could be obtained fairly easily. When archaeologists excavated the site of an Iron Age village at Ingombe Ilede in southern Zambia they found that it had been occupied for hundreds

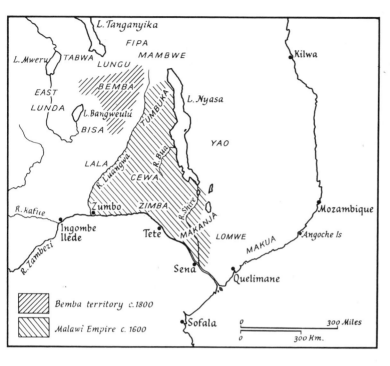

Bemba territory c.1800

Malawi Empire c.1600

of years before A.D. 1000, then abandoned until the fourteenth century, when it was reoccupied by a very advanced Iron Age people. Graves of this later period contained gold and copper ornaments, bead and cowrie shell necklaces, iron hoes, iron ceremonial gongs, cross-shaped copper ingots (probably used as trading currency), copper wire and tools as well as finely decorated earthenware pots and bowls. Clearly these people were skilled metal workers as well as long-distance traders. They may also have grown and spun their own cotton.

These first Iron Age settlers had reached a high level of development by the sixteenth and seventeenth centuries, when numerous bands of people moved in from the Congo. These newcomers were connected with Luba and Lunda rulers. They gradually conquered or absorbed the earlier inhabitants and established new social and political patterns.

The coming of new Bantu peoples from the west and north-west began in the sixteenth century and resulted either directly or indirectly from the establishment of the Luba and Lunda Empires. But the migrants who travelled eastwards from the troubled Congo region did not come in large groups to found empires. The clan was the most important social and political unit and larger states or   23

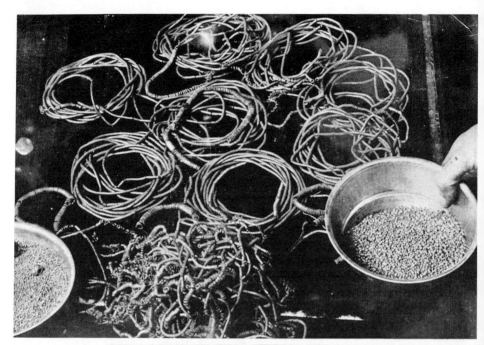

Gold ornaments from the Iron Age in Rhodesia. These ornaments from Dhlo Dhlo in Matabeleland are similar to those found at other sites in Zambia and Rhodesia. They indicate the existence of skilled metal-workers and an important trade network.

empires were not common. This does not mean that there was no change in the political life of this vast region between A.D. 1000 and 1800. It does mean that such changes as took place were the result largely of clan movements rather than mass migrations, and of the achievement of power by some clans over others.

A series of complex Bantu migrations, beginning perhaps as early as the fifteenth century, brought the ancestors of the peoples of the south and west of Lake Malawi to their present homelands. They are known collectively as the Maravi or Malawi. The migration pattern of these peoples is obviously very complex but we can distinguish the main outline of the origins of the more powerful groups.

According to Cewa traditions a chief whose title was Kalonga led his people into the region of the Bua River. When Kalonga had claimed his own territory he sent out some of his relatives to settle in other nearby areas. Of these the more important were Undi, from whom the Cewa people are descended, and Kaphwiti and Lundu, the founders of the Mang'anja people. Undi claimed territory to the south-west of Kalonga's. Kaphwiti and Lundu settled in the Shiré valley. Most of the Malawi chieftains continued to honour the Kalonga who had important religious functions and control of some of the important trade routes from the Zambezi valley to the interior.

Influence of the Portuguese

The Portuguese came to eastern Africa in the sixteenth century (see below, pp. 29–30) and had a considerable effect on the political situation to the north. In the second half of the sixteenth century the Kalonga's hold on his subordinate chiefs was weakening. Particularly troublesome were the Lundu branch of the Mang'anja in the southern Shiré valley. They had a reputation for ferocity and cannibalism and had extended their power over the Zimba and other peoples living near the Shiré and Zambezi Rivers.

In the 1570s groups of the Lundu's subjects (the name of the first chief was kept as a chiefly title) began to roam much farther afield. Some of the Lundu's war hordes attacked and destroyed the Portuguese posts at Tete and Sena and showed no mercy whatsoever to their inhabitants. Another band, perhaps 5,000 strong, reached the coast and marched northwards, overwhelming every village and trading settlement in their path.

Yet the Lundu remained the most powerful Malawi ruler until early in the seventeenth century. In 1608 Kalonga Mazura made an alliance with the Portuguese. He sent 4,000 warriors across the Zambezi to help the white men and their ally the Mwene Mutapa (see chapter 4). In return the Portuguese helped Mazura to deal with troublemakers in his own 'empire'. Chief among these was the Lundu. We know nothing of the conflict but it is obvious from Portuguese records that Mazura was victorious.

From this time the Kalonga greatly increased his territory until he had, in fact, created a personal empire. His object was the control of all the trade routes to the coast. He subdued the Lomwe and the Makua and dominated the area north of the Zambezi between the lake and the coast. The hinterland of the important Portuguese posts of Mozambique and Quelimane was under his control. He now felt strong enough to challenge the Portuguese. He demanded that they refer to him as 'emperor', a title they accorded to the Mwene Mutapa. In 1623 the Kalonga had tried to seize the empire of Mwene Mutapa, when its ruler died. Though he was foiled by Mutapa's Portuguese allies, Muzura gained a considerable amount of loot from his raid.

Once his position was secure Muzura settled to a long period of peaceful co-operation with his African and Portuguese neighbours.   25

A new overland trade route was established from the Zambezi to Mozambique and was frequently used as long as the Kalonga maintained control of the region east of Lake Malawi. But his control rested on military power, personal prestige and religious authority. Later rulers lacked the great Mazura's personal qualities. After his death around the middle of the seventeenth century the empire began to break up. By 1700 the various Malawi groups were following separate lines of development and were frequently at war with each other.

The Bemba

The Bemba travelled to their present homelands from the west, probably in the early seventeenth century. They passed to the north of Lake Bangweulu and moved south across the Chambeshi. As a result of quarrels some clans left the main Bemba horde soon after this. Some became the founders of a new group, the Bisa. Others set up ruling clans among the Lala. Turning eastwards the main group crossed Luangwa River and entered Cewa country. In clashes with the Cewa the Bemba leader, Chitimukulu (Chiti the Great) was killed.[*] Travelling northwards under new leadership the Bemba encountered the Fipa, an East African people of totally different origins and traditions. A long period of hostility with the Fipa followed before the Bemba turned westwards once more into the plateau land between Lake Bangweulu and Lake Tanganyika.

Here they found that the inhabitants were grouped in small communities which might be easily subdued and assimilated. Under these easier conditions the Bemba host split up into clan groups under the leadership of chiefs who set out each to conquer his own area of plateau land. They quickly overcame the early Iron Age farmers and pastoralists of the region and they absorbed much from the earlier cultures in the process (e.g. matrilineal succession, language variations and burial rituals). By the end of the seventeenth century the Bemba reigned supreme over a wide area and their power was still growing.

The Bemba clans recognised each descendant of Chitimukulu (whose name was used as a title by successive rulers) as a sort of 'paramount chief', having a unique ritual and political role to play

---

[*] Chitimukulu was killed by Mwase who was a chief either of the Cewa or Nsenga. Tradition states that Chiti's brother, Nkole wa Mapembwe, avenged the death before leading his people northwards. Chiti's body was buried at Mwalule, which is still the burial ground of his descendants.

in the life of the people. Bemba clans also came together under the leadership of the Chitimukulu in times of war. By the early nineteenth century the paramount chiefs increased their real power by successful military expeditions which increased their prestige and territory and by creating new chieftaincies for members of their own families. This centralisation made possible the great Bemba expansion of the nineteenth century.

The soil on the plateau where they lived was not very fertile and tsetse fly made it difficult to raise herds. The Bemba therefore took advantage of their central position to attack other communities. Thus Bemba groups raided the Tabwa for salt and (later) ivory, the Mambwe and Lungu for cattle, cloth and iron goods, the Bisa for salt and fish.

Frequently the size of a Bemba chief's following grew, not by conquest but by agreement. A Bemba clan would arrive in the locality of a small community. The local elders or clan leaders would realise the uselessness of resistance and would agree to talks with the Bemba. As a result they would accept the Bemba chief's authority. Their people would intermarry with his. After a time they would drop their customs in favour of Bemba ones. Thus without mass movement and without conquest a new Bemba territorial chieftaincy would be born.

Bemba clan migrations.

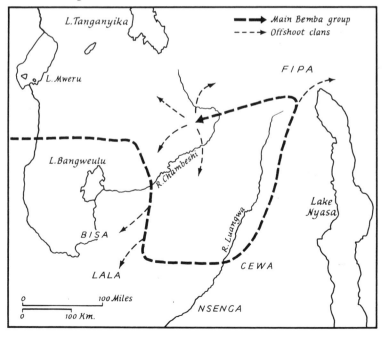

The Bisa

One of the more numerous peoples of what is now eastern Zambia were the Bisa. They lived by agriculture, pastoralism and trade. They were organised in small groups, acknowledging no chief or overlord. Around 1760 some of them were conquered by warriors from Kazembe and forced to pay tribute to the East Lunda chief. But the control exercised by Kazembe was very loose and the Bisa became not so much vassals as partners in long-distance trade.

The Yao

The Yao were also great traders and more about them will be said below. The earliest traditions give northern Mozambique as their homeland and they have only expanded northwards and southwards from there in comparatively recent times. The important unit of Yao society was the village, and chiefs were weak or powerful according to the number of followers they had.

Their land produced most of the things they needed and the Yao were largely self-sufficient. They obtained salt from burnt grasses. They tilled the land. They fished in Lake Nyasa and the many rivers of their homeland. They made their own barkcloth and pots. They obtained iron and made tools from the large deposits of ore in their territory. Thus well provided, it was perhaps natural that the Yao should become traders, exchanging their surplus goods for other items. As early as the sixteenth century the Yao had extended their trading activities to the coast. By 1800 they were becoming deeply involved in the slave trade.

Indian Ocean trade

It was the establishment of foreign merchants at the coast which stimulated trade. The 3,200 kilometres of coastline between Sofala and Mogadishu (in modern Somalia) border the Indian Ocean and for centuries the Indian Ocean had been one of the world's major trading areas. The main operators of commerce throughout this whole region were Muslim traders from Arabia, Persia and India. Most of their settlements were north of Cape Delgado. However, large trading ports were established at Mozambique and Sofala, and smaller settlements at places like Quelimane and the Angoche islands. Some Arabs penetrated inland along the Zambezi to set up trading posts at Sena and Tete. For the most part these peaceful foreign merchants were welcomed by the rulers of the lands where they settled. Many of them took wives from among the local Bantu peoples and over the centuries this gave rise to the development of a new community – the Swahili.

Between A.D. 1000 and 1500 these coastal settlements flourished. The supply of gold and ivory from the interior was erratic and trading seasons were seriously limited by the monsoon winds but the profits on trade were so good that the merchants were able to live in luxury. They built stone houses and mosques and decorated their homes with rugs, imported metalware and porcelain. They wore clothes of cottons and silks and ornaments of gold and copper. In the thirteenth century the rulers of Kilwa made themselves masters of the gold trade. A direct overland route to the gold lands was established via Lake Malawi and Tete. Dhows trading south of Cape Delgado had to pay tolls at Kilwa.

In 1488 the Portuguese sailor Bartholomew Diaz sailed round the Cape of Good Hope into the rich trading world of the Indian Ocean. By 1497 all was ready for the founding of Portugal's eastern empire. A soldier, Vasco da Gama, was put in charge of the first expedition. With three ships he travelled to the Cape. Sailing up the east coast he first encountered the Muslims, early in 1498, at Quelimane. Then he travelled on to the more important settlement of Mozambique. The Muslims reacted to the strangers with curiosity and courtesy – until

The Portuguese fort at Sofala.

they discovered that da Gama and his men were Christians. Then their attitude changed and the Portuguese explorers had to hurry on their way. Da Gama reported to his king that the African coast would have to be conquered if Portugal was to establish an eastern empire.

In 1502 the conquest began. Sofala fell under Portuguese rule in 1505 when Francisco d'Almeida visited the town on his way to take up his post as Portuguese Viceroy in India. His first relations with the leader of the Arab settlement were friendly and the Portuguese were allowed to build a fort. However, when the Muslims realised that their trade was suffering as a result of Portuguese interference they tried to throw the newcomers out. The result was defeat for the Arabs and their African allies. The Portuguese then appointed another man as Arab leader, whom they felt they could trust. Mozambique Island was attacked in 1507 and a fortress built there. This town became the centre of Portuguese administration south of Cape Delgado, and in 1509 an official known as the 'Captain' was appointed to be in charge of the area. Yet for several years Sofala was considered more important. Portuguese merchants and officials visited the town or settled there for some years and tried to control the flow of gold and ivory from the interior, though their influence both at the coast and in the interior was very limited.

4. Iron Age states
(4) Empires and kingdoms between the Limpopo and the Zambezi

The Shona kingdoms

For nearly a thousand years many different communities lived in the land between Zambezi and Limpopo, hunting, farming, herding, mining and trading. But in about A.D. 1000 this pattern of life was disturbed when a new wave of immigration began. Some of the Bantu had begun to leave the Congo forest and cross the Zambezi, probably coming through the Katanga region. They are thought to have all belonged to that particular branch of Bantu-speaking peoples known as the Shona.

Almost as soon as they arrived on the Rhodesian plateau, the Shona either drove out or ruled over the earlier inhabitants. Their warriors were fierce and skilful and it was almost certainly they who

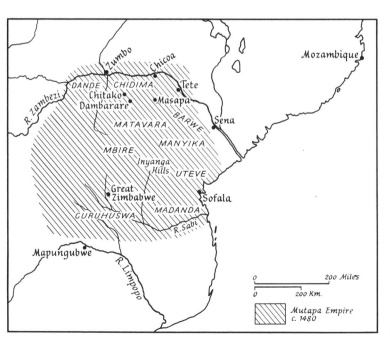

Bantu invaders fighting San hunters ('Bushmen'). In this expressive rock painting the invaders are seen surprising and overpowering the San by disguising themselves with bucks' heads and using their throwing spears with deadly accuracy.

defeated many of the Bushmen in battle and forced the survivors to flee southwards and westwards. Yet, the Shona seem to have been accepted much more peacefully by the Iron Age farmers and herders. The newcomers had strange powers and skills and the old herders and metalworkers readily accepted them as rulers.

It was the religious and political systems of the Shona that gave them their superiority. They brought with them powerful religious beliefs and impressive rituals and religious experts. They worshipped a god called Mwari, an all-powerful being who could only be approached through the spirits of the dead. These spirits, in turn, could only be approached by the chief and his religious experts. As Mwari completely controlled the life of the people – and particularly as he had power to give or withhold rain – you can see how much power the chiefs had over the people. The Shona built great enclosures which were both religious and political centres. As well as being the places where their chiefs lived, they were also the burial grounds for dead chiefs. Such a place was known as a *'zimbabwe'* (the word means 'a burial ground of the chiefs'.) By about 1300, the Shona began to build these enclosures in stone, partly to make them more impressive and worthy of Mwari, and partly to make them easy to defend. The

Great Zimbabwe. This photograph shows one of the more impressive stone buildings. It is usually called the Elliptical Temple.

ruins of many of these stone buildings can still be seen in Rhodesia. The most famous is Great Zimbabwe, where some of the Shona made their capital in about 1075, and where they began to build in stone in around 1350.

The Shona kingdoms were very well organised. As a state grew in size the chief would put men he could trust in charge of the different regions. As long as these 'governors' remained loyal no one could successfully challenge the authority of the chief.

But the Shona did not force their way of life on the other inhabitants of the plateau. On the contrary they learned much from the Iron Age people. They copied their pottery-making methods and they were greatly interested in their skill as metalworkers. They deliberately encouraged gold mining and the gold trade. They organised elephant hunts in order to gain the ivory which was much in demand at Sofala. Indeed, under Shona rule trade flourished as never before. Until the middle of the fifteenth century most of the Shona lived in the southern part of the country, towards the Limpopo. In fact, their most important centre was not Great Zimbabwe but Mapungubwe, which is actually south of the Limpopo. By about 1400 the whole region of southern Rhodesia seems to have formed a single Shona kingdom ruled from Mapungubwe. It was from this state that, during the next hundred years, the great Empire of Mutapa grew.

The king of this state was known as the Mambo and the Mambo was always chosen from the ruling family, the Rozwi. However, in about 1400, a change occurred and a new ruling group known as the Mbire took over. Under the new Mbire rulers, the Rozwi state of southern Rhodesia grew rapidly into the powerful Empire of Mutapa.

The Mutapa Empire

The first Mambo of the new dynasty was Chikura Wadyambeu but the man who founded the new empire was his son Nyatsimba Mutota, who came to the throne in about 1420. He immediately set out northwards on a military expedition with the aim of winning a much larger kingdom for himself. He wanted to gain control of the gold and ivory trade routes which were by now so busy that Muslim traders had come inland from the coast to deal directly with the African producers. There is a tradition that Mutota was told that Arab traders in the Dande country, around the Zambezi, had large supplies of salt and that the king immediately decided to set out with his warriors to obtain this much needed substance. Mutota also needed more land. The grasslands of southern Rhodesia – known as the Guruhuswa – were rich, but they could not feed the growing numbers of cattle which the flourishing Shona were gathering. The Mambo was a vigorous, ambitious and ruthless ruler. He was a great leader of men. When he set out on his career of conquest, his enemies were terrified. They fled before his warriors, whom they called *makorekore* – 'locusts'. To the mighty Mutota himself they gave the name *Mwene Mutapa* – 'master pillager'.

Mutota liked to think of himself as the master pillager so he added Mwene Mutapa to the official titles of himself and his successors. When Portuguese travellers came to the area in the next century, they thought the title referred to the whole empire and so they called the land ruled by Mutota's descendants *Monomotapa*.

Mwene Mutapa. A seventeenth-century Portuguese drawing of one of the rulers of Mutapa.

Mutota raided from Great Zimbabwe, which had once again become the Shona capital, to the Dande country. All the people his armies met were either conquered or hastened to accept Mbire rule. Mutota could not rule this enlarged empire from the far south, so he moved his capital to a new site, Chitako, near the Zambezi. The first Mwene Mutapa died in about 1450. His son, Matope, inherited the throne and carried on the work of conquest. He extended Mbire rule to the east, thus gaining complete control of the valuable trade routes. The provinces added to the empire were Madanda, Uteve, Manyika, Barwe and Chidima. By the time of Matope's death in about 1480 the empire stretched from the Zambezi to the Limpopo and from the Kalahari Desert to the Indian Ocean.

Trade in the empire grew rapidly. At the beginning of the sixteenth century one visitor reckoned that there were 10,000 Muslim merchants in the empire. This was certainly an exaggeration but it does give some idea of the scale of commercial activity in the Mwene Mutapa's territory.

Yet the Mutapa Empire was short-lived. Even from the beginning the Mambo was reliant upon the members of his family, whom he placed in charge of the various provinces. Frequently they gave trouble but the first two Mambos managed to overcome all rebellions. The crisis came after the death of Matope. The new ruler was Mavura who was carefully chosen from among Matope's sons according to the traditional Shona rituals. But within a few weeks he had been murdered by one of his brothers, Nyakuma, who seized the throne. The new Mwene Mutapa held his position for ten years but he had continual trouble with two other brothers – Changa, who ruled the Guruhuswa province from the old capital of Great Zimbabwe, and Togwa, who was Governor of Mbire. In 1490 these two joined together to challenge Nyakuma and succeeded in defeating and killing the Mambo in battle. Now Changa took over control of the empire, calling himself Changamire (he added to his name the title 'amir' which was given him by Muslim traders). He enjoyed supreme power for four years before being defeated in his turn by Nyakuma's son Kakuyo.

The old empire was now divided into two states: Mutapa in the north and what came to be known as the Rozwi Confederacy in the south (Changamire and his successors claimed to be the true representatives of the Rozwi dynasty, ruling from the ancient capital of Great Zimbabwe). For a while Barwe and Manyika remained part of the Mwene Mutapa's kingdom, while Uteve and Mandanda joined the Confederacy. But all of these regions eventually broke away to form independent Shona states. Of the two larger states that of the Changamires (later rulers kept the name as a royal title) was the more powerful and important. It controlled the gold bearing land, most of the important trade routes, the ancient capital and much of the best grazing and agricultural land. During the next two centuries, as the Rozwi state flourished, more buildings were erected at Zimbabwe and other large stone enclosures were built.

Portuguese penetration

For many years the Portuguese remained in their coastal bases, not daring to face the dangers and difficulties of the interior. Only in the 1530s, when Arab and African smuggling had seriously disturbed

Portuguese control of the gold trade, did the white men travel up the Zambezi and become involved in the relations between the Mutapa and Rozwi states.

The Portuguese penetration was at first a peaceful affair: the white men lacked the resources for armed conquest. First of all they established themselves in small groups in those places along the Zambezi and south of the river where Arab traders were already living. These were the towns and villages where fairs were held; centres where gold dust and other goods were collected for taxing by the Mwene Mutapa, and where trade took place between African and African and between African and foreigner. The Portuguese, like the Arabs, were welcomed at these fairs and within a few years they had come to dominate them. At Masapa, the leading fair, for instance, a Portuguese captain was appointed by the Mwene Mutapa to be in charge of the fair and to settle disputes between traders of all races. In 1531 the Captain at Mozambique founded a fair at the Arab settlement of Sena on the Zambezi and a few years later another was established 240 kilometres further upstream at Tete. These two towns became the main official Portuguese posts in the interior and were of both economic and political importance in the relations between the white king's agents and the black rulers of the Zambezi lands. The captains of the forts at Sena and Tete received grants of land from the Mwene Mutapa and were regarded in many ways by the local peoples as their chiefs.

But Portuguese contact with the peoples living between the Limpopo and the Zambezi was not controlled by royal agents of the government at Lisbon. From the mid-sixteenth century individual Portuguese adventurers obtained land from chiefs south of the Zambezi. These estates were known as *prazos*. They might be gained in a number of ways. They might be awarded by the Mwene Mutapa as a reward or payment for military assistance. They might be obtained from rebellious chiefs in return for aid in fighting against the Mwene Mutapa or local enemies. As the power of the ruler declined individual Portuguese adventurers took land by force. The Portuguese government encouraged its subjects to acquire large estates because it believed that by this form of colonisation a large area of Africa would come under the control of the Portuguese crown. It confirmed grants of *prazos* and made new grants. But it did not gain control of the land south of the Zambezi, for the *prazos* holders set themselves up as chiefs. Their power was based on large slave armies; they married African women; they kept up all the ritual associated with chieftaincy; they made alliances with local African rulers; they made war on neighbouring states and built up large 37 kingdoms for themselves. When, in the eighteenth century, the government in Lisbon tried to bring the area under closer control they found themselves opposed by the half-caste descendants of the first settlers who had become, in fact, rulers of new African communities. By that time some of the *prazos* were hundreds of thousands of hectares in size.

Mutapa, the Rozwi Confederacy and the Portuguese 1600–1800

The Mwene Mutapas of the sixteenth century welcomed the Portuguese largely because they hoped for their support in regaining the lost parts of their empire. There was, therefore, a steady increase in the power and influence of European traders, missionaries and *prazeros*.

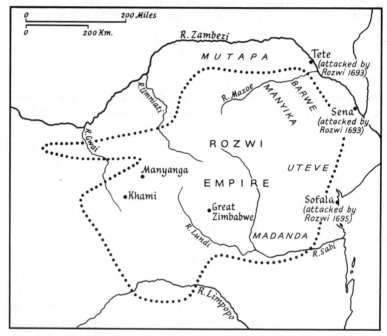

The Rozwi Confederation at its height c. 1700.

In the mid-sixteenth century two Mambos, Neshangwe and Chivere Nyasoro, re-established something of the former Mutapa greatness and even reconquered Mbire. But during the next seventy years the power of Mutapa's 'allies', the Portuguese, grew and the Mambos spent most of their time trying to maintain some degree of independence from the powerful foreigners. In the 1590s the Mutapa kingdom suffered another serious disaster when some of the Zimba came raiding, burning and plundering across the Zambezi and terrorised all the inhabitants of the state (including Portuguese and Arabs). Thousands of the Mambo's subjects fled to the Inyango hills and there built fortified, terraced agricultural settlements, the remains of which can still be seen. The ruler of Mutapa at this time was Mambo Gatsi Ruseri (1569–1627). Beset by civil wars, conflict with the Rozwi Confederacy, Zimba invasions and increasing Portuguese pressure, the Mambo found it impossible to rule his people efficiently and his reign was one of the most disastrous in the history of Mutapa. In effect he relied more and more on Portuguese support and, towards the end of his reign, signed a humiliating treaty which practically gave the Europeans control of his country.

In 1629 the next Mambo, Kapararidze, tried to regain national pride and independence by attempting to force the Portuguese out of his territory. But the Portuguese government was now pursuing a more positive policy towards its African possessions. The Portuguese were convinced that the gold mines of Mashonaland could be more profitably exploited and they also thought there were valuable silver deposits around Chicoa. They therefore attacked Kapararidze with a force including private *prazo* armies, government troops and warriors provided by Shona allies. The Mambo was overthrown and a puppet king, Mavura II (known after his Christian baptism as Dom Philipe I) was placed on the throne.

Meanwhile to the south the Changamires were strengthening and extending their state. In the 1680s Mbire was reconquered. Then Changamire Dombo raided southwards across the Limpopo sending the people of that region scattering before him. In about 1690 a new Mambo, Nyakambira, seized power in Mutapa. He was determined to drive the Portuguese out and turned for help to his powerful southern neighbour. United at last by their hatred of the white man, the two rival chiefs attacked Portuguese garrisons and trading posts, defeated their enemies in open battle at Maungo and advanced right up to the Zambezi valley. The foreigners retired to Tete and Sena where they managed to resist Shona attacks in 1693. Two years later Dombo even attacked the strong European fortress at Sofala.

Thus by 1700 the Portuguese were driven from the Rhodesian plateau, never to return, though further east the *prazeros* retained their power. But this was little comfort to Nyakambira. Though Dombo allowed him to continue to reign in Chitako, Mutapa was reduced to the state of a province of the Rozwi Confederacy. Dombo 39 returned to his capital and the Mutapa once more asserted a precarious independence, while relying heavily on support from the remaining Portuguese Zambezi garrisons. By 1720 the Rozwi state was at its height. The Changamires ruled an area almost as large as the Mwene Mutapas before them. For another hundred years they enjoyed their empire, feared alike by Africans and foreigners – until the 1830s, when their state was completely destroyed by invaders from the south.

5. Peoples south of the Limpopo

There were once two distinct linguistic groups of non-Bantu dwellers in southern Africa – the San and the Khoikhoi.

San hunters

The San were the direct descendants of Late Stone Age hunter–gatherers. The original San hunters (i.e. before they mingled with

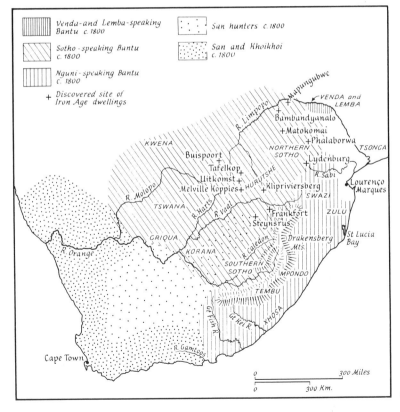

A San rock painting.

the Khoikhoi, which may have taken place a very long time ago) were light-skinned, small and had a physical characteristic called steatopyga (i.e. due to an excess of fat their buttocks stuck out notice-ably. See cave painting). They lived in groups of between twenty-five and seventy people, each band having its own territory (though the men hunted over a wider area in search of game). They lived in caves and rock shelters but when on the move they camped in the open. They were skilled in the use of bow and arrow and other weapons of stone, bone and wood, with which they caught all kinds of animals and fish. They kept dogs to help them in their hunting but had no other domestic animals. They dried out and stored any meat which they did not require immediately, for during the rainy seasons hunting was difficult. They ate honey from the hives of wild bees. Their knowledge of the habits of all kinds of animals was so detailed that they must have been among the finest trackers and hunters in the world.

From plants and snakes the San gathered poison to tip their arrows with, and the soil yielded wild seeds, berries, fruit and roots as well as insects, which the women dug for with pointed sticks. They ate their food raw or simply roasted, because they had no metal or earthenware pots in which to cook it. They covered their bodies with animal skins for warmth and decorated them with necklaces of eggshells or (in coastal districts) seashells. They painted them-selves for ritual dances. Dancing was important to these people. Round their camp fires they imitated the activities of the animals they understood so well. They also painted animals on the walls of their rock-shelters, and sometimes scenes of hunting and warfare. Hundreds of these paintings have been discovered in South and Central Africa but they are very difficult to date accurately, for the same kind of painting (which is quite different from the artistic traditions of other peoples of South and Central Africa) was practised by the San for centuries.

The San were originally spread over most of southern Africa. There were different kinds of San people. Some hunted on the plains and the edge of the Kalahari Desert, others lived in the mountains. Some dwelt along the river valleys while others lived at the coast and depended on the sea for some of their food. These groups developed different hunting and fishing skills. Their languages, though related, often differed so much from each other that San from different groups could not understand one another.

When newcomers crossed the Limpopo into south-east Africa (perhaps c. 1500), bringing with them new ways of life – herding and farming (see below, p. 45f) – there was no immediate clash between them and the San. The hunters lived alongside the Bantu and, in many

A rock painting showing a San–Nguni battle.

cases, lived in mixed communities with them. This relationship is known as *symbiosis*. The newcomers appreciated the San skills, not only as hunters but also as rainmakers. The San could obtain articles the Bantu wanted and so trade sprang up between the two groups: the San exchanged ivory, feathers and eggshell beads for cattle, iron and grain. The Thembu, who were iron smelters, employed the San as woodcutters to provide fuel for their furnaces. There was some intermarriage between the hunters and farmers and for a long time both sides benefited from their close relationship.

But the newcomers grew more numerous. They took over more land for their crops and herds, forcing the hunters to move into the mountains and the arid plains. In return the San sometimes raided Nguni settlements to steal cattle. So there were wars. Gradually the San were driven out of the bush lands east of the Drakensberg mountains. By 1800 there were few of them to be found in the eastern part of the region. As we shall see, by 1800 the arrival of the European at the Cape had also begun to put pressure on the San and the Khoikhoi, so that they were being driven out of the fertile areas of the south as well.

Khoikhoi herders

There are two distinct theories about the origins of the Khoikhoi-speaking peoples of southern Africa. Some historians believe that the Khoikhoi were Stone Age herders who were forced out of areas further north by Bantu farmers who took over their pasture for crop production. The other theory suggests that the Khoikhoi speakers are as ancient as the San, that they too were Stone Age hunter–gatherers, and that they learned from northern immigrants how to keep sheep and cattle.

There are similarities between both San and Khoikhoi languages on the one hand and languages spoken by small groups of people living in the Tanzania Rift Valley. These latter groups are known to be descendants of very early inhabitants of East Africa. What few traditions the Khoikhoi have about their origins speak of a movement from the east. Only when the west coast was reached, according to these traditions, did the Khoikhoi spread out over a wider area of southern Africa. These facts seem to support the theory of a northern origin.

On the other hand the herders and hunters of southern Africa are racially very similar and have been intermingling for a very long time. Furthermore it seems likely that cattle of the Sanga type, which originated in Ethiopia about a thousand years ago, were unknown in

44

southern Africa until some time between 1400 and 1500. By this time Khoikhoi herders were already living there and keeping sheep.

The Khoikhoi lived in clans of about 250 people and kept large herds of sheep and cattle. One such community would probably have about 2,000 beasts. Though each clan moved separately it belonged, with other related clans, to a horde which might number several thousand people. Sometimes hordes came together for trade or war. The Khoikhoi were nomadic and, in normal times, moved regularly from place to place every season. Like most cattle-keepers they rarely killed their own animals, normally slaughtering only for ritual purposes. They hunted for their meat, using techniques similar to those of the San. Otherwise they lived on milk, wild honey (they also made an alcoholic drink called 'mead' from honey) and wild vegetables.

They wore skins and loved to decorate themselves with ornaments. Ivory ornaments they made themselves but necklaces of copper and beads came through trade. The copper smelters were the Dama of Namaqualand to the north-west. Beads of European origin were obtained from the Ovimbundu of Angola and later from the Dutch settlers at the Cape. They rode on their oxen and used them to carry loads.

If some of the Khoikhoi did not start keeping cattle until the fifteenth century this would explain why few of them lived in the eastern part of the country. For, by then, Sotho and Ngoni agriculturalists had already begun to move into well-watered lands of south-east Africa. But there were large open spaces in southern Africa where the pasture was of reasonable quality and where wild animals could be hunted. In the seventeenth century, though the Khoikhoi hordes were large and there were thousands of San groups, South Africa was not very densely populated.

Early Iron Age dwellers in southern Africa

From the results of excavations at some of the sites indicated on the map below archaeologists believe that the Iron Age reached the area south of the Limpopo by about A.D. 1000 and perhaps earlier. At Matokoma ninth-century pottery fragments were found which were like pottery of the Rhodesian Gokomere culture (whereas the Gokomere people were established in Rhodesia by the fourth century A.D.). The Matokoma finds are however at the moment unique. There are distinct similarities between pottery discovered at Bambandyanalo and that made by potters of the Leopard's Kopje culture of Rhodesia. The men who lived at Bambandyanalo, Mapungubwe and other places 45 in the northern Transvaal were either descendants of the Leopard's Kopje people or, in common with them, were descended from earlier Iron Age inhabitants of Rhodesia. Remains of the same civilisation, known as the Uitkomst culture, have been found in other parts of the Transvaal and it is likely that these Iron Age peoples were still living over a wide area of the high veldt until the nineteenth century. The culture was an advanced one and is distinguished by fine pottery, tools and stone building.

A different, but probably contemporary, Iron Age culture has been disclosed by the excavation of sites in the western Transvaal (though this culture may have been more extensive). The Buispoort people were better at building in stone than their Uitkomst neighbours but otherwise their way of life was probably very similar. To both peoples metal working was important. They mined not only iron, but gold, copper and tin. But this did not, apparently, lead to the development of trade between the peoples of the high veldt. It seems that each community was able to produce most of the metal tools and ornaments it needed without having to rely on trade with its neighbours.

Evidence of Iron Age settlements has also been found in the Orange Free State and on the Natal coast. Pottery finds indicate some connection with the Buispoort culture and perhaps with the Uitkomst culture also. No dates have yet been attached to any of these discoveries and until archaeologists have explored the southern and eastern sites more fully it will not be possible to clarify the connection between the Iron Age peoples north of the Vaal and the early inhabitants of the Orange Free State and the coastal region.

What conclusions can we draw from the archaeological evidence and what does it tell us about the modern inhabitants of south-east Africa? Historians are fairly certain that early Iron Age peoples of the Transvaal were Bantu-speakers and that there is some connection between them and the two larger Bantu groups of modern South Africa, the Nguni and the Sotho. Pottery types and oral tradition connect the Sotho with Buispoort culture. Both were highly skilled craftsmen, metal-workers and builders in stone. The area where most Buispoort culture sites have been discovered (and where, incidentally, there is evidence of a dense population) is the very area which most Sotho traditions regard as the original Sotho dispersal point. Some Sotho groups probably developed distinctive customs as a result of contact with the Uitkomst people.

It is less easy to trace the connection between modern Nguni speakers and their early Iron Age ancestors. Perhaps they too were descended from the Buispoort people but underwent linguistic and cultural changes as a result of contact with Stone Age south Africans.

There is much that we still do not know about the origins of the four Bantu communities of southern Africa: the Nguni, the Sotho, the Venda and the Tsonga. However, their more recent history is a little clearer and we must now turn to consider this.

A Zulu dance.

The Nguni

By 1800 the Nguni-speaking peoples of southern Africa lived along the eastern edge of the region between St Lucia Bay and the Great Fish River. Inland their territory was bordered by the Drakensberg Mountains. Within the Nguni community there were many groups, each one speaking a different dialect. The more powerful of these groups, were the Zulu, Xhosa, Thembu, Mpondo and Swazi. It is not yet possible to describe the origins of all these major Nguni sub-divisions but we can say something about the general Nguni migration patterns.

The Nguni-speakers travelled from the north-west in a series of migrations. They travelled through the mountain passes probably in clan groups seeking pasture for their cattle, goats and sheep. They were farmers and hunters as well as herders but it was their cattle which they valued most highly. Their cows were of the Sanga type but differed in some ways from the animals belonging to the Khoikhoi. 47

The Nguni were already very mixed racially by the time they crossed the Drakensbergs, which suggests that they had travelled a long way, through land occupied by many different peoples. Some of their customs are similar to those of the non-Bantu herdsmen of the southern Sudan and it may be that some of the Nguni ancestors came from East Africa.

If they did come from so far north they must have begun their journeyings many centuries before their arrival in southern Africa. We know from the accounts of early European visitors that there were cattle-keeping peoples speaking Nguni dialects on the coast by the late sixteenth century. There is no reason to believe that they had just arrived there at that time. It is clear from oral traditions that before settling on the coastal plain some of the larger groups lived higher up the river valleys. It seems clear that many of the Nguni settlers must have been south of the Limpopo by A.D. 1400.

The Nguni were organised in small chieftaincies. They grew crops and kept cattle. Frequently chiefs raided or made war on each other. Sometimes chieftaincies split up and new leaders arose who took their followers away in search of fresh homelands. In this way the Nguni peoples spread out over the whole coastal lowland strip from St Lucia Bay to the Great Fish River. Towards the end of the eighteenth century the situation changed. The population continued to grow but most of the areas suitable for settlement had been filled. In the south further expansion was checked by Europeans. It was probably this situation of over-population which led to the remaining Khoikhoi communities being expelled and which, in the early nineteenth century, led to bitter warfare between several Nguni chieftaincies.

The Sotho

By 1800 Sotho peoples occupied most of the area north-west of the Drakensberg and Maloti Mountains between the Orange and Limpopo Rivers. Like the Nguni, they seem to have come in a number of migrational waves and like the Nguni they were a racially mixed people. They came from the north-west and their area of eventual settlement was decided by geography. To the west was scrubland and desert, to the south-east were the Drakensberg and Maloti Mountains while to the east and north-east lay a wide tsetse fly infested belt (see map on p. 41). The first Sotho-speakers probably settled in the watershed region of the Limpopo, Molopo and Harts Rivers. This original settlement may have occurred in the thirteenth or fourteenth century, or even earlier if the Sotho are descended directly from the people of the Buispoort culture. As the population increased various groups left the Sotho birthplace and dispersed over a wider area.

By 1800 some of the Sotho groups were the most skilful peoples of southern Africa. They made tools, weapons and decorative items out of metal, wood and ivory and fine clothes from animal skins.* By 1800 these goods had become important items of trade in parts of south-east Africa.

The Venda

The Venda are a very small population group, numbering about a quarter of a million people. But in terms of language and culture they are distinct from other south African Bantu. There are very close ritual and cultural similarities between the Venda ruling clans and those of the Ngonde and Nyakusa of northern Malawi. Probably some Ngonde chiefs left their homeland and began moving southwards sometime in the sixteenth or seventeenth century.

They arrived south of the Limpopo around the end of the seventeenth century. They found in the Soutpansberg Mountains a land of woods and grassland with many streams and rivers. It was similar to the land of their origin and thus perfectly suited their traditional way of life. So they settled. The earlier inhabitants of this land were primitive hunters who, apparently, had not even discovered how to make fire. Many Venda traditions tell of the ease with which these hunter–gatherers were conquered and either driven out or subjugated. The Venda had a magic war drum which, they believed, gave them victory over their enemies.

There must have been other reasons for the Venda's easy conquest of their predecessors. They were more advanced in every way. They had better weapons, better social and political organisation; they built in stone; and they introduced fire to the region.

The Lemba

The Venda probably learned some of their skills from the Lemba. The Lemba were a small group, quite distinct from the Venda but living in a symbiotic relationship with them. They had been conquered or absorbed into the Venda system at an earlier stage and were certainly more advanced culturally than their overlords, whom they called *Vha Senzi* – 'primitive'. The Lemba were fine craftsmen in wood, clay,

*The Sotho are especially famous for the *kaross*, a sleeveless jacket made of supple jackal or other hides, skilfully tanned and sewn.

49

gold, iron and copper as well as being skilled weavers. They traded
these goods with the Venda and with neighbouring peoples. Control
of Lemba trade was another reason for the wealth and, therefore,
power of the Venda rulers.

The Tsonga

The last Bantu group to be considered was probably the first to
arrive in south-east Africa. The Tsonga were living in the coastal
plain before the arrival of the Sotho, Nguni and Venda in neighbouring regions. The Tsonga people are the product of many migrations of small groups spread over a long period of time. These groups
came to speak a common language, though this language had and
still has several dialects. The Tsonga found themselves in a land of
rivers, lakes and coastal waters. It is not surprising that they became
expert fishermen, nor that fish became their major food. By the seventeenth century the Tsonga occupied a strip of territory from St Lucia
Bay to the Sabi River, but later the Mthethwa Nguni forced them out
of the the southern part of the coastal plain.

Being coast-dwellers the Tsonga were early on drawn into foreign
trade. The Portuguese trading posts at Laurenço Marques and Sofala
were largely dependent on the Tsonga for supplies of gold, ivory and
copper from the interior. Tsonga adventurers paddled hundreds of
miles up the Limpopo and other rivers obtaining these goods in exchange for iron hoes and imported cloth. Their contact with the
interior to the south-west was, however, limited by the existence of
a belt of tsetse fly-infected territory behind the coast.

This brief description of the main ethnic groups of southern Africa
is a very much simplified account of what was in fact a complex series
of interrelated societies. There is still a great deal that we do not know
about the relations between the thousands of sub-groups within the
San, Khoikhoi, Nguni, Sotho, Venda and Tsonga communities. Oral
evidence is difficult to collect and sift at the best of times. The terrible
upheavals suffered by most south African societies in the nineteenth
century have made it even harder to find traditions dealing with the
early history of those societies. Now we turn to consider another
migration movement – that of Europeans into South Africa. For this
we have much more evidence.

Dutch settlers

Five years after Diego Cão landed at the mouth of the River Congo
another Portuguese captain succeeded in finding the route round

Africa for which other sailors had long been searching. In 1488 Bartholemew Diaz sighted the south-east tip of the continent and named it the Cape of Good Hope, because now Portugal had good hope of establishing direct commercial contact with the Orient. But Diaz's discovery was not followed by Portuguese coastal settlement, as were discoveries in East and West Africa. Europeans who landed or were wrecked on the south coast reported that the region was only populated by small numbers of herdsmen. The Portuguese government realised from these reports that the Cape had no value as far as trade was concerned, so they concentrated on their settlements in Angola and Mozambique.

In the early seventeenth century the Dutch East India Company began trading with the lands and islands of South-East Asia. They needed ports of call on the long journey from Europe. Though they ousted the Portuguese from many of their posts they failed to dislodge them from their settlements in East and West Africa. So the Cape became important to Dutch shipping as a stopping place for fresh water and, in 1651, the governors of the Dutch East India Company decided to set up a refreshment station there so that passing ships could obtain food, stores and repair facilities.

On 6 April 1652 Jan van Riebeeck arrived in Table Bay with eighty followers to establish the new settlement. The European post was thought of purely as a refreshment station for Dutch ships and not as a colony. Van Riebeeck marked out an area of about 12,000 hectares for the settlements. No attempt was made to control or rule the local Khoikhoi population, and slaves were brought from Angola and elsewhere to do the hard manual work about the station.

Yet it was not long before the activities of the newcomers began to alarm and provoke the Khoikhoi. At first the herdsmen were prepared to trade their sheep and cattle with the Dutch. This did not produce enough livestock to meet the needs of all the long-distance trading vessels which called at the Cape. So, van Riebeeck allowed a number of his countrymen to farm land in the Liesbeeck valley. The local Khoikhoi were angry at this invasion of their grazing lands. They realised that the Dutch, 'kept in possession of the best lands, grazed their cattle where we used to do so, and that everywhere with houses and plantations they endeavoured to establish themselves so permanently as if they never intended to leave again, but take permanent possession of this Cape land (which has belonged to us during all the centuries)'.*

Their attempt to resist the white men led to war in 1657–8 and

* *The Early Cape Hottentots*, Van Riebeeck Society Publications, p. 14.

again between 1673 and 1677. War against European muskets could only mean defeat.

If the first and second Khoikhoi Wars were disastrous for the Africans they also discouraged the farmers. During the first decades of the settlement's existence there was much disagreement among the Dutch as to whether the Cape should be kept purely as a refreshment station or whether it should become an agricultural colony. But while the leaders argued the settlers decided the matter for themselves. Despite clashes with the local people and other setbacks more and more Dutchmen moved outside the Cape's boundaries to set themselves up as *boers* (farmers). There were three main reasons for this. First of all as the number of settlers increased and reared families they needed more 'living space'. Most of them had no desire to go back to Europe and they even disliked the restrictions placed on them by the Cape government. They wanted to move further inland where they could be 'free'. A second reason was the increasing importance of Cape Town. The amount of shipping calling there increased each year. Every vessel demanded stores of meat, grain and wine for the long journey eastward or westwards. With an increasing demand for farm produce the government could hardly restrict the spread of European farming. The slave trade was the third factor which influenced the growth of the colony. Slaves were imported mostly from East Africa but others came from Asia. Some of the local peoples were enslaved by white farmers after successful battles or raids with San or Khoikhoi communities. Slaves were used as manual workers, espec-

Table Bay in 1851. Table Bay had already become an important harbour frequented by the ships of many nations.

ially on arable farms. As the settlers penetrated further inland in search of land the Cape government extended the colony's frontiers to keep the adventurous farmers within its jurisdiction. And so, gradually, a new society came into existence, that of the Boers or 'Afrikaners'.

From the beginning racialism was a fundamental element in the thinking of the Boer settler. He despised the black man as an uncivilized savage and, being ignorant of the differences between communities, referred to all Africans as '*kaffirs*'.* Many settlers married or had sexual relations with African women but this did not lead to a mingling of races and cultures. It only produced a new group situated socially between the white and black communities. This was the 'Cape Coloured' people.

The settlers' church – the Dutch Reformed Church – provided a religious basis for racialist philosophy. Its doctrines were extreme Protestant and were largely based on the Old Testament. Its clergy taught that racial inequality was part of God's plan for the world and that white people were meant to rule over people of other colours. Towards the end of the eighteenth century, when other Christian churches in Europe and North America were condemning slavery and slave trading, the Dutch Reformed Church continued to give its blessing to these evils.

The Boers were largely cut off from all Western influences. They became a culturally-isolated and inward-looking community. Most of them were rough, hardy, ignorant men. The churches ran primary schools but apart from that there was no education and many settlers were illiterate. They developed their own language – Afrikaans – which was developed from Dutch, but included a few Portuguese, Khoikhoi and Malay words.† They were a stubborn and independent people and many of them were prepared to trek further into the interior whenever they felt that their freedom was being restricted by the government.

Early conflicts between Boers and Africans

South of the Vaal River there are no tsetse fly. This means that horses and oxen, as well as cattle and sheep, can flourish. This, in turn, means that men can travel easily over long distances on horseback and can

---

*The word *kaffir* originated with the Arab merchants of the eastern coast of Africa. They used it to describe infidels (i.e. non-Muslims). The term was taken over by many colonisers as a derogatory description of Africans.
† A number of slaves and immigrants came from Dutch colonies in South-East Asia.   53

take all their belongings with them in ox-carts. Long before the trek Boers set out in search of land and political freedom bands of the newcomers were wandering over a large area for reasons of trade. By the middle of the eighteenth century they were travelling as far as the Great Kei River (though the government forbade penetration beyond the Gamtoos River). They traded for ivory with the Thembu and they bought or stole cattle from the Khoikhoi and Xhosa. Though this led to frequent clashes between the settlers and various African groups, both sides benefited from trade.

It was the white farmer whose presence was really resented by the Africans. The Boers wanted large farms. It was every settler's aim to live where he could not see the smoke from his neighbour's chimney and 12,000 hectares was considered the smallest size for a holding.

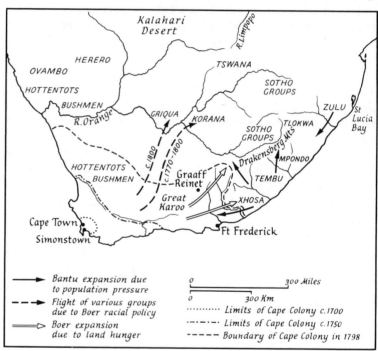

The expansion of Cape Colony 1652–1795. The Dutch East India Co. repeatedly moved the boundary to maintain control over settlers and stop conflict with Africans.

The trekkers were frequently in conflict with the Khoikhoi, though less so after 1713, when the latter's numbers were reduced by small-pox. By this time warfare with the San had become continuous and bitter. The Boers were determined to force the hunters out of their hunting grounds. The San retaliated by attacking Boer cattle and small groups of settlers with their deadly poisoned arrows. But the

54

small men of the bush could not win. By 1800 the San had disappeared completely from many areas, either killed or driven out by the more powerful white man.

Across the Great Fish River the settlers found a more formidable enemy. The southern Nguni, the Thembu and the Xhosa, were still steadily moving southwards and westwards as population increase forced them to seek new lands. From the middle of the eighteenth century fighting and raiding between Boers and Xhosa became frequent. The government tried to stop the conflict by forbidding farmers to settle beyond the Gamtoos River but this order was ignored. In 1778 the government accepted the situation and brought the eastern region as far as the Fish River into the colony.

This for the first time brought the Cape government into official contact with the Xhosa and only led to worse trouble. The following year, in revenge for the murder of one of their men, the Xhosa raided across the new boundary. The white government organized a small army to punish the invaders, which it did, killing many Xhosa and capturing 5,000 cattle. This First Xhosa (or Kaffir) War was the first of many.

The Kora, Gona and Griqua

The spread of white settlement in South Africa led not only to conflict with and destruction of the original inhabitants; it also led to the formation of new societies. These were people who, after living for some decades alongside the Afrikaners in the Cape, at last decided that they could no longer tolerate the white man's treatment of them. They therefore migrated eastwards and northwards in the closing years of the eighteenth century. Basically these people were Khoikhoi but some of them were the result of intermarriage between Khoikhoi and Dutch settlers. They had all adopted features from the European way of life. They rode horses and used guns. They trekked with ox-carts. They understood new methods of breeding and rearing cattle. Some were Christians, some spoke Afrikaans and a few could read and write.

Three main groups of these coloured peoples are distinguishable. The Gona lived in the eastern Cape. The Griqua and the Kora lived along the middle reaches of the Orange River. Their way of life was a mixture of hunting, herding, trading and brigandage. They lived in bands usually of between sixty and a hundred people, but frequently joined together into larger hordes for raiding or warfare. They hunted elephants and other animals and bartered ivory, skins and cattle for guns, ammunition and other necessities. These powerful groups were respected and feared by African and European alike.　55

6. The growth of long-distance trade

The growth of inter-community trade

The most important early trading centre yet excavated in the whole of sub-Equatorial Africa – Ingombe Ilede – is situated near large salt deposits. This is no accident; control of an important salt supply was obviously the basis of the Ingombe Ilede merchants' wealth and power. It brought traders long distances to their market. For salt was as important to early Iron Age Africans as it was (and is) to all men at all times. Many villages obtained their salt from lakes or plants but supplies gained in this way were small and of poor quality. The best supplies of salt, both for quantity and quality, came from salt lakes. The salt water was boiled or left in the sun to evaporate and the salt was then made into bricks. In this form salt was bartered from village to village and might end up a long way from the place where it was produced. But a long time before our period begins some people were probably travelling long distances to fetch their own salt from the salt pans.

Major long-distance trade routes c. 1800.

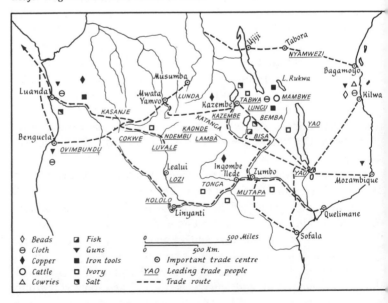

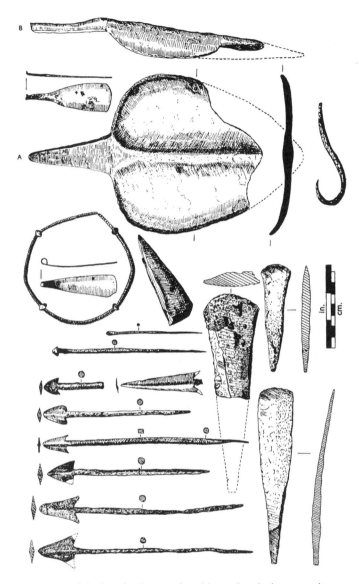

These are some of the iron implements found by archaeologists on a site at Khami, near Bulawayo. The large item near the top is a hoe. Other implements include spearheads and axes.

For farming, iron and iron tools were vital. Without axes and hoes it was very difficult to clear and till the ground. Like salt, iron was only produced in certain areas. The knowledge of how to smelt it and make it into tools was only possessed by certain clans which guarded their 57 secrets well. Sometimes the people living near iron deposits bartered lumps of iron-bearing rock for things they needed. But much more often they made tools themselves and used them as articles of trade. As well as hoes and axes they made arrowheads, spearheads, razors, ceremonial gongs and bells and chiefly regalia.

Like salt blocks, iron hoes became a widely accepted 'coinage'. Sometimes people acquired hoes through trade and melted them down to make into other tools and weapons. As time went by the iron-workers became more skilful, and at sites like Ingombe Ilede a variety of iron objects have been found.

Copper deposits are to be found right across the middle of Africa from the lower Congo to the lower Limpopo. Most of these deposits were being worked by the sixteenth century. By far the most important mines, however, were on the Copper Belt in modern Katanga and Zambia. At Sanga, in Katanga, archaeologists discovered graves of people who lived long before A.D. 1000 and who owned goods made of copper. Similar items have been found in sites over a wide area and these can only have reached the people who owned them by way of trade.

Iron Age copper goods seem to fall into two categories: decorative items and trade items. Wealthy Africans wore copper rings, bracelets, chains and bangles. At Sanga, Ingombe Ilede and other sites copper ingots, usually in the shape of an X have been found. These were used as another kind of currency.

Salt, iron and copper were thus traded between communities of Africans living many kilometres apart from each other. To this list we can probably add pottery, for most villages produced their own pots yet some craftsmen were so skilled that their pots were in great demand elsewhere. If these items, of which evidence remains, were traded over long distances, there is no reason to suppose that other perishable goods were not also carried along the caravan routes. Grain, cattle, hut-poles, skins – these and other items were important to Early Iron Age Africans. As they were not readily available in all areas at all times they must have been bought and sold.

As time went by certain trade routes became well defined and commerce became an importance part of life in many communities. Much of the region is well served by navigable waterways – the Congo, Zambezi, Limpopo, Orange, Vaal and their tributaries. These made the task of transport easier. Market villages and towns developed where people met regularly for the exchange of goods. Trade itself became a profitable occupation and certain clans specialised in it. Chiefs encouraged trade and profited by it in a number of ways. They collected tolls from caravans passing through their territory. They levied taxes on market transactions. They engaged in trade on their own account. Frequently they waged war on neighbouring rulers with the aim of bringing important markets or production centres under their control, thereby increasing their wealth. For instance when the Lunda ruler, the Mwata Yamvo, sent Cinyanta eastwards in the late seventeenth century, his main aim was to gain control of salt workings and copper deposits in the region of the upper Lualaba. As we have seen, this expedition led to the establishment of the East Lunda kingdom, known as Kazembe.

The impact of foreign traders

The Arabs were established in settlements by A.D. 1000, but rarely penetrated beyond the coast because the coastal rulers would not allow them to do so. The foreigners did travel up the Zambezi. They established trading posts in the valley, such as Sena, and did business in many of the towns and villages to the south. They brought with them cloth, beads and cowries to trade for gold, ivory and copper. Though they were few in number and their activities were strictly controlled by rulers such as the Mwene Mutapa, they did stimulate trading activities over a wide region. Beads and shells have been found at archaeological sites far inland, thus proving beyond doubt that these areas were linked to the coast by a long chain of commercial activity.

When they were disappointed they concentrated on ivory and slaves, particularly the latter as the plantations of the Americas and the West African offshore islands developed. Few Europeans cared to force their way deep into the continent and African rulers did not want white traders crossing their land. What happened was that some of the peoples in closest contact with the Portuguese, such as the Ovimbundu, went on trading and raiding expeditions into the interior. They took European cloth and beads and occasionally guns. Those trading nations which were powerful enough could dominate a long trade route. However where they came upon a well-organised and strong inland state they were at the mercy of its ruler and had to trade on his terms. The seventeenth and eighteenth centuries saw a considerable expansion of long-distance commerce and by 1800 well used caravan routes spanned the entire continent.

Trade routes. (1) Routes to the west coast

By 1800 three major trade routes had developed, which reached far into the interior. They had their coastal starting points in the ports 59 of Loango, Luanda and Benguela, and some of the traders had established firm commercial contacts with Musumba, the capital of the Lunda Empire.

These long-distance routes probably did not develop until the seventeenth century, when European demand stimulated African middlemen to penetrate further inland in pursuit of ivory and slaves. But Kongo and Angola had a vigorous commercial life before the Portuguese arrived. Salt, iron and copper all featured in this trade. Excellent rock salt was produced at Kisama south of the Kwanza River. Iron ore was found about 160 kilometres inland from Luanda. There were deposits of copper at Bembe in Kongo and north of the River Congo at Mindouli. People travelled long distances for these goods.

Let us look at the three principal west coast routes in turn. Starting in the north we have the route centred on Loango. Before Europeans arrived on this part of the coast the coastal peoples, the Vili, were already active participants in a trade with peoples of the hinterland. Articles of barter included palm oil, palm cloth, ivory, dried fish, copper, salt and redwood. Palm cloth had become a kind of currency. It was in the 1570s that the Portuguese began regular trading at the port of Loango and the Vili of Loango were quick to adapt their commercial activities to the demands of the foreigners. At the end of the sixteenth century the Dutch arrived and established a base at Loango. There was for many decades considerable rivalry between merchants from the two European countries but the local ruler, the Maloango, maintained a firm control of all traders, both Vili and foreigners.

The Europeans took an interest in all the traditional trade goods offered by the Vili, but in the early years their main concern was for ivory. Under the onslaught of hunters the elephant herds near the coast were depleted and many survivors retreated further inland to escape their attackers. This, probably more than anything else, was responsible for the lengthening of Vili trade routes. By the early seventeenth century their caravans were visiting Stanley Pool and the fringes of the Congo forest further north. There they exchanged salt, palm oil, cloth and cheap European goods for ivory supplied by pygmy hunters from the forest. The traders also crossed into the Kongo kingdom in search of ivory. Copper was also an important staple of the Vili trade. By the mid-seventeenth century they controlled the smelting and transporting of copper from the mines of Mindouli, even though these mines were in Teke country.

The Maloango grew rich and powerful on this trade. He maintained firm control of the markets and used the tolls to increase the size and improve the equipment of his army. His military power enabled him to extend his territory and exact tribute from vassal states as well as providing greater security for merchants. He prevented the Europeans from becoming too powerful and may even, for a time, have resisted their demands to open his port to the slave trade.

However, the demand for slaves increased and his own people as well as the foreigners wanted to participate in this lucrative trade. Now that the Vili trading empire had become so large, slaves were easier to obtain. Thus from the middle of the seventeenth century the slave trade expanded rapidly. By 1670 the Dutch were exporting about 3,000 slaves every year and a hundred years later the number of slaves exported by many nations had reached over 16,000 per year. By that time Vili traders were venturing deep into Kongo and they had trade contacts as much as 650 kilometres up the Congo River from Stanley Pool. They were in contact with peoples 400 kilometres inland to the north-east who supplied them with slaves in return for guns. To the south they traded with the Matamba, thus robbing the Portuguese of the Angola coast of some of their trade.

By the mid-eighteenth century Loanga was an extremely important port. Shipping from almost every European country called there. But it did not maintain its position of leadership much longer. The English and Portuguese set up bases at Cabinda and Malemba. The peoples of this part of the coast, the Kagongo and Ngoyo, were able to stop some of the caravans on their way back to Loango and divert them to their own coastal markets. But the demand was so great and the traders so active that there was profit for all. Guns, supplied without restriction by French, English and Dutch traders, were in widespread use and did much to enhance the power and prestige of inland leaders involved in the trade. Many of these leaders grew rich from the profits of the slave trade and from tolls levied on caravans passing through their territory.

Further south in Angola it was probably trade centred on the salt mines of Kisama which led to the development of the port of Luanda. Traders came from long distances to obtain salt and because the commercial activity round Kisama presented the possibility of penetration of the interior the Portuguese established themselves at Luanda. It may well have been a quest for salt which brought groups of Imbangala westwards into Angola in the mid-sixteenth century. The early seventeenth century in Angola was largely dominated by the attempts of the Portuguese and the Kasanje Imbangala to gain control of the Cuanza valley and the surrounding territory. Eventually, as we have seen, the Kasanje allied themselves with the white men against Ndongo. Clearly trade lay at the root of this alliance. The Kasanje (and the Matamba) controlled the area between the Kwanza and

Kwango Rivers. By trade and by exacting tribute from conquered peoples they obtained slaves and ivory, which the Portuguese were eager to buy. In exchange the Portuguese could offer guns (though Portuguese colonial governments, in the interests of security, tried to restrict the spread of firearms), palm cloth from Loango and salt (for by this time they controlled the Kisama mines).

The Kasanje and Mutamba were careful not to become too closely involved with the Portuguese; they did not want to share the fate of Kongo and Ndongo. In 1630 the Kasanje moved further east to an area where they would be more secure and from where they could control the Holo saltpans. Throughout the seventeenth and eighteenth centuries the Europeans made repeated attempts to force their way eastwards beyond the upper Kwanza but the Matamba and Kasanje proved too strong for them. They found it more satisfactory to deal with these people on a commercial basis than on a military basis.

So the Kwango River states were in a strong position to control trade between Central Africa and the west coast. By 1650 Kasanje merchants had reached the heart of the Lunda Empire and were trading in its capital. As well as trade goods the merchants introduced new crops such as manioc and maize to the Lunda. By the end of the century the Mwata Yamvo was regularly sending his own caravans to Cassanje. In the eighteenth century copper from the Kazembe-controlled Katanga mines was finding its way westwards. Though Portuguese power in Angola gradually grew, the white men had not succeeded in breaking the trade monopoly of the Matamba and Kasanje by 1800.

It may have been the traditional restless, warlike life of the Ovimbundu kingdoms which enabled them to take to slave trading with such ease. By the mid-seventeenth century some of these states had allied with the Portuguese and had obtained guns which they used in raids on their neighbours. Within a century most of the peoples of southern Angola had firearms, though the Bailundu and Bihé had emerged as the leading slave traders. By 1800 there were many trading settlements throughout Ovimbundu territory where Portuguese and pombeiros did business with the local people.

Beeswax and ivory were other important trade items. These mostly came from the Cokwe further east. The Cokwe were expert hunters and they also knew how to obtain honey and wax from the hives of wild bees which swarmed in the forests of their homeland. These goods were brought by Ovimbundu traders down to the coast at Benguela. But the Cokwe also fell victim to Ovimbundu slaving exploits as did other peoples east of the Kwanza. It was not until the nineteenth century that the Ovimbundu gained their reputation as 'the greatest traders of Bantu Africa' and began to travel right across the continent. But they had already penetrated deep into central Africa by 1800 and soon after were challenging the Imbangala for control of the routes to Mwata Yamvo.

(2) Routes to the east coast

Now we transfer our attention to the other side of the continent to see what commercial contacts the peoples of the Central African interior had with the east coast before 1800. There was one really important route along which goods flowed to and from the east coast and that was the Zambezi valley. Besides this there was a complex of routes to the north linking Kazembe with the Zambezi valley and the coast. These routes involved, principally, the Bisa, Malawi and Yao peoples. Further south there were Shona caravan routes which terminated at the port of Sofala. Beyond the Limpopo the peoples of south-east Africa had established important commercial contacts with Delagoa Bay. There were other routes in operation. For instance there was an active 'trade-chain' system among the peoples of northern Zambia and south-west Tanzania, through what is called the Lakes Tanganyika–Nyasa Corridor. However, we shall confine our attention to the four long-distance routes indicated above.

The Zambezi River provided contact between peoples of the coast and those of the far interior from a very early period. Excavations at Ingombe Ilede have provided evidence of what was probably only one of a number of important trading settlements in the Zambezi valley. Portuguese written accounts of the sixteenth century and later confirm that the peoples of the middle Zambezi carried out a thriving trade in ivory and copper (the gold presumably coming by way of trade with the Shona south of the river). Arab merchants were travelling up the river by the end of the fifteenth century, and probably much earlier, to exchange cloth, beads and shells for ivory and copper. The Tonga, Lenje and other peoples north of the river also crossed the Zambezi in canoes to trade copper with the people of Mutapa, probably in return for gold and salt. The Arab trade probably intensified early in the sixteenth century when the Portuguese captured Sofala and attempted to dominate the gold trade of the Mutapa Empire.

But bad days were coming for the traders of the middle Zambezi. The Portuguese decided to put a stop to Arab riverain commerce. They were annoyed by the gold dealers who were eluding them by sending their merchandise northwards to the Arab depots, instead of eastwards to Sofala. By the middle of the sixteenth century they had garrisoned Quelimane at the coast and established posts at Tete and 63

Sene. At the same time the Malawi dominated the northern bank of the lower Zambezi (see below, p. 24–5). All would have been well for the merchants if the Portuguese had themselves carried on the Arab trade. But the Portuguese were mastered by the desire to enrich themselves with gold and had little time for trade in other commodities.

However, the situation had already begun to improve. At the end of the seventeenth century most of the Portuguese had been driven out of Mutapa by Changamire Dombo. They were forced now to pay more attention to the area north of the river. In 1714 they set up a trading post at Zumbo and to it began to flow goods from the people living to the west, north and north-east.

The Lenje were the principal suppliers to the Europeans. They and their neighbours, the Soli, produced iron goods. These they traded for copper from the middle Kafue region and from the Lamba people further north. The Lamba, the Nsenga and many other peoples hunted elephant and most of the ivory found its way to Zumbo. Cloth and beads were still the main imports for which the products of this area were exchanged. The Lamba also traded with Kazembe and formed a link between the East Lunda kingdom and the traders of the middle Zambezi. But most of Kazembe's eastern trade was dominated by the Bisa. Some Portuguese expeditions trekked northwards from the river towards Kazembe but the rivalry of the white man was stoutly resisted by local traders and no permanent Portuguese bases were established away from the river. In the eighteenth century the Tonga seem to have established contact along the upper Zambezi valley with traders from the west.

The principal long-distance traders of the large area to the north of the middle and lower Zambezi were the Malawi, Bisa and Yao. The expansion of Malawi trade began in the late sixteenth century with the wars and raids of the Malawi chief, Lundu, from his base in the Shiré valley. As we have seen, Lundu, attempting to set up a kingdom independent of the Kalonga, extended his control over the Lomwe and Makua and over a wide area between the Shiré and the coast. Lundu probably also had economic motives for his empire-building. He wanted to escape from the commercial control exercised by the Kalonga, who for instance would not allow chiefs to trade in ivory without his permission. He also resented the Portuguese domination of trade on the Zambezi. In the early years of the seventeenth century he therefore established a direct trade route between the Shiré valley and Mossuril, on the coast opposite Mozambique.

Lundu's rebellion was subsequently crushed by the Kalonga but his conquests remained under vague Malawi control. For most of the seventeenth century the Malawi and their neighbours were able to trade north of the river quite free of Portuguese control. The main article of trade was ivory and the Europeans had to cross to Mossuril to exchange cloth and guns for it. This Malawi trading monopoly was broken in the eighteenth century as the Makua and their neighbours managed to escape from Malawi control and as the Yao to the north extended their trading activities.

Over the commercial world of what is now north-eastern Zambia the Bisa reigned supreme. Bisa society was organised in small groups many of which led a semi-migratory existence. It is not surprising therefore that trade played an important part in their life. They obtained fish from Lake Bengweulu and exchanged it with the Tabwa for salt. Iron, pottery, copper, cattle, and a variety of other goods passed through their hands and by the seventeenth century, if not before, they had become the major entrepreneurs. By the eighteenth century they were travelling as far as Tete and the Shiré valley and some Bisa communities had settled in Cewa country. About the middle of the century the western Bisa peoples came under the control of Kazembe and had to pay tribute to the East Lunda leader. From this time onwards the Bisa became Kazembe's important link with the Zambezi valley and the east coast traders. They took ivory from the Lunda and the Lamba and traded it at Tete for European and Indian cloth, beads and cowries. When the Portuguese began demanding slaves instead of ivory the Bisa chose the Yao as their trading partners instead, exchanging their goods at markets in the Shiré valley. Since Kazembe's kingdom was in regular contact with Musumba, it can be seen that the Bisa and Yao completed a trading chain which, by 1750, stretched right across the continent, bringing to the Lunda peoples in the heart of Africa a variety of foreign goods from east and west. These goods included guns, various kinds of cloth, procelain, umbrellas, mirrors, iron pots and tools. From Kazembe went copper from the mines of Katanga, which by 1800 was already famous in many countries for its excellent quality.

The last long-distance traders of the area north of the Zambezi whom we are going to discuss are the Yao. As we have seen these restless peoples were already important traders in the area east of Lake Nyasa in the sixteenth century. At first they exchanged their own produce, tobacco, hoes and animal skins with the Arabs and Swahili for salt, cloth and beads. The main market that attracted them was Kilwa. Then they began to carry coastal goods to their neighbours in the south-west, who gave them cattle in exchange. It did not take them long to discover that the Arabs and the Portuguese, who controlled most of the coast in the sixteenth and seventeenth centuries, valued ivory above all. This they obtained themselves by

The ruler of Kazembe. In this modern picture the ruler wears traditional regalia.

hunting or bought from the Malawi. In 1698 the Portuguese, whose power had long been in decline, lost control of the coast north of Cape Delgado. For a while Kilwa's importance as a port dwindled and the Yao had to seek a market for ivory elsewhere. They turned to Mossuril, no longer dominated by the Malawi. By the mid-eighteenth century the trade in ivory supplied to Mozambique by the Yao and Makua had become the basis of the island's economy. Between the years 1759 and 1761 Mozambique exported about 450 tons of ivory to India,* and most of this was provided by the Yao.

Later in the eighteenth century most Yao caravan leaders turned away from Mozambique and resumed trade with Kilwa and other towns to the north-east. There were three main reasons for this: the northern coast under the rule of Omani Arabs had become a flourishing trade area; cloth and other imported goods were cheaper there; and the Makua frequently disturbed Yao trade with Mossuril.

The ivory trade grew steadily as Yao activity increased. Regular contact was established with Bisa traders on the other side of Lake Nyasa. This trade was organised by small village chiefs who, by trading, grew rich and powerful. With much of their wealth they used to buy slaves, some of which they sold at Kilwa and some of which they kept to swell the ranks of their own followers. By the end of the eighteenth century the Yao had earned a name for themselves, not only as intrepid long-distance traders, but also as fierce slave raiders. Much of the area between Lake Nyasa and the coast had been laid waste by Yao slavers, supplied by the Arabs with guns.

Something has already been said about the Arab and Portuguese gold trade with the Mutapa and Rozwi empires. Now we must see how that trade formed part of the commercial life of the Shona peoples. Shonaland is richly provided with minerals. Iron, copper, tin and gold deposits are found over a wide area and salt can be panned in a number of places. This led to a flourishing internal trade throughout the area. It was probably the demand for salt which led to trade with the Muslims along the Zambezi and at the coast. Supplies of salt were not adequate and the salt pans were situated far to the west. It was probably sometime in the thirteenth or fourteenth century that the main gold trade route was established from Zimbabwe to Sofala, probably following the Lundi and Sabi Rivers. The reason for the development of regular trade was the growth of Rozwi power in the southern part of the region, around the Limpopo. Tribute reached the Mambos in the form of gold, copper, ivory and other goods. The rulers also controlled gold mining, which was carried out by slaves, and ivory hunting. When they had a large enough supply they sent a caravan to the coast. In return they received salt, cloth and beads. With these they could enhance their own prestige, reward servants and extend their power.

*The actual figure was 1,720 *bares*, and the *bare* had a fluctuating value, between 518 and 650 lb. Cf. A. E. Alpers, 'The Malawi Empire and the Yao', note 55 in H. N. Chittick and R. I. Rotberg (eds.), *East Africa and the Orient.*

The volume of trade increased with the establishment of the Mwene Mutapa Empire in the fifteenth century. Before this, trade had already been established by the Dande and others with Arab trading posts on the lower Zambezi. Perhaps there even existed a long trade chain by which Rhodesian gold found its way overland to Kilwa. It was the well-established gold trade to Sofala which so excited the Portuguese. But by the time they arrived this route had already dwindled in importance. When the Mwene Mutapa moved his capital further north (largely in order to control trade along the Zambezi) his control of the southern areas of the empire declined. The rival Rozwi line began to dominate the south and the old Mutapa Empire was split in two. The commercial result of these disturbances was that much less gold and ivory flowed to the Sofala coast.

From the mid-sixteenth century the Zambezi valley took over as the principal trade route serving Shonaland. In Mutapa the Portuguese established control over trade at the fairs, as we have seen. This lasted until Changamire Dombo's invasion of Mutapa at the end of the seventeenth century. Dombo continued to trade with the Portuguese, but very much on his own terms. He only permitted trade to Zumbo and allowed no Europeans into his territory. The Portuguese merchants therefore had to rely on their African agents – *mussambazes*. These made annual journeys to the goldfields, where they bought metal on the Changamire's terms. The Changamire demanded cloth, beads, alcohol and, above all, guns in exchange for gold. But although trade was under strict government control it flourished. The average annual output of gold exported from Butua (the most important mining area) alone was worth about £30,000 (in terms of modern value).

Though Zumbo was the most important trading port the fortunes of Tete and Sofala revived in the eighteenth century. The Manica seem to have been the entrepreneurs on the route to Sofala. They bought gold, copper, iron and ivory from peoples further inland and transported them to the coast. Other items known to have been sold in Manica markets are beeswax, rock-crystal, honey, cotton, skins and cattle.

7. New pressures
(1) The Mfecane

Dingiswayo, Zwide and Sobhuza

By the beginning of the nineteenth century important social and political changes were taking place among the northern Nguni. The basic reason for these changes was the growth of population which was leading to serious shortages of food and grazing land between the Drakensberg and the coast. This led the many chiefdoms and sub-chiefdoms of the northern Nguni to be in a state of almost constant conflict with each other. As you might expect, these troubles led to

Northern Nguni chiefdoms.

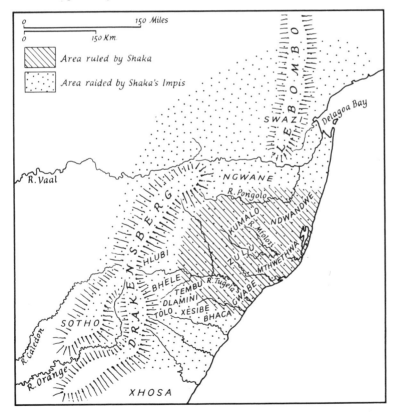

some chiefdoms growing stronger at the expense of others and three powerful Nguni states emerged in the northern area, the Ndwandwe, the Mthethwa and the Ngwane. Though the development of these states had been going on for some time we can point to three 'founders', each of whom did more than anyone else to establish the greatness of his chiefdom. They were Zwide of the Ndwandwe, Dingiswayo of the Mthethwa and Sobhuza of the Ngwane.

Zwide was an important chief in the area north of the Mfolozi River. He made war on his neighbours in order to add their lands to his own and perhaps also in order to control the trade routes to Delagoa Bay. As with Dingiswayo (see below) Zwide's strength probably lay in his reorganisation of the army. Traditional Nguni initiation ceremonies involved a period of ritual seclusion for young men about to be admitted to the full life of the society. This custom caused critical weakness in times of war. Some chiefdoms therefore abandoned it, requiring instead that their young men undergo military service in special regiments based on age-sets. Zwide probably made these age-set regiments the basis of Ndwandwe expansion. Conquered peoples also had to send regiments of young warriors to the army. Zwide fought successfully against the other two great emerging leaders of the region. Sobhuza was beaten and forced northwards into what is now Swaziland. Zwide's long conflict with Dingiswayo came to an end in 1817 or 1818. During a battle Dingiswayo left the main army to climb a nearby hill for a better view. Some of the Ndwandwe ambushed him and killed him. Zwide won the battle and Mthethwa power was destroyed. However, his success was short-lived. In 1819 he was defeated in battle by Shaka (see below) and his empire was broken up.

Sobhuza may have begun his career of expansion in order to protect his people against Ndwandwe and Mthethwa attacks. He took over a small chieftaincy in about 1815 and began uniting with his neighbours and reorganising his army. After his defeat by Zwide he led his people across the Pongolo River into the mountainous region beyond, where they could defend themselves more easily. More Nguni and Sotho chiefs joined him and it was from these mixed origins that the Swazi nation grew. Sobhuza died in about 1836 and was succeeded by his son Mswazi, after whom the people came to be called.

Dingiswayo seized power by ousting his brother from the leadership of the Mthethwa sometime after the death of his father (c.1800). He too changed the ritual and military customs of his people, forming powerful, united bands of young warriors. But he took the process further than any of his contemporaries. He took great care over the training of his regiments, or *impis*. Each had a distinctive dress and standard and every warrior was intensely proud of his *impi*. New techniques of warfare were worked out. Furthermore, Dingiswayo transformed the traditional raiding party or temporary army into a permanent or *standing* army. With this new, efficient fighting unit Dingiswayo extended Mthethwa authority over most of the neighbouring Nguni chiefdoms until his power was checked by the Ndwandwe. These chiefdoms became junior partners in a loose confederacy united by allegiance to Dingiswayo and fear of the army. As we have seen, Dingiswayo was eventually killed in battle against Zwide and his confederacy collapsed.

Shaka, king of the Zulus.

Shaka and the Zulus

This paved the way for the rise of Shaka. Shaka was born in about 1787, the illegitimate son of Senzengakona, the Zulu chief. The Zulus were a small Nguni group – perhaps 2,000 strong – who were soon to fall under Mthethwa control. During his childhood Shaka and his mother were rejected by his father's people and the young man became very bitter. He was determined to prove that he was a better man than his half-brothers by becoming the next chief. He joined Dingiswayo's army and soon proved himself a born soldier. Not only was he a brave warrior, he was also a clever tactician. He planned battles, training tactics and even devised new types of weapons and equipment. His ability was recognised: he was promoted to head of his *impi* and became a favourite of Dingiswayo. When in 1816 Senzengakona died, Shaka gained Dingiswayo's support in his claim for the chieftaincy. He marched back to Zululand with some of his followers, deposed the new leader without any difficulty, and became the Zulu chief. One of his great ambitions was thus fulfilled. As leader of the Zulus he began trying out his military ideas straight away. Warriors had to live under strict conditions until they were forty years of age. Training and discipline were very hard. For instance Shaka made his men fight barefoot, instead of wearing sandals as the custom had been before. Zulu warriors were taught to be fearless and ruthless and to kill women and children if ordered to do so.

Men trained in this way made very good soldiers but there were other reasons why Shaka's armies were so effective. The success of the Zulus in battle rested on four main tactics. First of all they used a short, stabbing spear, introduced by Shaka. This meant that after the enemy had thrown their spears the Zulus could quickly close with them and kill many with their own sword-like spears. Secondly Shaka always tried to surprise his enemies. He used spies, smoke signals and runners to gather information so that he could strike when his opponents were unprepared. Thirdly the Zulus used a variety of battle tactics which were varied according to prevailing conditions. The most famous of Shaka's battle formations was the 'cowhorn' formation. One or two regiments would engage the enemy while other regiments circled round at each side to enclose them, like the curved horns of a cow. Fourthly Shaka showed no mercy to defeated enemies. He was not prepared to allow them partial independence in a confederation; complete control was his object. He murdered chiefs and their heirs unless he was quite sure of their loyalty and he put his own trusted servants in charge of conquered territory.

Thus Shaka had already begun to expand Zululand before Dingiswayo's death. However, he was loyal to the Mthethwa chief as long as he lived. When Dingiswayo was killed in 1817 or 1818 his confederation broke up, but within a very short space of time Shaka was reforging it into a Zulu empire. He murdered the new Mthethwa ruler and put his own candidate on the throne. He won or forced the allegiance of those chiefs who had followed Dingiswayo. He trained their armies in his own way. He defeated powerful enemies like Zwide. The expansion of Shaka's state was extraordinarily rapid. By 1820 he controlled all the land east of the Drakensbergs between the Pongola and Tukela Rivers, and his men raided over a far wider area.

The Mfecane

This was the beginning of the Mfecane* – the 'turmoil', the 'time of troubles' – when, as one writer has put it, 'Every community throughout approximately a fifth of the African continent was profoundly affected, and many were utterly disrupted'.† Zulu raids started off a 'chain reaction' of violence. Shaka's hordes broke up the chiefdoms and confederations of their rivals. They devastated vast tracts of territory. Survivors were forced to flee over long distances to find new land and to escape from the Zulus. Bands of refugees wandered the countryside. Some were absorbed by other communities. The Fingo of southern Nguniland, for instance, originated in refugees who sought shelter among the Xhosa. But such immigrant groups only made the population problem worse. Most Nguni chiefs were not prepared to accept the homeless wanderers. What the refugees could not gain peacefully they tried to obtain by force. They banded together into armies to invade settled communities. Some failed and were destroyed. Others succeeded.

Some groups of wandering invaders came into being in a different way. When a powerful state such as Zwide's broke up, some of the generals, still ambitious, gathered a group of warriors together and began raiding for cattle and land on their own account. Some of Shaka's indunas left him in this way. As these men were successful more and more people followed them and they travelled over longer and longer distances.

Like ripples on the surface of a lake when a stone is thrown in, these invading groups spread outwards from the centre of the Mfecane. Where they were successful the raiders in their turn drove out others who moved further afield to clash with the inhabitants of yet more distant lands. In this way a complex series of violent migrations

---

*This is known by the Sotho as the *Difaqane*, 'the time of forced migration'.

† L. Thompson in the *Oxford History of South Africa*, Vol. I (Oxford, 1969), p. 345.

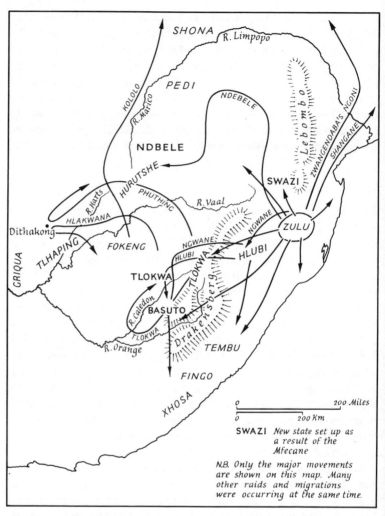

The impact of Zulu expansion.

occurred throughout south-east Africa and dominated the history of the whole area for over twenty years.

Shoshangane and Zwangendaba

One of Zwide's leading warriors was Shoshangane. Not long after his master's defeat Shoshangane began to collect a personal following. In about 1821 he began to move northwards. He attacked and over-
74 threw the Tsonga. He destroyed the Portuguese base at Delagoa Bay

and moved on into the coastal plain of what is now Mozambique. Here his people, the Shangane (or Gaza), dominated a wide region and were soon able to control trade between the coast and the interior. Leading as they did a life based on violence and warfare, the Shangane accumulated many prisoners. These became the basis of a revitalised trade in slaves with the Portuguese. Shoshangane's power was put to the test in 1828 when Shaka sent an army to invade his territory. On this occasion the usually victorious Zulus were defeated. With this threat past Shoshangane continued his empire-building. By 1830 he dominated most of the area between the lower Zambezi and Limpopo Rivers. Many Shona groups had been absorbed or driven out and Shoshangane was collecting tribute from Portuguese traders at Sofala, Tete and Sena.

Zwangendaba's early career was similar to Shoshangane's. He, too, was one of Zwide's lieutenants and he, too, fled northwards along a path similar to Shoshangane's. Indeed, for some years he and his followers lived close to the Shangane settlements north of Delagoa Bay. But in 1831 Shoshangane drove him out. Zwangendaba was forced into the territory of the Rozwi, with results which we shall discuss fully in chapter 10. All we need say here about Zwangendaba is that his wanderings make one of the more remarkable pages of African history. With his steadily growing band of followers he travelled over 3,000 kilometres from his original home. When he died in about 1848 his bones were laid to rest near Lake Rukwa in what is now Tanzania.

Mzilikazi

In about 1818 Shaka took control of a small Kumalo chiefdom whose ruler was Mzilikazi, and Mzilikazi became a leader in the Zulu army. In 1822 Shaka sent Mzilikazi on a raid into Sotho country. The raid was successful and the warriors returned driving many head of cattle before them. But Mzilikazi refused to give up all the spoils of war to his overlord. Shaka was angry and made plans to have Mzilikazi murdered. Mzilikazi fled, taking with him two or three hundred warriors and so became a wandering warlord, plundering and devastating in the eastern Transvaal north of Swaziland. He was very successful and conquered many of the Sotho communities. As his fame and power grew other Sotho leaders placed themselves under Mzilikazi's protection, while Nguni and Sotho refugees flocked to his camp. Soon Mzilikazi's mixed following became known as the Ndebele.

Despite his power and success Mzilikazi was afraid of the Zulus. He found it difficult to settle and was always moving his camp north-

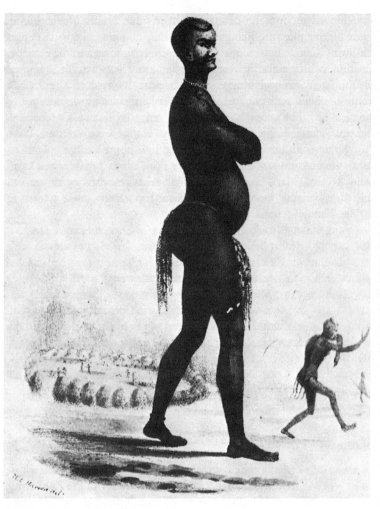

Mzilikazi, king of the Ndebele.

wards or westwards to put more distance between himself and Shaka.
He had cause to be afraid. The Zulus frequently invaded his territory
even after Shaka's death (1828). In 1832 Mzilikazi did establish a
more permanent settlement near the source of the Marico River. It
was a fertile area and a good base for his military operations. From
here his armies and raiding parties fought over most of the Transvaal
and beyond. By this time Mzilikazi dominated an area of some
7,500,000 hectares between the Limpopo, the Molopo, the Marico and
the Vaal, and in raids further afield his armies came into conflict with
the Pedi, the Shona, the Griqua and many others. The next stage of

Mzilikazi's story is bound up with the history of the Boers and will be dealt with later.

Moshweshwe

Another great leader thrown up by the Mfecane was Moshweshwe, the founder of the Basuto (or Lesotho) nation. His father was a village headman in one of the small southern Sotho chieftaincies south of the upper Caledon River. By the time the Mfecane burst, sweeping away much traditional authority, Moshweshwe was a mature young man of renowned bravery and wisdom. Men readily flocked to him

Moshweshwe, chief of the Basuto.

during the time of troubles and by 1824 he had built up a large following. In that year he established his headquarters in the mountain stronghold of Thaba Bosui. Here his people were safe; Zulus, Tlokwa and Ngwane all tried to capture Moshweshwe's stronghold and all failed. He never sought conflict with the marauding groups passing through the country. He always preferred to establish friendly relations with other powerful chiefs. But when resistance was necessary, he resisted and his mountain base proved impregnable. Moshweshwe became known as the invincible King of the Mountains and groups of homeless Sotho from many shattered communities joined the ranks of his followers.

Moshweshwe encouraged all who wished to place themselves under his protection. He married into other chiefly families and he made alliances. A far-seeing politician, he knew that in such troubled times he must base his power and security on three foundations: an impregnable capital, a large following and good relations with his neighbours. His reputation spread rapidly. Even powerful chiefs like Mzilikazi respected Moshweshwe and seldom invaded his territory more than once. In the 1830s Moshweshwe became the dominant personality in the region between the Orange and the Caledon. His people came to be known simply as the Basuto (i.e. BaSotho – *the* Sotho).

Kololo

The last group of migrants we shall be able to consider is the Kololo. These were an offshoot of the Fokeng. When in 1822 the Fokeng were forced northwards across the Vaal they split up under various leaders. The inhabitants of seven or eight villages attached themselves to Sebitwane and under his leadership joined in the raiding of the area between the Vaal and the Harts. But in about 1831 Sebitwane decided that little was to be gained from constant warfare with Sotho and Tswana groups. His people needed land and security. So Sebitwane marched northwards in search of a new home. What happened to him and his people we shall see in chapter 10.

This is not the end of the Mfecane: in chapter 10 we shall be considering the impact of migrants, such as the Ngoni and Kololo, who burst upon some of the Central African peoples north of the Zambezi. We have completed the history of the Mfecane in southeast Africa but it would be wrong to leave this tragic episode as just a story of population movement. It was, in fact, a period of devastation and horror perhaps unparalleled in the history of the continent. Villages were burned, farmland was laid waste, men and women died of starvation, many wandered the country alone or in small groups seeking food and shelter, some even became cannibals.

The Zulus 1824–35

To return to Zululand, we pick up what was happening there under Shaka and his successors. As Shaka's power grew his character deteriorated. He became a tyrant, concerned only with enforcing his own will. He seldom listened to advice; he forced his subordinates to carry out his policies, even when they were bad policies; when his subordinates failed they were punished – usually by death. He kept his armies ceaselessly on campaign. He ordered people to be put to death without adequate reason. He was merciless to his enemies, cruel and unpredictable to his friends.

But Shaka was the first great African leader in the south to establish close relations with Europeans. In 1824 a British settlement was founded at Port Natal. It was a small settlement and the white men were mainly concerned with hunting and trading for ivory. This, of course, brought them into contact with the Zulus and, before long, with Shaka. Shaka extended his protection to the white men. He valued their technical and medical skills; he was fascinated by the presents they brought him; and he realised the importance of their firearms. He signed treaties with the settlers which, they claimed, gave them possession of land around Port Natal. Like most 'treaties' signed between African leaders and early European settlers, each side understood something quite different by the agreement. We may be sure that Shaka had no intention of giving up any of his sovereignty to a few strangers whom he could crush easily if he so chose.

The relationship between Shaka and the British settlers worked to the benefit of both. Shaka's prestige was enhanced and he benefited from the skills of the white men. In 1826, for instance, when his warriors had failed in a raid on some of the Kumalo, Shaka asked the British for help. This time, supported by a small force from Natal armed with guns, the Zulus were successful. The British, for their part, were able to wander freely throughout Shaka's dominions gathering ivory.

The end was now drawing near for Shaka. Some of his subject chiefs had already defected. Many of his army leaders were tiring of his tyranny. Members of his own family were plotting his overthrow. In 1824 an unsuccessful attempt was made on his life. After that Shaka became even more suspicious and cruel towards those close to him. In 1828 another plot was hatched by one of Shaka's aunts and two of his half brothers. On 24 September the two half brothers, 79

Dingane and Mhlangana, stabbed Shaka to death. Proceeding with their well-laid plans the conspirators then murdered the army commander, and other officials and relatives known to be loyal to the late chief. This done Dingane disposed of his partner in crime, Mhlangana, and had himself proclaimed chief. Most of the Zulus accepted the change of régime with relief, believing that Dingane would be a more moderate ruler than his predecessor. The army, having just returned from their defeat at the hands of the Shangane, were glad of Shaka's overthrow since it undoubtedly saved them from being punished for having failed.

Dingane's reign started quietly enough but the new king lacked Shaka's authority and military prowess. He was unable to stop the decline of the empire and more and more subject chiefs broke away from his control. Seeing the disintegration of his dominions Dingane panicked. He made shows of force and violence in many parts of his territory. He tightened his control over political and military leaders. He became as much a tyrant as Shaka had been.

His relations with the white men also deteriorated. He began his reign determined to preserve the mutually beneficial friendship with the Natal settlers. He even permitted Christian missionaries to begin work among his people. But times were changing. More and more

Natal c. 1850.

Europeans arrived in Natal. Because they were armed with guns and had their own small armies of Africans and coloured people, Dingane found that he could not always control their activities within his territory. Trading disputes between Europeans and Zulus became common. Dingane's enemies began to seek and to be granted refuge in Port Natal. The British made requests to their home government for colonial rule to be established over Natal. Fearful of the growing power of the foreigners, Dingane tried to restrict their activities but this only stirred up the resentment of the white men. This was the situation in the 1830s when Dingane and other African leaders were faced with a new problem – the migration of Afrikaners out of Cape Colony into the Bantu lands of south-east Africa.

8. New pressures
(2) The spread of white settlement in the south

Britain acquires control of Cape Colony

As we have seen, the gradually growing white colony in southern Africa had its problems. There were conflicts with the original San and Khoikhoi inhabitants of the Cape and with the Xhosa of the eastern frontier. There were also differences between the Boers, the settler farmers, and the government of the colony, the Dutch East India Company. These difficulties, especially the conflict between frontiersman and official, grew worse when the British government took over control of the Cape. This occurred in 1806 as one result of a European war.

The coming of the British had created an 'eternal triangle' of hatreds and misunderstandings. First of all there were the Africans who resented the encroachments of the white man. Then there were the Afrikaners, who believed themselves by right of racial and cultural superiority as well as by right of conquest to be the true heirs to the soil of southern Africa. The British had little in common with the Boers beyond colour of skin. They considered themselves to be responsible for all the inhabitants of the colony, black and white. They wanted to prevent racial conflict and opposed slavery.

Conflict with the Xhosa

On the eastern frontier there were no less than nine wars with the

Xhosa Wars

1779 1789 1799 1811–12 1819 1834–5	Disputes over the Great Fish River boundary
1846–7	Resistance to annexation
1850–3 1877–8	Risings against British rule

Xhosa between 1779 and 1878 (these used to be called the 'Kaffir Wars').

Land hunger among the Xhosa and their neighbours was becoming intolerable. As well as the wastefulness of traditional farming methods and the growth of population there was, from the 1820s, a growing refugee problem as northerners fled from the Zulu *impis*. So Xhosa pressure built up in the region of the Great Fish River (the official eastern boundary of the colony) at the same time that Afrikaner settlers were pressing eastwards in search of grazing land and trading opportunities.

Relations between black and white on the eastern border were by no means always hostile. Xhosa sought refuge within the colony in times of famine or war and some settled permanently on the Zuurveldt, west of the Fish River. Many of these refugees sought work as farm-hands and servants. Christian missionaries were working in Xhosaland from early in the nineteenth century and, although the coming of a new religion created some enormous problems for the leaders of African society, the growing number of converts did help to break down the cultural barrier between black and white.

But competition for land and cattle increased. In 1835, for instance, the frontiersmen claimed to have lost 60,000 cattle in Xhosa raids (probably an exaggeration) and they took 14,000 cattle from the Xhosa in reprisal raids. Other causes of trouble were arguments over

Trade waggons arriving in Grahamstown, 1850. This gives some indication of the very profitable trade in ivory and skins from Xhosaland.

trade and runaway slaves and servants, who escaped into African territory. But always the struggle for grazing land was the underlying cause of conflict between the two communities.

The Xhosa Wars

After the first war of 1779 (p. 55) the Africans were simply pushed back across the Great Fish River; there was no permanent settlement of the border problem. Ten years later as a result of wars in Xhosaland, a group of Xhosa under the leadership of Ndlambe seized some of the frontier farms. The Boers naturally turned to their government for military help but the new *landdrost* (chief officer), Honaratus Maynier, had more sympathy for the Xhosa than for the settlers. He restrained the frontiersmen from launching a reprisal raid and told Ndlambe's people they might stay if they settled peacefully alongside the white men. The Second Xhosa War, therefore, marked a victory for the Africans.

The frontiersmen complained that the government would neither allow them to deal with the 'Kaffirs' themselves nor send sufficient troops to the frontier to protect them. In 1799 the settlers of Graaf-Reinet rebelled against the British government (see below, p. 97) and the Ndlambe took the opportunity to strengthen his position by uniting most of the local people under his leadership and driving out more of the settlers. A force was sent to restore order. It put a stop to the fighting but did little else.

The new British administration was determined to achieve a permanent settlement. It brought out a large number of new emigrants from Britain and planned to settle some of them in the eastern part of the colony. The way to peace and economic development, the Cape Town government decided, was to push the Xhosa back beyond the Great Fish River, garrison the frontier with an adequate force and populate the Zuurveldt with more white farmers. Thus, in 1811 and 1812 a large government force pushed Ndlambe and his followers back into an already overcrowded Xhosaland and set up frontier garrisons.

In 1818 Ndlambe increased the size of his following and turned against his overlord, Ngqika. Ngqika considered himself an ally of the British and, when he was defeated by his enemies, he appealed to the Cape government for help. Glad of the opportunity of dealing a blow at the victorious and dangerous Ndlambe, the British sent a powerful force across the Fish River. The campaign went on for some months and Ndlambe did much damage along the border before famine forced him to abandon the conflict and flee into hiding. The British persuaded most of the Xhosa to recognise Ngqika as 'paramount chief' and Ngqika agreed to withdraw all his people beyond the Keiskamma. The area between the Fish and the Keiskamma was declared neutral territory.

All this did was to deny a large area of land to two land-hungry people. Neither Ngqika nor the Cape government could enforce it, particularly when the Mfecane transformed the Xhosa land problem into a land crisis. Xhosa clans living in what came to be known as the Ceded Territory refused to move. White and black herdsmen filtered back into the forbidden land. Government policy was inconsistent and failed to prevent a renewal of border raiding. Generally speaking it was the Boers who were more successful in this creeping warfare. Better armed, and sometimes supported by their government, they gradually encroached on the Ceded Territory.

In 1834 the West Xhosa leaders, Macomo and Tyali, alarmed at recent Cape annexations of African territory, decided to make another bid to secure the ancient Xhosa frontiers. At the head of 12,000 warriors they invaded across the Fish River. For a while they were successful. Then, early in 1835, reinforcements arrived to aid the harassed frontiersmen. The invaders were pushed right back to the Great Kei and beyond. Large numbers of cattle were taken as a punishment and the Cape Governor, Sir Benjamin D'Urban, decided to annex all the land between the Great Fish and the Great Kei Rivers. This territory was now called Queen Adelaide Province and its capital was at Kingwilliamstown. But D'Urban did not have the full support of the British government. A committee was appointed to examine relations between the white and black races in southern Africa. Its report condemned fresh annexation of African land. In October 1836 Queen Adelaide Province was abandoned. The old situation was virtually restored.

Population increase among the Xhosa, as well as loss of land and cattle, placed intolerable strains on traditional farming methods. Political authority was breaking down largely because of the humiliating treaties and agreements forced on chiefs by the colonial power. As times grew harder extremists received more and more popular support. Some reacted against missionary teaching and sought a return to traditional religion. Witchcraft revived and 'prophets' appeared frequently. So disputes and problems continued on the eastern frontier, the Cape government from time to time trying to minimise them by making fresh treaties with recognised chiefs.

Seventh Xhosa War

The worst and the most important of the Xhosa wars was the Seventh

Xhosa War, sometimes known as the War of the Axe, which broke out in 1846. There were seven major causes of this war. First of all there was the old trouble of border raids. The young warriors involved in attacks on border farms were now armed with guns and were a more serious threat than the raiders of earlier years. After an incident in 1844 in which an Afrikaner farmer was killed, the authorities decided on the military occupation of the Ceded Territory. The second cause of the war also arose from the incident just described. The Governor, Sir Peregrine Maitland, travelled to Xhosaland and made a new series of treaties with the chiefs. These obliged the Xhosa to accept the setting up of new forts and garrisons in the Ceded Territory. They permitted white farmers to reclaim stolen cattle any time and anywhere in Xhosaland. They laid down that any Xhosa suspected of a crime against a British citizen was to be tried within the Colony by a white court. They attacked several Xhosa traditions and forbade the chiefs to enforce pagan customs on Christian converts. Naturally the chiefs were alarmed at the encroachment on their land and the attack on their authority contained in these treaties. The third cause was the activities of extremists on both sides. Maqoma, who had been the regent of the Ngqika Xhosa during Sandile's minority, felt deprived of power when Sandile was installed as chief. He compensated for this by leading Xhosa extremists, complaining of Sandile's weakness and demanding action. Some of the settler leaders on the other hand believed that a final showdown was called for with the Kaffirs. They wanted the Xhosa expelled from the area west of the Keiskamma so that the fine land of the Ceded Territory could be available to white farmers.

The failure of the government to pursue a single policy or even to understand the problem stands as the fourth cause of the war. Between 1834 and 1855 there were seven governors of Cape Colony and each had his own ideas about the border problem. Furthermore, nearly all the men appointed as governors were soldiers by profession. They did not understand African society or African problems. For them the border question was a military question, which had to do with 'troublesome natives' and not with ancient peoples trying to cope with new economic and political situations. Governments also changed fairly frequently in London. Colonial secretaries were not usually very knowledgeable about or interested in southern Africa and few of them tried to exert a strong influence on affairs in the Cape.

The fifth cause of the war was the building in 1844 of Post Victoria in the middle of the Ceded Territory. The Xhosa resented the fort's existence. Troops from the fort raided Xhosa villages and Xhosa warriors attacked the fort. However, the Cape government believed that the presence of Post Victoria would deter the Africans from fresh outbreaks of violence.

All these other causes of war were aggravated and made worse by the sixth – drought. In the early 1840s there were serious failures of the rains. This forced black and white into closer contact. Farmers on both sides of the border wandered far afield in their search for pasture. Hungry Xhosa poured into the colony looking for jobs which would enable them to get food, shelter and pay. From time to time the government clamped down on this contact between black and white and this led to protests from both sides.

But the last and most important cause of all was the land problem. The Xhosa feared that if they did not resist settler pressures they would lose all their land to the white men.

In 1846 two incidents occurred which led to war. In January the government decided to move Post Victoria to a site near Block Drift. Towards the end of the month surveyors began work on the site of the new fort but by mistake they started surveying on the wrong side of Keiskamma River – in Xhosaland. Immediately the word spread that the Colony was planning a takeover of Xhosa territory. In March a police escort taking a prisoner to Grahamstown was attacked by a Xhosa band of chief Tola's. The prisoner was accused of stealing an axe (hence the name the War of the Axe). Colonel Hare, Lieutenant Governor of the Eastern Cape, now believed that it was 'impossible to refrain any longer from punishing the systematic violation of justice and good faith on the part of the Kaffirs'. On 1 April he declared war.

Hare sent an inadequate force into Sandile's country. This was attacked and put to rout by a great tide of Xhosa and Tembu who, now that all restraint was cast aside, swept on into the Colony attacking farms and military posts with great boldness. Throughout Xhosaland missionary stations were destroyed and Europeans put to flight. But Hare called up reserves and an army of 14,000 colonial troops soon changed the course of the war. The Xhosa fell back. Most of their land was occupied and thousands of head of cattle taken.

The governor decided that this time the land would be permanently annexed and mostly settled with European, Fingo, Khoikhoi and 'friendly' Xhosa farmers. This was exactly what the Xhosa had feared and they therefore refused to stop fighting. But they could only prolong the sufferings of their people by further resistance. The fighting became more savage. Many Xhosa were forced by starvation to surrender. The war became, in the words of one of the missionaries, 'a war of extermination'. In December 1847 a new governor, Sir

Harry Smith, annexed all land as far as the Kei and called it British Kaffraria. Smith called the chiefs together and symbolically exploded a waggonload of gunpowder before their eyes. 'There go the treaties,' he shouted. 'Do you hear? No more treaties. I make no treaty. I say this land is mine.'

As a result of this decisive war Xhosaland was shattered. The authority of most of the chiefs was destroyed once and for all. The only independent Xhosa were those living beyond the Kei. In British Kaffraria the best land was taken from the local people, who were moved into special locations. Over 25,000 Ngqika Xhosa had died or fled between 1846 and 1848.

The last Xhosa wars

Disorganised and bewildered, the Xhosa were ready to listen to anyone who promised them salvation. Such was the image of the self-styled war doctor, Mlanjeni. He persuaded large numbers of the Xhosa that if they made the necessary sacrifices and took the war medicine he gave them they would be protected from the white man's guns and would therefore be able to prevail over their enemies. Emboldened by this teaching and encouraged by difficulties the British were experiencing in other parts of South Africa, the leading chiefs felt able to resist the colonial authorities towards the end of 1850. They refused to attend a meeting which Smith called. In retaliation Smith deposed Sandile and set up another man as chief of the Ngqikas. Sandile's people naturally refused to recognise the change of leadership. War began and most Xhosa on both sides of the Kei joined in, as did many other discontented African groups. Faced with widespread resistance the colonial forces were unable to deal with it quickly. Fighting continued for two years and was carried beyond the Kei into the territory of the Xhosa chief, Kreli. Peace was finally made in February 1853 and once more the Xhosa had to pay for their defeat with cattle and land.

In Kaffraria more Europeans were settled until the fertile land represented a 'chequer-board' of black and white farms. Groups of detribalised Fingo and Mfengu were also settled on new land. The colonial government made a pretence of supporting the authority of Xhosa chiefs but these now became salaried officials of the government and more and more of their tasks were taken over by European advisers.

Many Xhosa now turned for help to traditional religion and prophets. Mhlakaza, a prophet and adviser to one of the Xhosa chiefs, promised supernatural aid in sweeping the white man into the sea

Xhosa with their cattle.

if the Xhosa would renounce witchcraft, sacrifice *all* their cattle, destroy their grain and refrain from sowing the next season's crops. The prophet's message spread like a grassfire across Kaffraria and the dreadful cattle-killings began. Some 200,000 animals were slaughtered. The crops were not planted. Grain stocks were destroyed. By February 1857 the people were starving. But the supernatural army which was supposed to arise to deliver European cattle and produce into their hands did not materialise. The government tried to organise relief but could do little to feed so many people. Thousands died. Thousands more migrated into Cape Colony in search of work and food. An unofficial census of a large area of Kaffraria estimated that the population had dropped from nearly 105,000 to about 37,600 during 1857.

Under the governorship of Sir George Gray (1855–62) some moves were at last made to help Africans in white-controlled southern Africa to adjust to a new way of life. African schools were founded and the first large hospital for Africans was built. But drought, lack of money and the activities of some of the white farmers made the work of government in British Kaffraria almost impossible. In 1866 the territory was incorporated into Cape Colony and was known thereafter as the Ciskei.

Meanwhile, across the river in the Transkei a situation was 89 developing which led to the Ninth (and last) Xhosa War. In 1857 Kreli, the leading Xhosa chief, had been forced beyond the River Bashee with his people, and police had been sent to patrol the Transkei in order to keep the eastern border of Kaffraria peaceful. Some Fingo were allowed to settle in this area, and when in 1865 Kreli was allowed to return to some of his former territory, he was angry to find the Fingo 'dogs' there. In 1877 hostility turned into warfare. The Cape government supported the Fingos and when they came into conflict with Kreli's men the Ninth Xhosa War had begun. Soon Xhosas and Tembus within the colonial boundaries had taken up arms and the whole of the south-east from the Fish to the Bashee was in turmoil. Inevitably the tide of battle was turned by the Europeans and their Fingo allies and, in June 1878, the war came to an end. In the Ciskei the pattern of reallocation of land to white farmers was repeated. Some of the chiefs were dismissed or imprisoned (Sandile had been killed in the fighting). In the Transkei European settlement was not allowed but the people were brought under close control by the appointment of magistrates to supervise their affairs.

By the end of the Xhosa Wars the settlers had been prevented from destroying the Xhosa and taking all their land, but the Xhosas' way of life had been destroyed. They were spread all over the British-ruled south. Many were working for low wages on European farms. Others were trying to practise traditional methods of agriculture on plots of land which were too small, and thus continued to sink further into poverty.

The Khoisan

Another problem of equal importance was the Khoisan peoples. As we have seen, after an initial attempt at resistance, some remained in what was fast becoming a 'white man's country' and adapted themselves to the European's way of life. They learned to handle horses and guns. They became workers on Boer farms. They served the government as mounted soldiers in the frontier districts. There was considerable racial mingling between the Khoisan and the white immigrants. Though treated as inferior by the white man these people were theoretically free. Some used their freedom and trekked out of the colony to form their own Kora, Gona and Griqua communities. Others were not so fortunate; they were enslaved by the white settlers and were forced to work, usually under appalling conditions, for the new masters of the land. Throughout the first half of the nineteenth century most of the San hunters retreated further and further into the interior, frequently falling a prey to the attacks of Boers and Griquas until they found some security in the arid Kalahari, where no herdsmen would wish to despoil them of their sparse hunting grounds. There were, however, some San who adapted themselves to the white man's way of life. For instance, the first London Missionary Society workers who arrived in 1798 were greeted at Cape Town by a group of San who asked them to start a mission in their land 400 kilometres away.

The end of slavery

After 1806 there were two different attitudes towards the indigenous people of the Cape. The settlers of Dutch origin with their bigoted racialism considered all black men as inferior creatures. Their law recognised slavery and they regarded the keeping of slaves as one of their inalienable rights. The British rulers believed that all men are equal. Slavery had already been stopped at home and there was growing agitation for its abolition throughout the British Empire.

One year after Britain's takeover of Cape Colony the government in London passed a law putting an end to the slave trade. In 1812 circuit courts were set up to travel round the frontier areas to examine charges of ill-treatment of slaves and servants (these courts were contemptuously referred to by the frontiersmen as the 'black circuit'). In 1815 Frederick Bezuidenhout, a farmer at Slagter's Nek, refused to stand trial before the circuit judges. A small force of Khoikhoi soldiers was sent to fetch him. Bezuidenhout fired at the soldiers and was shot resisting arrest. The local Boers were outraged. A minor rebellion broke out as a result of which thirty-two Boers were banished from the frontier district and five were hanged.

Many Boers realised that the government was determined to uphold its policy towards the Africans and supported this policy over the next fifteen years or so by improving the conditions of slaves. They hoped by so doing to prevent the total abolition of slavery in the Cape. New regulations were introduced restricting enslavement, governing conditions and terms of service and requiring slave owners to keep a punishment book which could be examined by the authorities. In 1826 a 'Guardian of Slaves' was appointed whose job it was to see that all the regulations relating to slaves were enforced. During these years the governors found themselves caught between a British government determined to enforce sweeping regulations concerning slavery and a body of Cape farmers urging them to take notice of their special circumstances before introducing new legislation. In 1830 an Order in Council was passed at Westminster which forced on Cape Colony a new set of regulations governing the treatment of slaves, some of which could not be enforced. The Afrikaners were outraged and there were riots at Stellenbosch. But anti-slavery forces were gaining in strength and, in 1833, an Act for the abolition of slavery throughout the British Empire, was passed through the parliament in London. The Boers could now accept a slaveless existence or leave the colony in search of new lands where they could continue to adopt their own attitude towards the 'blacks'.

To ease the situation for slave owners the new Act allowed them to keep their slaves for five years as apprentices. After that time the former slaves were to be free to seek other employment. In 1841 a Masters and Servants Ordinance was brought in which introduced new regulations binding upon employers and employed on a basis of complete racial equality.

Free Khoisan and Coloured peoples

The situation of the free Africans of the colony also improved during the first half of the century. At the beginning of the century they were free in little but name. They had no land and so needed to work. Therefore their employers could pay them low wages and treat them badly. Furthermore if a servant ran away he could be caught and forced to return to his master. Numbers did run away and in 1799 quite a few ex-servants joined the Xhosa in their war against the frontiersmen. The end of the slave trade in 1807 only made the Boers more determined than ever to maintain a tight grip on their servants. But again they found themselves confronted by a British adminstration determined to cancel out the racial inequalities operating in the colony. They also found themselves up against some of the missionaries, who exposed the cruelty of the employers and got themselves soundly hated by the Boers for their interference. But their interference forced governors to act. In 1809 the Earl of Caledon issued his 'Hottentot Proclamation'. This laid down rules about conditions of labour but also restricted Khoisan movements by not allowing them to travel from one region to another without a permit.

The settlers were also bringing pressure to bear on the governors. In 1812 they persuaded Sir John Craddock that something more must be done to restrict the movements of African workers and to provide a permanent labour force. The result was a proclamation that any Khoisan child who was born on a Boer farm and lived there for eight years might be apprenticed by the farmer for a further ten years. This was designed to keep not only the child, but also his parents on the farm.

But in the same year the missionaries scored another victory with the setting up of the 'black circuit'. These courts revealed that great injustices were being inflicted on coloured servants and, despite protests and riots, many Boers were tried and sentenced by the circuit judges. The introduction of trial by jury in 1827 was another step towards securing equality before the law for Africans. A fresh burst of activity by the London Missionary Society missionaries in the mid-twenties led to the most important step forward in gaining humane treatment for the African population. This was Ordinance 50 of 1828, sometimes known as the 'Hottentot Charter'. This prohibited labour contracts of longer than one year. It stopped the forced apprenticeship of children. It removed the obligation of Africans to carry passes. Above all it introduced legislation against the colour bar in southern Africa by establishing the principle of the equality of all races before the law.

One unfortunate result of Ordinance 50 was an increase in vagrancy (people wandering the countryside without homes or jobs) and cattle raiding, as some Africans took the opportunity to leave harsh employers. With this problem in mind, a settlement was made for 250 Khoikhoi and Coloured families on land taken from the Xhosa in the Kat River valley. Established in 1829, this settlement flourished for twenty-two years. Then, in 1851, some Khoikhoi joined in the Eighth Xhosa War in the hope of gaining complete political freedom. After the war the lands of the rebels were confiscated and allocated to European farmers. The Kat River rebellion did not prevent the Khoisan and Coloured peoples from making an important political step forward two years later. When the colony gained self-government it was on a multi-racial franchise, with the wealthier Africans being allowed the vote.

But though the black and Coloured communities enjoyed political and legal equality with the whites they were still regarded as socially inferior. They served the community in many capacities. Some of them became wealthy farmers. Many of them sent their sons and daughters to school. But the Europeans refused to recognise them as equals. They expected 'respect' from the 'natives'. They would not make integration work.

The Griqua and Kora

The Griqua and Kora settled in four major groups: around Griqua-town were the followers of Andries Waterboer; at Campbell lived Cornelius Kok and his people; around Philippolis lived the East Griqua of Adam Kok; to the north of the Caledon River the Kora had settled. Within these communities there were always two types

Griqua and Kora territory.

of people: the more responsible, who wished only to settle to a peaceful life of farming and trading; and a wilder element, the Bergenaars, who preferred a life of raiding and brigandage, usually against their African neighbours to the north and east. The Mfecane, by creating conditions of chaos in the area to the east and north-east of the Griqua settlements increased the tendency towards raiding. The numbers of the Bergenaars increased and the Kora lived almost exclusively a life of violence.

The activities of the Griqua and Kora were of little concern to the Cape government until about 1830. Missionaries went and lived among these people and experienced some success in their religious and educational work. Apart from them and some of the frontier Boers with whom they traded, the Griqua and Kora had little contact with the white man. But by 1830 many of the Boers had moved across the Orange and leased grazing land from the Griquas. In 1826 the northern Cape boundary was moved up to the Orange. In 1835 the

94

Great Trek of the frontier Boers began (see next chapter) and the Africans who had already made their 'trek' found their grazing land and their water holes overrun by Afrikaners. The missionaries supported the Griqua and urged the colonial government to protect them from the Boers. They also suggested that the British should give official recognition and support to the Griqua leaders so that they could control the Bergenaars. But the British were reluctant at this stage to extend their authority beyond the Orange River.

The first tentative move by the colonial government to try to stabilise the situation came in 1834. Then the governor, Sir Benjamin D'Urban, made a treaty with Waterboer, who in return for an annual salary agreed to keep order in his territory and to co-operate with the Cape government. But nothing was done to help the East Griqua and their leader Adam Kok III, who were bearing the brunt of the Boer invasion. The rulers of the Cape were too concerned about the eastern frontier.

At last, in 1843, Governor Napier made a treaty with Adam Kok similar to that made earlier with Waterboer. But the Boers in Kok's territory had by now become so powerful and so numerous that the treaty provoked a crisis. They had no intention of recognising Kok's authority over them and they certainly did not recognise the authority of the Cape governor, from whose jurisdiction they had fled. Fighting broke out and colonial troops had to be sent to Kok's aid (1845). Now a British resident was stationed at Philippolis and regulations laid down concerning land transactions between Griqua and Boers. But since neither Kok nor the resident had any means of enforcing his decisions the position remained unchanged.

From this point the fate of the East Griqua and neighbouring groups was bound up with Britain's changing policy towards the Trekker Boers. In 1848 the governor, Sir Harry Smith, annexed all the land between the Orange and Vaal Rivers as the Orange River Sovereignty. This attempt to control the Boers and their relations with Africans brought the East Griqua within British protection and for a few years they enjoyed peace and security. Then, in 1854, the British changed their policy. By the Bloemfontein Convention they withdrew to their old boundaries leaving Kok and his people to the mercy of the independent Orange Free State. Soon the smaller Kora and Griqua communities had disappeared as the Boers leased, bought or took their land. To prevent this happening to his people Adam Kok sold up his territory in 1861 and led his people in another trek, this time across the Drakensberg. He founded a new capital, Kokstad, and a new Griqualand East. Here, for a few years at least, his people were able to enjoy the land in peace.

9. New pressures
(3) The Afrikaner invasion

[We objected to] the shameful and unjust proceedings with reference to the freedom of our slaves; and yet it is not so much their freedom which drove us to such lengths, as their being placed on an equal footing with Christians, contrary to the laws of God, and the natural distinction of race and colour, so that it was intolerable for any decent Christian to bow down beneath such a yoke; wherefore we rather withdrew in order thus to preserve our doctrines in purity.

Anna Steenkamp, Piet Retief's niece (1876)

... the motives of this emigration are sufficiently obvious ... they are the same motives as have, in all ages, compelled the strong to encroach on the weak, and the powerful and unprincipled to wrest by force or fraud, from the comparatively feeble or defenceless, wealth or property or dominion ... Opportunities of uncontrolled self-indulgence and freedom from the restraints of law and settled society, are, it would appear, in all countries, irresistible temptations to the inhabitants of the borderland of civilization.

Lord Glenelg, British Secretary for War and Colonies (1837)

As you can see from the above quotations many reasons have been given for the Great Trek, some of which contradict others.

Reasons for the Great Trek

We can distinguish three main reasons for the Great Trek and a number of lesser ones.

The first reason was the relations between the Boers and the British. As we have seen, the Afrikaners were a culturally backward people. Most of them were descended from poorly-educated Dutch immigrants who had left Europe in the middle of the seventeenth century. They were largely untouched by the new religious and political ideas which had emerged in Europe since then. The Afrikaner was 150 years behind the times. He believed in rigid class and racial distinctions. He believed in slavery. He had a strict, puritanical faith which buttressed his beliefs with prejudice and absolved him

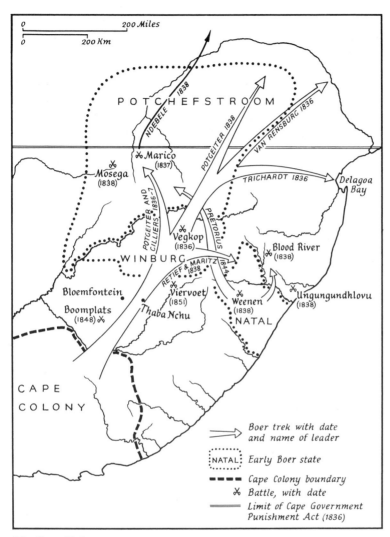

The Great Trek.

from the responsibility of trying to see anyone else's point of view. Even by the eighteenth century the Afrikaners had encountered little challenge to their beliefs or interference with their way of life.

But relations between government and governed grew steadily worse after the British took over Cape Colony. In 1799 trouble flared up again at Graaff Reinet over the arrest of a certain van Jaarsveld for forgery. His friends released him from prison and tried to involve other people in their stand against authority. The pocket rebellion was soon suppressed by government troops but this did not make an end of resentment towards British rule in the outlying parts of the colony.

In 1820 the first British settlers arrived and were given plots of land in the Zuurveld, which had cost the British government £50,000. The Afrikaners were alarmed at the British official immigration policy as it seemed the beginning of an attempt to undermine the Boer way of life. Most British settlers moved to the towns and became tradesmen or officials. In the centres of administration they began to exercise an influence out of all proportion to their number. They complained about the existing legal system, which usually favoured the Afrikaner land-holder. In 1827 the Charter of Justice introduced trial by jury and a basically British judicial system (though most of the actual laws remained unchanged). Between 1823 and 1828 Dutch was replaced by English as the official language. Afrikaner leaders made periodic appeals to the government to set up an elective legislative body. In 1834 a Legislative Council was set up, but membership of this council was entirely at the governor's discretion. All these factors made many of the Boers feel that Cape Colony was no longer their country; that it was being changed to conform to a British pattern; that the only way to preserve their own culture was to obtain independence of British domination by leaving the Cape.

The second major cause of the Great Trek was the Boers' attitude towards Africans. No religious doctrine was believed in more enthusiastically than that of the inferiority of the non-white races. 'The people wills to agree to no equality between coloured and white inhabitants either in Church or in State' – so stated the constitution of the South African Republic in 1858. The doctrine of the divinely ordained subjection of 'the sons of Ham' was founded upon certain Old Testament texts.

There was, of course, a practical side to the Afrikaner's attitude towards Africans – he needed workers. Few Khoisan or Xhosa farmhands were prepared to tie themselves to an employer for long periods of time and they usually left their employer if they felt they were not being well treated. So the Boers wanted their workers to be forced to stay – bound by bonds of slavery or by long-term contracts. The British rulers abolished both. Many farmers now experienced a serious labour shortage.

A connected problem was that of vagrancy and crime. Frontier farmers undoubtedly suffered a great deal from stock thieves. Some of these were Xhosa raiding across the eastern border. Others were unemployed Khoikhoi. Until the promulgation of Ordinance 50 in 1828 there was some control over the movements of Cape Africans, who were not allowed to leave their jobs without written permission from their employers and, if found wandering without passes, could be arrested for vagrancy. From 1828 onwards the Boers had far less control over black workers. They claimed that vagrancy and stock thefts had increased (which was probably true, though the amount of the increase was undoubtedly exaggerated), that the government would not allow them to go after cattle raiders and punish them

Trek Boers crossing Cradock's Pass in 1840.

(which was certainly true) and that the government, having forbidden the farmers to keep law and order in their own way, was incapable of keeping law and order itself (which was largely true in some of the outlying districts). In 1834 one of the first acts of the new Legislative Council was the passing of a vagrancy law. It empowered officials to arrest suspected vagrants and force them into work either for the government or for a private employer. But missionary activity forced the British government to veto the proposed law. The Boers now had visions of large numbers of ex-slaves and servants wandering the colony without any control by the white men.

The third main reason for the Great Trek was the attitude of the Boers to the land. They had never lost the basic belief that the land was theirs for the taking and they resented government attempts to regulate land allocation and the size of farms. Before the British takeover there had been little attempt at control. Most cattle and sheep farms were held on licence from the government. Licences were obtained for a very low annual recognition fee. In 1813 a new system of (higher) rents was introduced and the government tried to prevent the perpetual migration by splitting up existing farms among the heirs on the death of the existing farmer. The Boers resented bitterly this attack on their traditional freedom. The rumour, in 1832, that the government was going to make no more grants, but that all farmland would have to be bought at auction, persuaded many Afrikaners to leave the colony. Others still hoped to acquire new land with government help. They were delighted when D'Urban annexed the Queen Adelaide Province in 1835 and had high hopes of good farmland being available for white settlement. When the British government abandoned the province they were disillusioned. They believed the authorities would never do anything about their need for land and that they would have to find new lands for themselves.

There were a number of other minor reasons for the Great Trek. Firstly there was the emancipation of the slaves and the way it was carried out. The Boers disliked losing their slaves but they hoped at least for reasonable compensation as the British parliament had voted £20,000,000 to be paid to the former slave owners throughout the empire. The difficulty was that this money had to be claimed in London. Most Boers, therefore, either had to forgo their compensation or claim it through agents, who took their own commission. So the farmers faced loss and delay in obtaining what they considered their rights.

The activities of the British missionaries were another source of agitation to the Boers. The missionary societies and particularly the L.M.S., under the leadership of Dr Philip, knew that the Boers took every opportunity to compete with African herdsmen for pasture and water. They knew that the Boers were trying to turn some of the border chiefs against the Cape government in order to stir up war from which, in turn, they hoped to benefit. They reported these things back to Cape Town and London. The missionaries were not always right over details, but in persistently drawing attention to the racialism, bigotry and greed of the Afrikaners they were right in principle.

Another factor which encouraged the Great Trek was the belief

Dr John Philip. The great upholder of African interests was 43 when he arrived in South Africa in 1819 and he devoted the next thirty years of his life to serving the people in his care. He drew the attention of Europe to what was happening in South Africa, especially in his book 'Researches in South Africa' (1826). His activities turned most of the settler population against him but he did succeed in influencing British government policy at an important stage in the occupation of South Africa.

that the land to the north-east was empty. Large tracts of land had been depopulated by the Mfecane. Boer spies sent to the area reported that beyond the mountains lay a broad belt of well watered grassland with only a sparse African population. Most attractive of all was the area now known as Natal, virtually empty due to the activities of Shaka and Dingane.

The first trekkers

The trek began as a trickle in 1834 and had turned into a flood by 1836. In preparation the Boers had laid in large stocks of gunpowder and ammunition. Most of the trekkers gathered themselves into large groups under chosen leaders for their journey into the unknown. The first large groups were those led by Louis Trichardt and Janse van Rensburg. Setting out separately in 1835, they joined forces near the Vaal River the following year and journeyed together some distance towards their goal – the region of Delagoa Bay. Then they separated again, van Rensburg's party hurrying north-eastwards. By the time they reached Tsonga country the trekkers were severely weakened by disease. In the lower Limpopo valley a Tsonga force fell on van Rensburg's party and destroyed it completely. Trichardt's followers were harassed by tsetse fly and mosquitoes and were further exhausted by the difficult crossing of the Lebombo Mountains. They finally reached Delagoa Bay, where Trichardt and many of his colleagues died. The remnants eventually sailed for Natal to join other Boer families.

102   *The Battle of Vegkop, 1836.*

Trek waggons crossing a river.

Potgieter and Cilliers

Early in 1836 a party led by Andries Potgieter and Sarel Cilliers set out from Thaba Nchu (a Rolong settlement north of the lower Caledon River, which became a kind of base camp for the trekkers). They moved north into the territory dominated by Mzilikazi and the Ndebele. They made alliances with local chiefs against the much feared Ndebele. Mzilikazi had no welcome for people who came apparently equipped to take over the land. He sent a force of 5,000 warriors to attack the Boers at Vegkop. The Ndebele captured all the Boers' sheep and cattle and inflicted heavy casualties. But the trekkers were able to survive by forming their waggons into a large circle, called a *laager*, and using them as a barrier from the shelter of which they could fire at their assailants. With the help of Chief Moroka of the Rolong, who loaned them oxen, Potgieter and Cilliers' party got back to Thaba Nchu.

The trekkers decided that the Ndebele would have to be driven out or cowed and another leader, Gert Maritz, assisted by Rolong allies, fought two major battles against the Ndebele. In the first at Mosega they destroyed the settlement and captured 7,000 cattle. The second encounter took place near Mzilikazi's capital on the Marico River in November 1837. The Ndebele put up a fierce resistance and 103 were only defeated after a nine-day battle. 1837 was a bad year for Mzilikazi. As well as the appearance of a new threat, the Boers, there was fresh activity from his old enemies the Zulus. For months he had been contemplating another move; the defeat at Marico was the last straw. Dividing his people into two groups, he trekked northwards across the Limpopo. (We shall follow the history of the Ndebele in later chapters on Central Africa.) His Sotho subjects and their dispossessed neighbours reoccupied land they had been forced out of by the Ndebele. But they found themselves up against the Boers who claimed the land by right of treaty and conquest.

Potgieter now (1838) advanced deep into the conquered territory and founded the town of Potchefstroom, which soon became the centre of a Boer republic of the same name. Some of his followers remained south of the Vaal and established the state of Winburg. Potgieter's followers found that supplies were difficult to obtain and for this reason Potgieter decided to move towards Portuguese-controlled Delagoa Bay. In 1844 he moved eastwards, but discovered the same problems that had destroyed Trichardt's attempt to settle in the same area. In 1848 Potgieter was on the move again, this time northwards into the Soutpansberg. The farming there was poor but the Boers found a profitable sideline in the ivory trade.

Here the trekkers met up with the Sotho, Venda, Tsonga and Pedi who were recovering from the effects of the Mfecane, particularly the raids of Shoshangane. As they reoccupied their lands they found that fresh invaders, the Boers, were encroaching on them. Conflict began in 1854 when Makapane, a Sotho chief, destroyed a hunting party from Schoemansdal. The Boers reacted with an attack on Makapane's followers and killed about 3,000 of them. They raided Venda and Tsonga villages for slaves, some of which they sold to the Portuguese. The Africans reacted by raids on white farms. The authorities at Schoemansdal tried to restore order and confidence by controlling their own extremists, but those extremists refused to be controlled. In 1867, after an attack on the Venda strongholds with the assistance of reinforcements from the south had failed, the Boers withdrew from the Soutpansberg.

Zululand and Natal

Since 1824 there had been a small colony of British traders at Port Natal (Durban), to whom Shaka had extended his protection. Dingane continued this relationship, trading with the white men and allowing them to travel in his territory on trading and hunting expeditions. But gradually his attitude changed. There were four main reasons for this. First of all the numbers of the British and their African followers gradually increased. Groups fleeing from the Zulus went to Natal and put themselves under the protection of the merchants. By 1835 there were only thirty white men at Port Natal but they had 2,500 Africans under their control, some of whom they had armed with up-to-date guns. A second and related reason for Dingane's mounting hostility was that some of the Africans protected at Port Natal were fugitives from Zulu justice, and the merchants refused to hand them over. Thirdly, reports of white land-grabbing reached Dingane from the Xhosa frontier. Fourthly, the Zulu leader heard that in 1834 the merchants had asked the British government to annex Natal. (In the following year they renamed Port Natal as Durban in honour of the Cape governor.) The worsening relations led to some minor clashes between armed parties of Zulus and 'Natalians', but in 1835 an attempt was made to recreate peace and friendship. In return for a promise by the merchants to return all future fugitives to him Dingane agreed that he would continue to protect the Natal settlement. At about the same time he agreed to allow Christian missionaries into Zululand. Unfortunately some of the merchants broke their side of the bargain the following year. Dingane, furious, broke off relations with the British and closed the Tugela River frontier to them. This was still the situation when, at the end of 1837, the first Boer trekkers crossed the Drakensberg.

This party was led by Piet Retief and Gert Maritz. Leaving the main party to negotiate the Drakensberg passes Retief went on ahead in the hope of establishing friendly relations with the merchants at Durban and with Dingane. The first object was easily achieved and Retief went on to Ungundhlovu, Dingane's capital. The Zulu chief welcomed Retief's party and told the Boer leader that he would consider favourably his request for land if Retief, as a gesture of goodwill, would raid Tlokwa territory to recapture some cattle, horses and guns recently taken by Sekonyela's men. Delighted, Retief set out on the mission and sent word to the main party of trekkers who immediately descended from the Drakensberg to the upper valley of the Tugela.

Dingane was now in a difficult position and it was by no means easy or safe for him to meet his side of the bargain with Retief. The advance of the white man was proceeding with alarming rapidity. The British in Natal were making fresh requests for land. The Boers had defeated Mzilikazi and occupied most of the region beyond the Drakensberg. Now hundreds of them had entered his territory before he had given permission. If he agreed to Retief's request for land would the matter rest there, or would the Zulu, like the Xhosa, find their territory gradually nibbled away by the white man? If it came to full-scale war between the Zulu and the Boers Dingane knew well that many of his African enemies would side with the Boers. Several of his councillors urged him to drive the newcomers out. A display of strength, they said, would get rid of them once and for all.

It was probably the insolence and stupidity of some of the white men that finally made up Dingane's mind. First Gardiner, one of the missionaries, reminded Dingane that he had already promised to the missionaries some of the land that Retief wanted. Then alarming news came that Retief had, by a trick, captured Sekonyela and, with the great Tlokwa chief completely in his power, had easily got back Dingane's cattle, guns and horses. When Retief returned he angered Dingane by refusing to hand over the recaptured horses and guns along with the cattle. Finally, when the Zulu chief hesitated over the land grant, Retief threatened him with vengeance from the white man's god if he failed to co-operate. Dingane decided to kill the Boers.

On 4 February 1838 he made an agreement ceding Durban and its hinterland to Retief. Two days later during a farewell party the Boer emissaries were surrounded by warriors, dragged to the execution hill outside Ungungdhluvu and battered to death. Before news of the murder could reach the main Boer encampments a Zulu host swept down upon them. At Weenen they massacred 500 of the intruders at night. Most of the others were warned in time to form *laagers* and beat off the attack. In April Durban was burned to the ground and the European survivors were forced to take refuge on a ship in the harbour.

The Boers were determined on revenge. In November 1838, Andries Pretorius took over the military command of the Boers and, within days, was leading an armed force into Zululand. On 15 December the Boers made their *laager* on the banks of the Ncome River and were there confronted by 10,000 Zulu warriors. Though vastly outnumbered the white men had guns and a cannon. With these they wrought havoc among the *impis*. At the end of the day 3,000 Zulu lay dead, while not a single Boer had been killed. From that day the Ncome was known as Blood River.

The great empire built by Shaka never recovered from this defeat. Dingane's hold on conquered chiefdoms weakened and, in 1839, his own half-brother, Mpande, rebelled against him. He led a large band of warriors across the Tugela and threw in his lot with the Boers. The next year he and his men joined Pretorius in an invasion of Zululand. Dingane sued for peace – in vain. His envoys were put to death. He was forced into the northern part of his country where he fought a last, hopeless battle against the invaders. Defeated, he fled into Swaziland, where he was captured and murdered by some of the traditional enemies of the Zulu nation.

The Boer republic of Natal

The Boers now claimed all territory between the Tugela and the Mzimkhulu. Soon they had spread over most of this area, founding farms and pasturing their cattle. Mpande co-operated with the white government to the south and thus avoided any fresh invasions of his territory. He reigned for thirty-three years and they were years of recovery and consolidation. Mpande reasserted his control over the whole area between the Tugela and the Pongolo and successfully defended his northern frontiers (though he lost some of his western lands to the Boers).

A new capital was built for the republic at Pietermaritzburg and a government was set up. The farmers wanted labourers and servants and so a new form of slavery was started. It was called 'apprenticeship'. Under this system children and young people were made to serve to the age of twenty-five for men and twenty-one for women. Large numbers of Africans, mostly refugees returning to their former lands, now flocked into Natal. The Boer government saw them as a possible threat to the white community and determined to control them very firmly. It passed a law that no more than five African families might live on one farm and that the rest should be herded into reserves in the south of the country. But the republic did not have the resources to carry this programme out and the Boers found themselves living in the midst of a large, mobile African population.

The Basuto and the Boers

Another African community to be seriously affected by the Great Trek was the Basuto of Moshweshwe. In 1833, at Moshweshwe's invitation, members of the Paris Evangelical Missionary Society began work among his people. In the same year he gave Moroka's Rolong permission to settle at Thaba Nchu. Moshweshwe regarded Moroka as his vassal but the Rolong chief later claimed that the Thaba Nchu land had been ceded to him outright.

Before the new mixed community had had much chance to settle down, the Boer trek began. Some of the first migrants obtained temporary grazing rights from Moshweshwe. When Moshweshwe asked them to move on they refused. In desperation he turned to the Cape authorities for help. The British were reluctant to involve themselves beyond the existing frontiers of the colony as we have seen but, in 1843, they signed a treaty with Moshweshwe. Its terms were similar to those of the treaty signed at the same time with Adam Kok. Moshweshwe's sovereignty was recognised and he was made an annual payment by the Cape government. The treaty did not work. Basutoland boundaries with Griqua, Rolong and Boer states were ill-defined. Boers within Moshweshwe's territory refused to accept his authority. The chief asked in vain for a British protectorate to be established.

The Cape government did suggest a compromise. Moshweshwe was to designate certain areas in which land could be sold or leased to Boers, and Britain was to provide a Resident to control the activities of the settlers. This arrangement, formalised in 1846, was also a failure. Neither Moshweshwe nor the Resident at Bloemfontein had the power to enforce it. The problem became steadily more complex and incidents between Boers and Basuto more frequent. In 1848, as we have seen, Governor Sir Harry Smith took the logical step of annexing Transorangia as the Orange River Sovereignty.

The problem of the frontiers now fell to the British Resident in the Sovereignty, Henry Warden, for solution. In 1849 he made his deci-

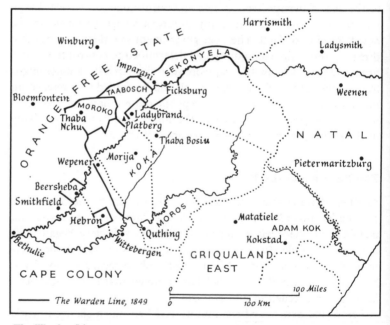

The Warden Line.

sion by creating a frontier known as the Warden Line. This pleased nobody and fighting broke out in earnest in several places, despite Moshweshwe's continued attempts to keep the peace. In June 1851

Warden, who was not very sympathetic towards Africans and made little attempt to understand their point of view, lost his patience with what he considered African defiance of his authority. He determined on a showdown with Moshweshwe and gathered a large force for a punitive attack on Basutoland. In a battle at Viervoet Warden suffered a crushing defeat and hurried back to Thaba Nchu. Now the whole area was plunged into anarchy. Moshweshwe's people and allies, elated by success, were uncontrollable. The Boers no longer respected Warden's authority.

In the following year the new Cape Governor, Sir George Cathcart, decided to restore order. In order to restore confidence in British military power, he personally led an army across the Caledon at the end of 1852. He captured many cattle but was driven off by Moshweshwe's men. Now the wise chief made a diplomatic move which saved his people from further attack and enabled Cathcart to withdraw without losing face. He offered peace and promised to control his people in future. Cathcart thankfully withdrew. It was of little importance; in just over a year Britain had ceded her rights in the area to a Boer republic, the Orange Free State.

But before that, Moshweshwe's long struggle with Sekonyela had come to an end. In 1853 the Tlokwa allied with some Korana groups to raid Basutoland. Moshweshwe's army made a surprise night attack on the Tlokwa mountain stronghold. The enemy fled. The majority of the Tlokwa accepted Moshweshwe's peace terms, which were that they might stay in their land if they recognised his overlordship. But Sekonyela would not humble himself. He fled to Cape Colony, where he died three years later.

Moshweshwe had now disposed of all serious rivals and was indisputably the most powerful man in Transorangia. The leaders of the new Boer republic were therefore happy to accept Moshweshwe's offer that the two states should live side by side in peace. And so it happened – until 1858. Then disputes over the boundary grew into war. The Boers penetrated Basutoland but when they came face to face with a large army drawn up before the impregnable Thaba Bosiu they retreated and made a peace based on a compromise over the border issue. Like most compromises it satisfied neither side.

Fighting inevitably broke out again, this time in 1866. Still the Boers could not make a successful attack on Moshweshwe's stronghold, but this time they used different tractics. They wasted the land and kept the Basuto penned up in their strongholds in an attempt to starve them into surrender. By this time the aged Moshweshwe's strength was failing (he was about eighty) and his sons were already disputing the succession. With the aid of the missionaries he sent a message to Cape Town renewing his request for British protection. In March 1868, when all seemed lost, the British High Commissioner proclaimed that 'the Basutos shall be British subjects; and the territory of the said tribe shall be British Territory'. Moshweshwe had to agree to some of his land being ceded to the Boers but he knew that his people and territory were now secure. Happy in this knowledge he died in 1870, in the same month that British and Free State authorities fixed the Basuto–Boer frontier in the convention of Alival North.

110   *Sekonyela.*

British–Boer relations

When the wilder Boer elements began to leave Cape Colony in 1834–5 some of the British authorities were delighted. By leaving British colonial territory these racially-minded Afrikaners had eased the Cape's frontier problem. But there were others, mainly the missionaries, who were alarmed at what the trekkers would do to the Griqua, the Basuto and other African groups they came in contact with. These urged the British government to try to control the trekkers in some way. The result was the Cape of Good Hope Punishment Act of 1836. This declared that all former inhabitants of Cape Colony were British subjects and still under the jurisdiction of Cape courts unless they went beyond the 25° S line of latitude. The Act provided for the trial of suspected criminals provided they could be returned to the Cape together with witnesses of their offence. It was virtually impossible to put this law into effect over most of the area concerned, though in 1837 a magistrate was appointed to the British community at Durban.

The next problem posed by the trekkers was their establishment of the Natal Republic. The British community at Durban had for years tried to persuade the British government to annex the area but the ministers in distant London could see no reason for taking on this additional colonial burden. The appearance of the Boers in 1839 changed the situation. Merchants at Durban complained that the Boers would interfere with their commercial rights. Some politicians were worried about allowing the Afrikaners to control Durban and the neighbouring coastline. For a few months in 1838–9 a small British military force was sent to Durban to keep an eye on the situation but apart from that the Cape government did nothing to hinder the Boers. However, pressure from the interventionists increased. In 1840 Pretorius ordered a raid against the Bhaca to the south, allegedly to punish them for stealing cattle. The Boers returned from the raid with 3,000 cattle and several 'apprentices' (i.e. slaves). The Cape government feared that the Boers might provoke fresh trouble in the eastern border district. Alarm increased in the following year when Pretorius announced his policy of pushing 'surplus' Africans into reserves in the south of the republic. On hearing this Governor Napier immediately gave the order for the military occupation of Durban.

The Boers naturally resisted what they considered an invasion of their territory. There were clashes between military contingents of both sides. When British reinforcements arrived the republicans were forced to give up the struggle and come to terms. In August

1843 most of the leaders accepted the British terms. Natal became a British possession (formal annexation was confirmed by the British government in 1845) and most of the Afrikaners trekked back across the Drakensberg in search of freedom.

Until the arrival of Sir Harry Smith as Governor and High Commissioner in 1847 no action was taken to involve Britain beyond the Orange River. Smith believed firmly in British culture and he saw annexation as the only way of extending it and of restoring peace to the border regions. When he crossed the Orange he found the Boers divided and most of the chiefs anxious to place their people under British protection. After little consultation with the parties concerned Smith declared Transorangia a British colony in February 1848. Some of the Winburg Boers were angry and Pretorius crossed the Vaal from Potchefstroom at the head of a small army determined to drive the British out of trekker lands. There was a battle at Boomplats in August which proved an easy victory for the British. The Vaal now became a real dividing line between determined, republican, anti-British Boers and 'loyalist' Boers, who had become disillusioned with the trekker movement and desired the security of British protection.

Smith now returned to Cape Town, leaving the new province in the hands of a Resident and twenty-two paid white officials. They had no financial help from outside and a quite inadequate military establishment. When the Resident, Warden, was soundly defeated in battle by Moshweshwe in 1851, British authority collapsed and there were threats of another Transvaal invasion.

In 1852 the Colonial Secretary sent two commissioners to hold discussions with the Afrikaner leaders. They met a delegation headed by Pretorius and after two days of talks the Sand River Convention was signed. By this treaty Britain disclaimed all rights to the allegiance of Transvaal Boers, agreed not to enter into alliances with any African chiefs beyond the Vaal and agreed to supply the Boers with arms and ammunition. The Colonial Office had also decided on withdrawal from the troublesome Orange River Sovereignty, despite the fact that it was peopled mostly by Africans and Boers who wished to be under British protection. A commissioner was appointed in 1853 to make the necessary arrangements with the Afrikaners. But the commissioner, Sir George Clark, had difficulty in finding Afrikaner representatives willing to negotiate a complete British withdrawal. At last Clark 'appointed' some Boer 'representatives' of republican sympathies and with them he drew up the Bloemfontein Convention of February 1854. The British gave the Boers complete freedom and relinquished all treaties with African leaders except Adam Kok (and even the Kok treaty was amended so as to be almost valueless to the Griquas).

In 1866 British Kaffraria was annexed to Cape Colony and this date may be taken as marking the end of a phase for the white communities in South Africa. There were now four self-governing white states. Cape Colony and Natal Colony (which became separate from the Cape in 1856) were British dependencies with multi-racial constitutions. The Orange Free State and the South African Republic were white-dominated Afrikaner states.

10.   New pressures
(4) The impact of the Mfecane north of the Limpopo

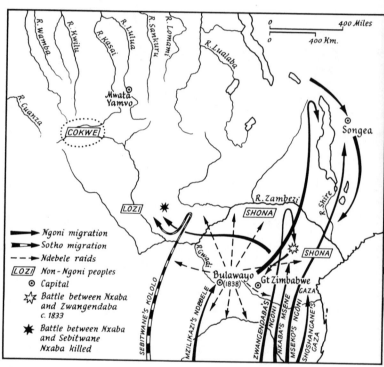

The Mfecane north of the Limpopo.

The Shangane

When Shaka's Zulu explosion fragmented Nguni society, three groups moved northwards out of his reach. They were the followers of Shoshangane, Zwangendaba and Nxaba. Shoshangane's people settled in the region of Delagoa Bay until 1828, when, like Mzilikaze's Ndebele, they found that there still was not enough room for safety between themselves and the Zulu. So they moved further north into the highlands bordering the Sabi River. But Zwangendaba and Nxaba were already in the area with their followers and there was fierce competition for the land. The ranks of the Shangane had been swollen by groups of Ndwandwe and other peoples defeated by the Zulus and it was partly due to superior numbers that Shoshangane was able to triumph over his rivals, defeating first Zwangendaba (c.1831) and then, shortly afterwards, Nxaba.

Once these other migrants had been forced out Shoshangane found it a comparatively easy task to conquer the peoples of the lowlands to the east. From his stronghold at Chaimite he despatched *impis* to invade the Manica, the Ndau, the Chopi and other peoples of what is now Mozambique. You will recall that in the eighteenth century this was commercially a flourishing region. Rozwi and Portuguese merchants met to exchange goods at inland and riverside markets as well as at the coastal trading centres. The Shangane did not destroy this commerce but they did dominate it. The Rozwi rulers were powerless to defend the fringes of the empire because they were in the process of being smashed by Ngoni and Ndebele marauders. The Portuguese *prazo* owners fled and their estates languished. Shoshangane attacked the major Portuguese settlements and trading posts. In 1833 Lourenço Marques was looted. In 1834 the Portuguese captain at Inhambane tried to halt the Shangane advance. He and most of his men were left dead on the field of battle. In 1836 the Sofala garrison was destroyed. Sena and Tete were brought under Shangane control and forced to pay tribute. By 1840 Shoshangane had established an empire stretching from the Limpopo to Inyanga, an empire usually known (after Shoshangane's grandfather) as the Gaza Empire.

After the death of Shoshangane in the late 1850s two of his sons, Mzila and Mawewe, disputed the succession. Though Mawewe inherited from his father, Mzila was able to raise a successful rebellion against him and became the new chief. This struggle occurred in the southern part of Gaza territory, for Mawewe had returned to the former homelands of his people near Delagoa Bay. His new capital was Biyeni. Mawewe fled to Swaziland but refused to accept defeat. With the aid of the Swazi he tried to regain his throne, while Mzila turned to the Portuguese for help in retaining it. The Swazi and the Portuguese continued to interfere for many years in Gaza's affairs and the Portuguese claimed that Mzila had placed his land under their protection. Mzila at last decided to withdraw from the troubled area. He returned to the Sabi highlands and set up his capital at Manklagazi. The Gaza Empire flourished during Mzila's reign. But before his death in 1885 the chief had already seen the beginnings of a slow Portuguese recovery which was to result in the colonial conquest of his territory before the end of the century.

Zwangendaba's Ngoni

The Ngoni led by Zwangendaba were, perhaps, the most remarkable of Bantu emigrants from south-east Africa. For ferocity and barbarity in warfare they had few equals. But even more worthy of note is the distance they covered. Always raiding and fighting, sometimes settling briefly, usually on the move with their families and livestock, the Ngoni smashed their way for over 3,000 kilometres through East–Central Africa between 1819 and 1845.

After his defeat by Shoshangane, Zwangendaba led his people westwards and thus entered the Rozwi Confederacy. This state was still prospering under the rule of the Changamire dynasty, a culturally advanced civilisation, until it was smashed by Zwangendaba's horde. The Shona were no match for the fierce Ngoni, with their new battle tactics. Great Zimbabwe was sacked in 1831 or 1832. The survivors, including the reigning Changamire, Chirisamaru, fled. The pursuing marauders then attacked Dhlo Dhlo, killing, destroying and looting. According to tradition Chirisamaru made his last stand in his hill fortress near the modern Inyati. This was captured by the Ngoni after a three-day siege during which they used a captured Portuguese cannon. When all his warriors had fallen or fled the Changamire allowed himself to be captured. He was then put to death after suffering the cruellest tortures. The dynasty came to an end and thousands of Shona men, women and children were murdered or enslaved by the restless Ngoni masses. Having ranged over most of the empire in search of cattle, captives and loot, they trekked northwards and crossed the Zambezi on 19 November 1835* into Nsenga country where they created havoc for the next four years. Then they fell upon the Cewa and Tumbuka and raided in the area to the west of Lake Nyasa for about another four years.

One reason why the Ngoni were unable to remain long in any one place was that their numbers were growing all the time. At every stage of the migration captives were incorporated into the host. Indeed, by 1840 there were more non-Ngoni than Ngoni in Zwangendaba's following. As the Ngoni burned and destroyed wherever they went it was not long before they had used up all the food to be obtained in the area they were staying in and so had to move on. Occasionally the Ngoni encountered states which were too powerful for them. Such were Kazembe and the Bemba state of Chitimukulu. After initial skirmishes with these peoples Zwangendaba decided not to risk further encounter but to concentrate his warlike efforts on smaller and more

*The event can be dated precisely because it occurred during an eclipse of the sun and the dates of these rare phenomena are all known.

Ngoni warrior.

fragmented societies. Such a society were the Fipa of the area between Lake Tanzania and Lake Rukwa. They in their turn were conquered and for a time the Ngoni settled on their land. There Zwangendaba's long journeyings came to an end; he died in Ufipa sometime between 1845 and 1848.

After the death of their leader the Ngoni split into five groups. Two of them continued northwards; Mpezeni, one of Zwangendaba's sons, 117 with a large following set off south-westwards. Driven off by the Bemba they marched back into the country of the Nsenga and submitted this region to a second conquest. Mpezeni remained the master of a large area north of the middle Zambezi until the 1890s.

Mombera, another of Zwangendaba's sons, led the main fragment of the nation southwards along the way they had come. In what is now northern Malawi he defeated the powerful Kamanga kingdom (c.1855) and made himself all-powerful over an area bordered by Lake Nyasa and the territory of the Cewa and Bemba. For twenty years Mombera's mixed following prospered and multiplied in this region. But it gradually proved more difficult for the chief to control his people. From 1875 there were many attempts at secession by various racial groups within the empire. Some succeeded but most failed and Mombera managed to preserve his state almost intact until the colonial era.

The third group consisted of the followers of Ciwere Ndhlovu, a Nsenga warrior who rose to high rank in Mombera's army. From Kamanga, Mombera sent a large advance party southwards down the western side of Lake Nyasa, and he put Ciwere in charge of this party. When his army reached the good pastureland near the south-western edge of the lake, Ciwere decided to stay. He also decided he was far enough away from his overlord to make a bid for independence. Ciwere added to his Ngoni and Nsenga following by raids on the surrounding Cewa and established what was, in fact, a Cewa state with a foreign ruling dynasty.

The Maseko and Msene Ngoni

After his defeat by Shoshangane (c.1832) Nxaba's horde split into two. One group, the Msene, led by Nxaba, went westwards in the wake of Zwangendaba while the remainder, known as the Maseko, moved northwards under the leadership of Ngare. His horde, growing steadily larger as a result of raiding and warfare, crossed the Zambezi, then the Shiré. Marching still northwards through the country of the Yao and the Makua to the east of Lake Nyasa, the Maseko eventually reached the Songea district of what is now southern Tanzania in the early 1840s. There Ngare died and was succeeded by Maputo.

At Songea they were joined in about 1850 by the Gwangwara, one of the factions of Zwangendaba's horde. Before long the two groups were at war. Maputo was killed and his followers scattered. The main body of the Maseko moved south once more. Passing round the southern end of Lake Nyasa they settled in the highlands west of the Shiré River in the 1860s. For a quarter of a century the Maseko dominated and frequently devastated the Shiré valley and highlands, closing the Yao trade routes and inflicting heavy defeats on the Kololo. In 1896 the Maseko armies were defeated by the British and their chief, Gomani, was executed.

Like Zwangendaba's people the Msene raided Rozwi settlements and helped to destroy the empire. Then Nxaba turned against Zwangendaba and defeated him in battle. The Msene continued to move westwards, enjoying considerable military success. Then near the Zambezi they ran into another migrant group, the Kololo, led by Sebitwane. The Msene were drawn into a position where they were cut off by the rising waters. There Nxaba and his horde perished by starvation or drowning.

The Kololo

The Kololo had reached the Lozi flood plain after many years of wandering through what is now Botswana. In the 1830s they settled along the Kafue River, but they were driven westwards from there by the Ndebele. They thus came to the Barotseland flood plain occupied by the Lozi, which they reached at the time of the annual flood, when all but a few areas of high land were under water. The Lozi attacked in their war canoes, believing that they would be able to force the newcomers into the water and destroy them. But they had reckoned without Sebitwane's cunning. He ordered his men to pretend to retreat, luring the Lozi to follow. When the pursuers had been tricked into leaving their boats far behind, the Kololo suddenly turned and destroyed their enemies before they could escape.

Sebitwane now conquered the whole Lozi kingdom with the exception of a small group under the leadership of some members of the Lozi royal family who fled beyond his reach. But Sebitwane did not want to crush the Lozi completely. He knew that if they were to enjoy their new homeland in peace the Kololo must live alongside and intermarry with the local people. Sebitwane himself took Lozi wives. He allowed many Lozi headmen to maintain their positions of authority and he incorporated Lozi warriors into his army. Thanks to Sebitwane's wise policy there was peace and harmony in the land for many years.

Lozi support also helped Sebitwane in two more conflicts with the Ndebele. Still seeking land and angered by his earlier failure to defeat Sebitwane, Mzilikazi launched two more attacks in the 1840s. Both were driven off with heavy losses. From that time Sebitwane ruled his people in peace until his death in 1851.

Within a few years almost all that Sebitwane had worked for collapsed. There were four main reasons for the rapid decline of the Kololo nation. The first was malaria. Sebitwane's followers had come from a region where there was no malaria, but in the humid Zambezi valley malaria-bearing mosquitoes breed freely and many of the Kololo caught the disease. Unlike the local people, who had developed partial immunity to malaria, the affected Kololo became seriously ill and many died. Shortly before his death Sebitwane moved his capital to a higher, healthier spot at Linyanti, but by this time he had already lost many valued warriors and officials.

The second reason for the collapse of Sebitwane's achievements lies in the character of his successor, Sekeletu. This man completely lacked his father's judgement and ability and he came to the throne unwillingly. As well as his defects of character he had to endure a worse affliction – leprosy. When this disease fell upon him he was convinced that its cause was witchcraft. He became suspicious and cruel, capturing and punishing both real and imagined enemies whom he believed to be in some way responsible for his misfortune. He turned against the Lozi with bitterness and completely reversed his father's policy of integration between the two peoples of the kingdom.

The third reason was the recovery of the Lozi. Largely as a result of Sekeletu's harsh policies many of the Lozi turned back to their old royal family for leadership. In 1860 a large group of Lozi rebelled and joined their chief, Masiku, in exile. Masiku died soon afterwards, but his successor, Sepopa, watched the steady disintegration of the Kololo kingdom and waited for his opportunity to invade his weakened foe.

That chance came in 1865. In that year Sekeletu died and the Kololo, instead of preserving their unity in order to resist the Lozi, indulged in a succession dispute which split the tribe. This failure of the Kololo to agree on a leader was the fourth reason for the kingdom's collapse. While the Kololo were fighting each other Sepopa struck. Thousands of Kololo men were slaughtered and thousands of Kololo women taken as wives.

So, after less than half a century the great Kololo empire collapsed. Its members were killed or dispersed. But something of these fine people did survive. In 1851 David Livingstone visited Sebitwane and subsequently a number of young Kololo men accompanied the missionary down the Zambezi as porters. In 1860 sixteen of these men decided to remain in the Shiré valley. They married local women and soon became the leaders of the local community. Using their traditional military and administrative skills these Kololo organised resistance to the Yao and Ngoni, for many years defending the people of the Shiré valley from slave traders. They remained a major influence in the area until the colonial partition of the 1890s.

The Ndebele

After his defeat by the Boers in 1837, Mzilikazi decided to move his people northwards out of range of both Boer and Zulu raids. After months of wanderings and many battles, the Ndebele settled in the region of the modern town of Bulawayo. This was near the heart of the old Rozwi empire, but the Rozwi had already been defeated and dispersed by the forces of Zwangendaba and Nxaba. The Ndebele fused with the local people and established firm control over what is still known as Matabeleland. Beyond this Mzilikazi's warriors raided over a wide area between the Limpopo and the Zambezi.

The Ndebele dominated all people who were weaker than them-

The Ndebele migrations.

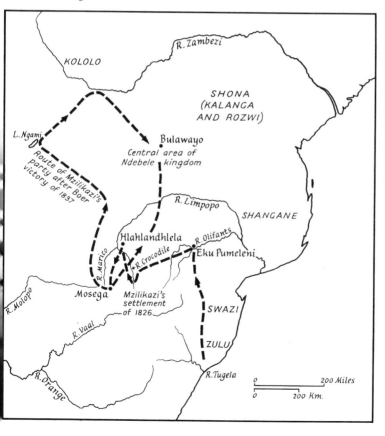

selves. Where they encountered stronger people, there they made their boundary. After some years of hostility, peace was made with the Boers in 1852. Similarly Mzilikazi made an alliance with Shoshangane in the east because the Shangane were strong enough to repel Ndebele raids. No treaty was made with the Kololo but after the failure of his attempts to defeat Sebitwane, Mzilikazi decided to send no more invading armies across the Zambezi. Gradually warfare became less frequent. More and more of Mzilikazi's subjects were able to follow the peaceful pursuits of trade and agriculture. Encouraged by the peace and good order of the Ndebele state and by the king's great hospitality, white men from the south and the east came to Mzilikazi's land in increasing numbers. The ageing chief warmly welcomed missionaries and allowed them to work among his people. Others came to hunt, to trade in ivory and skins and to look for valuable mineral deposits.

The newcomers brought new problems. Some quarrelled with Ndebele traders. Some introduced diseased cattle to Ndebele pastures. Some wanted to negotiate exclusive mining rights on Ndebele land. Though the work of government became more difficult Mzilikazi retained his grasp of affairs almost until the end of his long life. During his last twenty years he was frequently ill and in pain but he did not die until 1868, when he was past seventy years of age.

It was only after months of intrigue and civil war that Lobengula managed to win his father's throne. But once he had secured his position he soon reunited the Ndebele. Unfortunately it was his fate to rule at a time when European interest in Matabeleland was growing.

11. New pressures
(5) Commercial expansion in Central Africa

Between 1800 and 1880 more and more states became involved in long-distance trade as both African and foreign merchants penetrated farther into the continent. The introduction of guns and ruthless slaving broke the power of once great kingdoms while other, previously obscure, communities grew rich and powerful by taking a leading part in trade.

Portuguese Angola

Up to 1822 Angola continued as basically a producer of slaves for the Brazilian plantations. In 1822 two heavy blows fell: in Luanda the

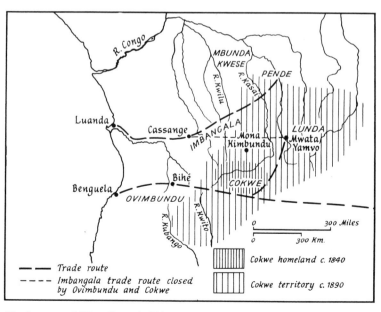

Trade routes of West Central Africa.

government was overthrown by revolution; and in Brazil another revolution freed the country from Portuguese rule. The first of these revolutions led to eighteen years of political chaos in Angola. The second destroyed the traditional pattern of Angolan commerce.

The slave trade still went on. Ships still carried African men and women to Brazil and to São Tomé. After the introduction of cocoa growing to São Tomé in 1822 the island needed more slaves than ever for plantation work. But the Angolan dealers no longer had a monopoly of the trade to South America. The trade in slaves was doomed for other reasons. Portugal was coming under increasing pressure from other European countries to stop. The government in Lisbon resisted this pressure as long as possible. In 1815 the Portuguese agreed to prohibit slave trading north of the equator and only to allow the trade within her own territories. This meant that trade with Brazil was still legal. The independence of Brazil removed this legality but not until 1836 was slave trading prohibited to Portuguese subjects by law. That law was ignored – and successfully ignored – by European and African slave dealers for a few more years but from 1840, under stronger, firmer governors, authority and order were restored and the slave trade gradually dwindled.

The government tried to find other types of commerce to sustain the economic life of the colony. Cotton and coffee plantations were established but they enjoyed only temporary success. The Portuguese also tried to gain control of the trade routes to the interior. Between 1855 and 1866 they reconquered Kongo in order to exploit the Bembe copper mines and control trade on the lower Congo. But the resources of the area were inadequate to pay the costs of administration so the white men withdrew. Between 1848 and 1863 there were various unsuccessful campaigns against the Imbangala aimed at controlling their markets and trade routes. By 1863 they had driven the Portuguese out of their territory and resumed complete commercial control once more. By contrast the Ovimbundu remained on good terms with the Portuguese. They continued to trade with the Europeans and went on commercial ventures organised by them. They continued to be the main suppliers of slaves to the Portuguese until well into the 1880s.

In the late 1860s rubber was discovered, and from 1870 there was a rapid development of new trade. This provided the Portuguese and their associates with a valuable substitute for slaves. Portuguese and Ovimbundu traders hurried to make fortunes out of the boom. Commerce flourished once more in Angola as it had not done for nearly a hundred years. The rubber boom came just in time for the Portuguese. In the 1880s other European nations began to lay claims to

African colonies. With the wealth obtained from rubber Portugal was able to cling onto and extend her traditional sphere of influence.

The Imbangala, Ovimbundu and Cokwe

The changing pattern of trade at the coast brought changes to those peoples who ventured far inland to keep Angolan markets supplied.

The Imbangala found their position challenged by other commercial rivals – the Ovimbundu and the Cokwe. The struggle with the Ovimbundu for control of trade with the Lunda kingdoms had been going on for decades. By 1850 the Imbangala were no longer able to dominate the old route. Instead, they struck north-eastwards and established trading links with the Pende. The decline of the slave trade was another blow to the Imbangala, for slaves had been their main trading commodity. Here, the rise of the Cokwe (described below) came to their aid – temporarily. The Cokwe were fine hunters and could be relied on for a good supply of elephant tusks. In return for ivory the Cokwe demanded slave women. The Imbangala were therefore able to buy slaves and ivory from the Lunda and Pende, then exchange some of their slaves with the Cokwe for more ivory for sale to the Portuguese and their agents at Cassange. As the Cokwe increased their commercial activity and their power the Imbangala found them less co-operative as trading partners. First the Cokwe taxed their caravans heavily. Then, in the 1870s, they forced the Imbangala out of the direct route to Mwata Yamvo.

The Ovimbundu were the most energetic and adventurous long-distance traders on the western side of the continent. Moreover they were clever enough to adapt their commerce during a century of dramatic changes. By 1800 they already controlled the southerly routes to the interior and their centre of Bihé was one of the biggest slave markets in tropical Africa. Slaves formed the staple of Ovimbundu trade at this time. The men of Bihé brought beeswax and skins from the interior and they were accomplished elephant hunters. However, until 1834 the Portuguese king had a monopoly of the ivory trade. This depressed prices and checked Ovimbundu dealings in ivory.

In the middle years of the century there was a growing world demand for ivory. This, and the removal of the royal monopoly on the ivory trade stimulated Portuguese and African dealings in elephant tusks. The Ovimbundu slave trade did not stop when the Portuguese demand slackened off. They found a growing interior market. Stimulated by the lower prices now asked for slaves, expansive and vigorous societies such as the Kololo, Lozi and Cokwe purchased as many slaves as the Ovimbundu and other traders could supply. The search for ivory and slaves drew the Ovimbundu caravans ever deeper into the interior. By 1860 they were bartering slaves and ivory at Tete on the lower Zambezi.

The expansion of trade in the interior brought new wealth to individuals and groups within African society. It introduced new and better crops such as maize and cassava to a wide area. On the other hand it spread the use of firearms which led to increased raiding and warfare.

The Cokwe learned a great deal about commerce from the Ovimbundu. They were already the finest elephant hunters east of Kwango, and when they obtained guns from the Ovimbundu they made a bid for commercial independence. By 1860 they had stopped the Ovimbundu from slave raiding in their territory. Before long they were able, as the leading suppliers of ivory and wax, to impose their own terms on Ovimbundu dealers.

The Ovimbundu were quick to realise the importance of rubber. They discovered rubber trees east of the Kwanza and in Cokwe territory. As the demand for and the price of African rubber increased, more and more Ovimbundu engaged in the trade. By the 1880s a 'rubber boom' was in full swing.

Trade probably provided the main reasons for Cokwe expansion. Hunters had to go further and further afield in pursuit of elephants as the animals nearer home were killed or fled. Later, the same problem occurred with rubber. The Cokwe killed off thousands of rubber trees by tapping them too severely. They then had to search farther from home for more trees. Trade also brought the Cokwe the guns that made expansion possible.

Cokwe conquest began in earnest in the 1850s probably stimulated initially by a search for beeswax. By 1875 they dominated much of the area between the Kwito and Kubango Rivers. They had their most devastating effect in the north and north-east. There the Cokwe penetrated and helped to destroy the already crumbling Lunda Empire. They spread steadily northwards and had dominated the area around Mona Kimbundu by the mid-1870s. Their advance continued and ten years later they reached the land of the Pende, where they were halted. Further east, trading and raiding took the Cokwe across the Kasai River in 1866. They soon gained a reputation as warriors and in 1875 one of the contenders for the Lunda throne invited the Cokwe to help him. They did so and thereby gained a firmer foothold in Lunda territory. The Lunda nation was by this time hopelessly divided and no Lunda group was powerful enough to throw the Cokwe out. The newcomers now raided widely on their own

A Cokwe mask. This expressive mask was made for use at secular games and entertainments.

account and added greatly to the strife and chaos of the 1880s. When, in 1885, a large Lunda army was gathered to expel the invaders it was utterly defeated by the Cokwe, who had more guns.

Cokwe power was at its height about 1890 but soon afterwards the tide began to turn. In 1892 a united Pende, Mbunda, Kwese army soundly defeated the Cokwe in a major battle on the bank of the River Kwilu. Four years later a new Mwata Yamvo reunited many of the Lunda and successfully confronted a Cokwe army. The Cokwe now withdrew east of the Kasai. However, they were still a powerful and energetic people. It was only the arrival of colonial forces which finally destroyed their power and independence.

The Lunda Empire

Until well into the nineteenth century the kingdom of the Mwata Yamvo continued to be a strong, expansionist state. Between 1800 and 1850 Lunda rulers frequently raided neighbouring states and added fresh territory to the empire. Under Yaav ya Mbany who reigned from about 1760 to 1810 the empire reached its greatest extent. Another long reign was that of the ruthless Naweej II, who ruled from 1810 to 1852.

During the next half century the Lunda Empire was almost completely destroyed. The two main causes of this disintegration were the growth of long-distance trade and a series of succession disputes. Long-distance traders began to reach the capital during the reign of Naweej II. He encouraged merchants and even gave them permission to raid in parts of his territory for slaves. But the Lunda Empire could not derive much benefit from commerce. Their land was right in the centre of the continent, at the end of the trade routes from the east and the west. If they wanted caravans to call they had to attract them by offering slaves and ivory cheaply. If they wanted guns they had to pay a high price for them. They simply could not compete on equal terms with peoples nearer the coast. What therefore happened during the second half of the century was that neighbouring peoples grew richer and more powerful as a result of trade. They had more guns and were better able to resist the famed Lunda warriors.

If there had been unity within the empire and strong leadership the rulers might have been able to resist these new pressures. But throughout the second half of the nineteenth century the empire was torn by a series of succession disputes. Rebellions, assassinations and depositions were frequent as rivals fought for the throne. In the thirty years from 1857 to 1887 the Lunda had ten different rulers.

In 1886 the Cokwe drove Mwata Yamvo Mudiba from his capital and sold the people of the town into slavery. A year later they were back again, this time to place a new ruler, Mushiri, on the throne. Before the year was out they had turned against Mushiri and driven him from the capital. For more than ten years the Lunda Empire was in Cokwe hands. They devasted a great part of it and sold thousands of Lunda into slavery.

In 1898 Mushiri and his brother, Kawele, returned from the distant corner of Lunda land where they had taken refuge. They carefully

Brutality on the slave trail. Scenes like this were common when Africans displeased Arab traders.

organised resistance to the Cokwe and finally led an army against the invaders. After a three-day battle beside the Lulua River the Cokwe were defeated. But before the Lunda were able to take advantage of their victory a new threat appeared. This was the Congo Free State. The Congo Free State armies overthrew Mushiri and placed a rival on the throne as Muteba III. For many years the two brothers fought valiantly against the colonial forces and Muteba's warriors, but in 1909 they were captured and killed.

The Bemba

As the Bemba succeeded in their career of aggression they became more and more involved in trade. They forced the Bisa out of some of their trading areas. They gained control of the salt pans at Chibwe. When the Bisa were driven out of some of their traditional trading areas they carried on their activities elsewhere. They bought ivory from the Lamba and took it to trading posts on the middle Zambezi, where they exchanged it for European cloth and other imported goods. They travelled to Katanga for copper and in the east their activities extended as far as Cewa country. But their direct route from the Shiré valley to Kazembe was blocked by the Bemba. The Bisa 129 took a full share in the trade boom of the mid-nineteenth century. By 1867 they were dealing in all manner of goods including slaves (they had not originally been slave traders). The Bemba did not destroy Bisa trade on the plateau: They simply controlled it. Most of the trade goods which had found their way to Kazembe were now bought by Bemba chiefs.

The most important commodity the Bemba gained from trade was guns, most of which came from newcomers to the north. In the 1840s Arab and Afro-Arab traders from the east coast as well as Nyamwezi traders from what is now central Tanzania began to reach Kazembe via the Tanganyika–Nyasa corridor.

Most of the Bemba expansion occurred during the reigns of two great Chitimukulus, Cileshye (c. 1840–60) and Citapankwa (1866–87). Cileshye seized the throne from a weak king and united the chiefs firmly behind him. Citapankwa was a great warrior and during his reign the Bemba became richer and more powerful than ever. Citapankwa's successors were lesser men, unable to preserve Bemba unity but the Bemba remained the masters of the plateau until the end of the nineteenth century.

Kazembe

To the west Kazembe's kingdom continued to expand throughout the first half of the century. For most of that time, from 1805 to c.1850, the throne was occupied by Kazembe IV (Kibangu Keleka). It was he who welcomed the first Nyamwezi traders in the early years of his reign and who, in 1806, also welcomed Angolan *pombeiros* from the other side of the continent. Trade flourished along the routes running to and from his empire. In the 1840s Arab and Nyamwezi traders began to arrive more frequently in the East Lunda Empire, attracted in particular by the copper of Katanga. Difficult times arrived after the accession of Kazembe VI (Cinyanta Mussona) in 1854. Trade with the Bisa became more difficult as Bemba power grew, while new developments threatened Kazembe's westerly caravan routes.

One man was responsible for this. His name was Msiri. He was a Nyamwezi trader and he arrived in the Kazembe kingdom in 1856. Cinyanta allowed him to move on to Katanga and here he settled with his followers, who came to be known as Yeke. Msiri established good relations with the local chiefs. By treaties, by commerce and by raiding he steadily built up his following and his power. By the time of Cinyanta's death in 1862 Msiri had already established a degree of independence from the Kazembe. He was trading with caravans from Mwata Yamvo and Angola without the permission of his overlord.

Msiri's influence was demonstrated in 1865 when two Lunda princes tried to raise a rebellion against the new Kazembe, Mwonga Nsemba (1862–70). Kazembe's representative had to turn to Msiri for help in crushing the insurrection. Mwonga Nsemba was angry and worried when he realised how powerful this Nyamwezi trader had become. He reacted by killing all easterners in his territory. This only provoked the Arab and African traders to retaliate. Between 1868 and 1870 they waged war on Kazembe, finally defeating him. Mwonga Nsemba hurried back to his capital only to find that he had lost the support of his people, some of whom murdered him shortly afterwards.

The political structure of the East Lunda kingdom now collapsed. Rivals vied for the throne and did not hesitate to seek the support of Msiri, or any other African or Arab leader who had followers and guns. By 1871 Msiri ruled all the old Kazembe lands west of the Luapula. He monopolised the trade in ivory, copper and slaves throughout this region. His caravans travelled to the east and west coasts. He established his capital at Bunkeya and called himself King. The only people for whom Msiri showed respect were other powerful Arab and African traders from the east. He had to maintain good relations with them because they were in a position to threaten his supply of guns. The Kazembe and other chiefs continued to resist Msiri's extension of power but he remained without any serious rival until 1890.

Arab and Afro-Arab Traders

It was the growing world demand for ivory and the development of clove plantations on the islands of Zanzibar and Pemba, for which slave labour was required, which encouraged African long-distance traders (foremost among whom were the Nyamwezi) and coastal merchants to travel to new regions. The easterners devastated an increasingly wide area in their search for ivory, slaves and (later) copper. Two factors made them particularly terrifying. One was their supply of guns. The other was the fighting methods they had learned from the Ngoni, who, as we have seen, used techniques derived from Shaka's innovations among Zulus. Ngoni warriors were particularly brutal and most of them owed allegiance to no one except their warlord. The same characteristics were seen among the Yeke and other bands of trader–warriors. An African or Arab trader would hire a band of mercenaries (known as *ruga-ruga*) and set off on a 'commercial' venture. But strict trading was reserved for areas where the chiefs were powerful. Elsewhere murder and pillage were the usual

An Arab massacre of Manyema men, women and children which occurred at Nyangwe. It was only one of many unnecessary acts of brutality.

methods of obtaining ivory, slaves and other goods. By way of illustration we will consider the career of one of these traders – Tippu Tip.

Tippu Tip

Hamed Bin Muhammed el Murjebi was an Afro-Arab from Zanzibar. He gained his nickname of Tippu Tip because of a nervous twitching of his eyelids. During the 1850s he made many trading journeys in what is now Tanzania and gained a reputation as a ruthless and crafty dealer in ivory and slaves. He was also bold and adventurous. In 1867 he entered the Tabwa territory, though he knew that the leading Tabwa chief, Nsama, had cheated and even killed other Arabs. In one battle he overthrew Nsama, captured his capital and took possession of the king's enormous store of ivory. Tippu Tip's victory over Nsama was an important turning-point in the history of the region. It showed the Tabwa, the Bemba, the East Lunda and others how powerful the newcomers were. Two years later Tippu Tip went into East Lunda territory and arrived at the time when Mwonga Nsemba was turning against the easterners. Tippu Tip, in league with other Arabs, attacked the Kazembe's army and was largely responsible for the defeat, flight and subsequent death of Mwonga Nsemba.

Tippu Tip now moved far away to the north-west, still in pursuit of untapped sources of ivory. Among the Tetela, where no Arab had ever been, he gained himself a chiefdom by trickery. He raided widely and increased his territory. He received tribute of elephant tusks from chiefs who acknowledged his authority. He had to set up depots to house his immense stores of ivory. In the early 1870s the Arabs of Kasongo and Nyangwe recognised Tippu Tip as their overlord. This gave him control of Manyema and Rua territory. Tippu Tip now ruled an immense personal empire which stretched westwards from Lake Tanganyika as far as the Lomami and which was only limited in the north by the Congo forest. He and his deputies ruled this area until the coming of the white man. Then, rather than give up his hunting grounds and his way of life, he allied with the Belgians and became for a while a colonial governor based at Stanley Falls. Not until 1890 did Tippu Tip leave Central Africa to spend the last years of his life in wealthy retirement at Zanzibar. Though he was the most celebrated of the trader–rulers of the late nineteenth century, he was only one among many.

Tippu Tip.

The Yao

The expansion of trade on the Swahili coast benefited the Yao traders and enabled many of them to become powerful local leaders. By 1800 powerful rulers were organising frequent caravans to the coast and beyond Lake Nyasa.

The most famous Yao leader of all was Mataka Nyambi. He was born in about 1800. As a young man he rebelled against his overlord and with a few kinsmen formed a separate village. He took to a life of trade, first exchanging baskets for hoes, then using the hoes to obtain slaves. At last he had enough followers to be able to take up slave raiding on his own account. He was successful and before long his activities extended over 'the whole of Yaoland and the lake, practically the whole of that part of Africa, and he became the Sultan Che Mataka, the supreme ruler'.*

Mataka established his headquarters at Mwembe, which grew into a sizeable town. He was, apparently, a bloodthirsty tyrant who ordered executions and mutilations on the slightest provocation. Such fear did he inspire that few of his subordinates ever dared to rebel against him. This was as well, for like other Yao leaders, Mataka had no administrative system to hold his empire together. He is said to have had 600 wives, and when he died sixty young boys and girls were sacrificed and buried with him. He was able to pass on a large, united empire to his successor.

A state of almost perpetual war existed in Yaoland and the surrounding area. The great Yao states were always raiding the communities around the lake and along the Shiré valley. They were frequently at war with each other. For much of the century they were in conflict with the Ngoni. In the 1840s the Maseko Ngoni fought their way northwards as far as Songea. For twenty years they carried out sporadic raids in Yaoland. Then in the 1870s, when they were forced out of Songea by the Gwangwara, they turned southwards and marched into the Shiré highlands. The resulting chaos and insecurity did much to change Yao social customs. By the middle of the century large tracts of good farmland were deserted. The people preferred to live in large, defensible villages and towns. With this new urban life went a new sophistication. The Yao took to copying the ways of the Swahilis and Arabs. They dressed like the coast men. They learned their language and they began to adopt their religion – Islam.

* D. Livingstone, *Last Journals* (London, 1874), p. 83.

Peoples of the Lake Nyasa–Shiré Highlands Region

'One of the dark places of the earth, full of abominations and cruelty'* – that was how one European visitor in the late nineteenth century described the area which is now Malawi. As well as the Ngoni invasions the peoples living to the west and south of Lake Nyasa suffered repeated raids from Arabs, Yao, Bemba, Bisa and the Afro-Portuguese *prazeros* of the lower Zambezi region. This densely populated and fertile region became one of the major sources of slaves in the whole of Africa. Probably about 20,000 men, women and children every year were carried off to east coast ports.

Most communities were destroyed or absorbed but some offered successful resistance. The most notable example of this is provided by the Cewa chief, Mwase wa Kasungu. He controlled the trade route to Kota-Kota and was thus able to force the Arabs there to sell him guns. With these he resisted an Ngoni invasion in the 1860s and then made an alliance with the Ngoni leader, Mbelwa. The Tonga united in the face of Ngoni pressure and, though at great cost, they maintained their independence. In the Shiré valley the situation was more confused. Attacked from all sides by powerful enemies, many of the peoples of this area were prepared to follow anyone who could inspire them and lead them to victory. This was how the Kololo warriors introduced to the area by Dr Livingstone managed to establish themselves as chiefs in the Shiré valley. Two other individuals who became leaders among the Nyanja were Chibisa, an ex-slave, and Belchior, a former Portuguese soldier.

The Portuguese and their allies on the lower Zambezi

In the east the decline of Portuguese power and influence which began in the seventeenth and eighteenth centuries was continuing. The garrisons were undermanned. The Europeans had neither the power nor the money to enable them to extend their rule inland. But had they had the initiative and the equipment for territorial expansion they would have found it difficult to overcome rulers like Shoshangane and Zwangendaba.

The Ngoni invasions almost destroyed completely the power of the Portuguese and their inland allies. Many *prazo* owners were driven off their estates or gave up and went home because of the disturbed state of affairs in the interior. Of those who remained, many had to pay tribute to Shoshangane. But the gradual dwindling of the number of *prazeros* left those remaining more powerful. They accumulated

*J. W. Jack, *Daybreak in Livingstonia* (London, 1901), p. 18.   135

more territory and more followers. They acquired more slaves and also opened up new trade routes. The authorities were powerless to control the activities of their own subjects. In any case many officials were themselves actively involved in slave dealing. When Dr Livingstone visited the area in the 1850s and 1860s he was appalled to find white men and their agents trafficking in human beings while the government did nothing to restrain them.

As well as raiding their African neighbours, the *prazeros* raided each other. This not only added to the unnecessary bloodshed and chaos in the lower Zambezi area; it also concentrated power in fewer hands. Weaker *prazeros* were forced out and their lands taken over by their rivals. By 1860 the region was dominated by four family groups. The names of these families were Portuguese but there was by this time little else about them that was Portuguese. Continued inter-marriage with the local people had made the *prazero* families almost completely African. The family heads had taken on most of the trappings of chieftaincy. The *prazos* had become powerful African communities, dependent on slavery and slave trading, able to defend themselves against all enemies – black and white.

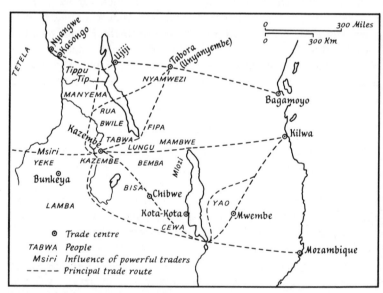

Eastern trade routes in the late nineteenth century.

In the second half of the century the Portuguese government mounted a number of expeditions to explore the hinterland. More money was granted for administrative development and engineering works at the coast. In the 1860s and 70s Lourenço Marques began to develop from a small garrison town into the thriving city and port it is today. On the Zambezi there was a deliberate attempt to make Portuguese authority above Sena a reality. After several attacks government troops eventually wrested control of Tete from the local *prazero* in 1887. Zumbo, which had been closed as a trading post in 1836, was reopened in 1861. In 1889 it was made the administrative centre of a new colonial district.

12. The growth of European interest in Africa

For about seventy years the whole of the area we are concerned with was under European rule. It is this period of colonial control that we shall be dealing with in this section. As we have seen, foreigners of Portuguese, Dutch and British origin had gained control of some areas but by 1880 less than a quarter of southern and Central Africa was in the hands of white men. It was not at all clear that the foreigners would maintain control in all areas, let alone extend their authority. Many African groups were putting up stiff resistance and most of the white colonies received little active support from their governments in Europe. After 1880 this situation changed. European powers became engaged in a 'scramble' for African territory and within a few years there was no part of the continent south of the Congo forest which was not ruled from London, Brussels, Lisbon or Berlin.

European interest built up slowly during the middle years of the century. Men came as missionaries, explorers, hunters, prospectors and adventurers. Apart from the missionaries they all hoped to make a profit out of the natural resources of the continent. They wanted to find ivory, skins and precious metals. However, it was the discovery of diamonds which really began the industrial development of southern Africa.

Diamonds

Diamonds were first discovered on the Orange River near Hopetown in 1867. There was no immediate rush to the region but the situation changed a few months later when diamonds were discovered along the banks of the lower Vaal. By the beginning of 1870 prospectors were flocking to Hebron and Klipdrift. But within a year attention had shifted southwards to a far richer diamondiferous area – the Dry Diggings (modern Kimberley). Soon claims were being made and concessions sought by excited miners. There were three main claim-

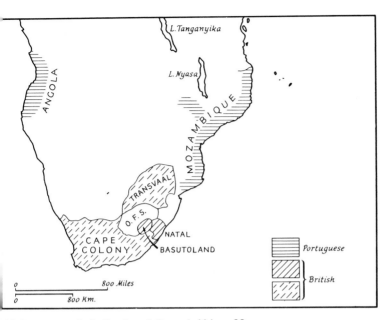

(a) *European rule in South and Central Africa 1880.*
(b) *European rule in South and Central Africa 1895.*

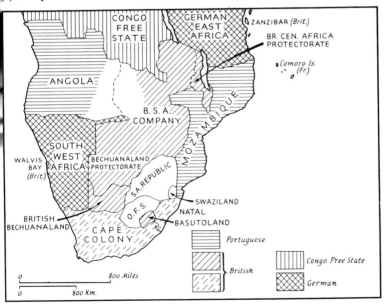

ants: the Orange Free State, the South African Republic and the Griqua leader, Waterboer. The rival claims were based on a complicated series of written and verbal treaties as well as actual occupa- 139

Early gold mining.

tion. In 1868, M. Pretorius, president of the South African Republic suddenly claimed an area westwards from the Republic as far as the Kalahari Desert. Fierce protests were made by the British, the Portuguese, various African leaders in the area and missionaries. Pretorius was forced to withdraw but he was still determined to gain part of the diamond-mining area for his country. In 1870 he assumed authority over the area to the north of the lower Vaal and issued a diamond-mining monopoly to three of his friends. There was another outcry and Pretorius again backed down but not before the miners at Klipdrift had declared the area an independent republic, in the hope of avoiding any further interference.

The leaders of the two Boer states now tried to gain control of the diamondiferous area by peaceful negotiation with Waterboer, and Rolong and Tlhaping leaders. When these talks at Nooitgedacht broke down Waterboer asked for British protection. Now it was the turn of the Orange Free State leader, J. H. Brand, to take decisive action. He annexed the area west of the Vaal, known as the Campbell Lands. The miners at Kimberley, as well as Waterboer, protested against this action and the Cape government announced that the Free State had no jurisdiction over British subjects in the disputed territory. It was now the end of 1870 and the situation was becoming tense. Brand wanted the issue to be put to the arbitration of independent foreign judges but Britain refused. The last thing Britain wanted was for European powers to become interested in South Africa. By the following April armed Cape and Free State forces faced each other along the lower Vaal.

The man who was most responsible for the final outcome of the dispute was Sir H. Barkly, the new Cape Colony High Commissioner. He had strong imperialist beliefs and knew that Britain's position in

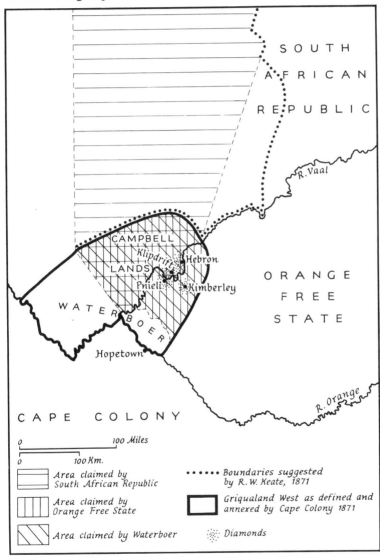

The disputed diamond producing area, 1869–71.

South Africa would become seriously weakened if the Boer states gained control of the diamond mines. He persuaded Pretorius to accept the arbitration of R. W. Keate, Lieutenant-Governor of Natal, on the border dispute north of the Vaal. Then he persuaded the Cape parliament to agree to Waterboer's request for his land to be annexed. Keate made his report in September. His recommendations excluded the Klipdrift area from the South African Republic and included the Campbell Lands in Waterboer's territory. Keate said nothing about the land east of the Vaal where Kimberley and the richest mining area lay; he had not been required to make judgement on this. But, in October, when Barkly carried out the annexation of Waterboer's territory he included the whole of the disputed area in the new province of Griqualand West. The Boers were furious at what they considered yet another example of British treachery and deceit, but there was little they could do to reverse the situation.

Political developments in South Africa 1871–84

As we have already seen, the British put an end to Moshweshwe's conflict with the Boers by annexing Basutoland in 1871, and further east the Xhosa were finally quelled in 1877. Even then relations between Africans and settlers were far from peaceful. The South African Republic was involved in a dispute with the Zulus over the Blood River boundary. To the north they were having trouble with Secocoeni, the Pedi chief, who refused to acknowledge Boer rule and who would not allow the Republic to build a railway to the coast across his land.

The British government wanted to break out of the repeating cycle of events – Afro-Boer conflict, British intervention, British annexation. The British Colonial Secretary, Lord Carnarvon, thought that the idea of federation might be acceptable to the South African Republic. The government at Pretoria was in financial difficulties. When campaigns against the Pedi failed the government was no longer able to rely on the support of its own electors.

Under these circumstances Sir T. Shepstone, the Secretary for Native Affairs in Natal, was sent to the South African Republic to try to persuade the government to agree to annexation. The government was in no position to resist and in April 1877 Shepstone simply declared that the Transvaal was a British territory. The Boers under the leadership of Paul Kruger, the former Vice-president, protested loudly but could offer no effective resistance. Soon the attention of all the Europeans in South Africa was diverted to a new problem in the Zulu War.

After the death of Dingane the sting went out of the Zulu military force. Mpande, the next ruler, followed a policy of peaceful co-operation with his white neighbours and this was largely the attitude taken by Cetshawayo when he became king in 1873. But during the thirty-three years since Dingane's death the main problem of the Zulus – land hunger – had grown worse. Zululand was now encircled by white-controlled territory so that state expansion was impossible. Even the existence of a Zulu army, which was once more raised to a peak of size and efficiency by Cetshawayo, was regarded with disfavour by the government of Natal.

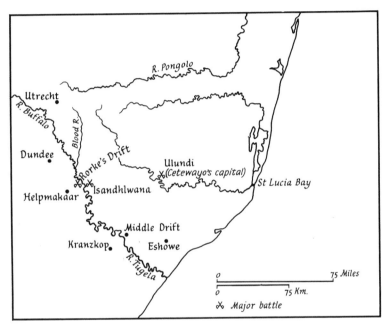

The Zulu War, 1879.

The Zulu War

In 1877 Sir H. B. Frere was appointed as Governor of Cape Colony. He was determined to bring about the desired South African federation and he was convinced that a firm line with the Zulus would help win the Boers over. In the middle of 1878 Frere asked for more soldiers to be sent from England so that he could put a speedy end to the Xhosa War and also overawe the Zulus. At the same time he appointed a commission to decide on the Blood River lands dispute between Cetshawayo and the Transvaal. To his annoyance the commission reported in favour of the Zulu leader. Frere could not go 143

Cetshawayo.

back on this but he inflicted severe conditions on its implementation: the Zulu army was to be disbanded; Boer farmers from the Blood River lands were to be compensated; a British Resident was to be stationed in Zululand; and a large payment was to be made in cattle as a fine for certain border incidents. It was impossible for Cetshawayo to comply with this ultimatum and to retain any real freedom. Frere had orders from London to avoid war with the Zulus but, when Cetshawayo failed to respond to the ultimatum, he ignored his instructions and launched an invasion of Zululand in January 1879. On the 22nd a British force of 1,800 men was attacked by Cetshawayo's *impis* at Isandhlawana. Four hundred were left alive. Alarm and anger spread through the Cape; the divisions between Boer and

Briton became deeper and some African leaders raised the standard of revolt against their white masters. But Cetshawayo was only interested in protecting his own territory; he did not attack Natal. British reinforcements arrived and in July a European army fought its way through to Cetshewayo's capital, Ulundi, and defeated the Zulus.

The British government was determined not to annex Zululand; all they wanted to do was make Zululand 'safe'. Cetshawayo was deposed and exiled. There was to be no new chief; instead the people were divided into thirteen chiefdoms ruled by leaders selected by the Governor of Natal. A British Resident was to be appointed. Most of the Blood River Lands were to be ceded to the Transvaal. The members of the royal clan were reduced to the status of commoners. The result was anarchy. Law and order broke down without a central authority to enforce them. The Resident had no power to enforce his will on the Zulus. Conflicts arose between new rulers and members of the royal clan. In a desperate bid to restore order the British sent Cetshawayo back to his country in 1883 but he was forced out by his enemies and died soon afterwards. For another four years the British refused to annex Zululand but then they realised that it was the only way to restore peace and stability to the land.

But by that time Britain had once more lost the Transvaal. The event that sparked off the first Anglo-Boer War was an attempt by British authorities to seize the goods of a Transvaaler who had not paid his taxes. The local people banded together and threw the colonial officials out. In December 1880 the Boers elected three leaders, Kruger, Pretorius and P. Joubert, and proclaimed their independence. The war, if such it can be called, consisted of a number of skirmishes and one minor battle (Majuba Hill). The British government had no desire to continue the conflict. Peace talks between the two sides began and the result was the Pretoria Convention which came into effect in October 1881. By this agreement the 'Transvaal State' came into being. It had complete internal self-government under British 'suzerainty' (a term which was rather vague but which involved ensuring the laws of the new state were brought into line with those of the British colonies, particularly where the rights of Africans were concerned, and installing a British Resident at Pretoria).

In 1884 the terms of the Pretoria Convention were considerably amended, in the Transvaal's favour. It resumed the name 'South African Republic'. Its territory was increased towards the west. It gained complete control over its internal law-making. The British Resident was reduced to the status of a consul. The Republic gained much more control over foreign affairs. The South African Republic was, in effect, independent. The idea of federation was dead. British 145 and Boer attitudes had hardened and each wished to pursue their own way of life. The Africans would have liked to have been able to pursue their own way of life too but that was scarcely possible. As the white men demanded more and more land the Africans found their territory either annexed or its boundaries firmly fixed by the invaders.

The Battle of Isandhlwana, with Lord Chelmsford's advancing column.

Cecil Rhodes

The economic development of South Africa gave rise to a new pheno-menon – the wealthy, powerful businessman. The wealthiest and most powerful of them all was Cecil Rhodes. Cecil Rhodes was also the best example of another new phenomenon – the imperialist. Rhodes came to South Africa in 1870 at the age of seventeen for the sake of his health. Within a year he was on the Kimberley diamond field making a quick fortune for himself. He was a clear-thinking and far-sighted young man. He knew that mining would become more difficult and more expensive as men had to go deeper into the earth to find the diamonds. When several of the small mining companies ran into difficulties Rhodes was ready. He bought them up and amalgamated them into what became De Beers Consolidated Mines Ltd. By 1890 De Beers had a monopoly of South African diamond mining and Rhodes was a multi-millionaire. From the first he was interested in politics and in 1880 was elected to the Cape parliament. His attitude to the complex problems of South Africa was quite clear: he believed Britain should rule all of it. He admired the Boers and believed that British and Boer territories could be amalgamated by common consent. Rhodes was a complete imperialist. He was convinced that Britain stood at the summit of all human civilisation and that by extending her empire she could extend that civilisation all over the world. When Rhodes was a student at Oxford he heard these words from one of his lecturers. They made a great impression on him and may be considered as Rhodes' motto:

... youths of England, make your country again a royal throne of kings, a sceptred isle, for all the world a source of light, a centre of peace ... This is what England must do or perish; she must found colonies as far and as fast as she is able ... seizing every piece of fruitful waste ground she can set foot on, and there teaching her colonists that their chief virtue is to be fidelity to their country.*

As far as Africa was concerned Rhodes wanted to see a wide belt of British territory extending from the Cape to Cairo and he urged this policy more insistently when other powers began to vie with Britain for control of parts of the continent. He was prepared to make his vast wealth available to the British government to help to realise his dream. We shall see in the next chapter how Rhodes took a lead in British expansion in Central Africa. At this stage it is important to realise how influential Rhodes was. His intense patriotism inspired his fellow countrymen in South Africa and in Britain.

Rhodes played a part in the British occupation of Bechuanaland. This was another example of the by now traditional cycle of events — border conflict, reluctant British intervention, annexation. In 1881 a conflict sprang up between two Rolong chiefs, Montsioa and Moshete, around Mafeking. Further south the Tlhaping Mankoroane attacked the Korana settlement led by Massouw. Moshete and Massouw were successful largely because they were helped by armed men from the Republic. The victorious chiefs rewarded their allies with grants of land and the two Boer states of Goshen and Stellaland came into existence. This alarmed some sections of British opinion because

*John Ruskin quoted in André Maurois, *Cecil Rhodes* (London, 1953), p. 44.   147

the new Boer lands spanned the route to the northern interior. Kruger saw Goshen and Stellaland as useful bargaining pieces and at the London Convention in 1884 he agreed to persuade the settlers to withdraw from most of the new territories in return for concessions from the British government (see above, p. 145).

But complications came from an unexpected source. In 1882 German traders had established a base on the south-west coast of Africa at Angra Pequẽna. Now, in 1884, Germany suddenly annexed the whole of Namaqualand. This caused the South African Republic leaders to have second thoughts. There was the possibility of important trade connections with the Germans and perhaps even a direct railway link with the coast. The British government saw their economic control of the Boer republics and their free road to the interior threatened. The situation needed very careful handling.

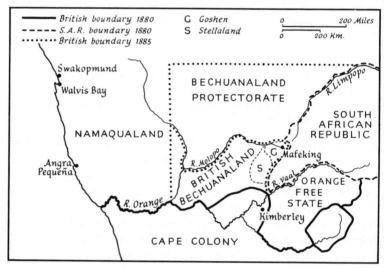

Occupation of Bechuanaland.

While high-level talks between the British and German governments took place in Europe, Rhodes was sent to discuss the problem with Kruger as Commissioner in Bechuanaland. It was felt that Rhodes understood the Boers and would be able to reach agreement with them. But some of the settlers resisted a settlement and so a British show of force was necessary. Five thousand troops marched into the disputed area. The settlement terms included the complete takeover of the area south of the Molopo River as the colony of British Bechuanaland and the establishment of a British protectorate over the rest of Bechuanaland as far as 22° N and 20° E.

Events in Europe

Throughout most of the nineteenth century Britain had been the most economically advanced country in Europe. She had pioneered the Industrial Revolution and transformed herself from an agricultural country to a manufacturing nation with the world's first sprawling, grimy industrial cities. She had the best and biggest merchant navy in the world. British ships carried raw materials from many lands to Britain and manufactured goods from Britain to many lands. The search for materials and markets had led to the building of the British Empire, the biggest empire the world had ever seen. But British governments were always reluctant to add to that empire. It was their experience that colonies cost a great deal to administer, entailed heavy responsibilities with regard to subject peoples and ultimately sought independence. Britain had lost the United States of America in this way and by 1880 most of her larger colonies were self-governing. So Britain's leaders preferred to encourage traders to establish their own links with other lands. The British navy helped to make the sea routes safe. For this bases such as Cape Town and Mauritius were important. Occasionally Britain sent military or naval assistance to their subjects who were having difficulties with the natives of a particular locality. Sometimes this intervention led to unofficial political control (as in Zanzibar), sometimes it led to conquest and colonization (as in Lagos). But as long as Britain led the world economically the British government believed that such involvement should be kept to a minimum.

While Britain was establishing her lead the major European nations were absorbed in political problems. Germany and Italy, for instance, were evolving from a number of small states into new nations, while France experienced six major changes of government, four revolutions and two invasions between 1814 and 1871. But by 1871 these upheavals were past. By this time, too, the Industrial Revolution was having a great effect on the continental powers. They now began to be in need of markets and sources of raw materials. Their captains and merchants began to challenge the supremacy of Britain's captains and merchants. Europe also had a population problem. During the second half of the century millions of men and women were driven by poverty or hardship to seek what they hoped would be a better life in another land. But the most powerful forces at work in Europe were nationalism and national rivalry. Germany and Italy, the new nations, were determined to prove their power and glory. France, humiliated by a crushing military defeat in 1870–1, was determined to reassert her ancient greatness. Britain was determined to yield none of her commercial and maritime supremacy to any rival power. These conflicting nationalisms, as Europe's leading statesmen knew, could lead to diplomatic clashes or even war. No one wanted this, least of all Europe's leading political figure, Otto von Bismarck, Chancellor of Germany. He needed peace and stability in Europe so that the new Germany could develop rapidly. As a part of his policy of keeping the peace in Europe he encouraged other nations to turn their ambitions towards other parts of the world – including Africa.

Concern and curiosity about Africa had been growing steadily between 1850 and 1880 but after the latter date there was a dramatic upsurge of interest in the 'Dark Continent'. In all the leading European countries there were groups of imperialists urging their governments to annex parts of Africa. They urged all sorts of motives for colonisation – the wealth to be gained from the exploitation of ivory, gold, diamonds, copper, etc.; the need of Africans for Christianity; the urgency of delivering Africa from the scourge of the slave trade; the wonderful opportunities for industrious immigrants. But all of them had the same thought in the back of their minds, 'if we don't colonise, someone else will'. Still the statesmen paid little attention to the imperialists.

By 1880 Britain and France had a number of colonies (most of them small) around the coasts of Africa. Portugal, or course, still had her possessions in Angola and Mozambique. The first events in the scramble for Africa accurred when rival colonial ambitions clashed in Egypt and the Congo.

Clashes in Egypt and the Congo

Egypt assumed a new importance for Europe in 1869 when the Suez Canal was opened. This provided, for the first time, a short route for cargo and passenger ships travelling to and from the East. The canal was controlled by an international company of which the Egyptian government was the largest shareholder. The ruler of Egypt, Khedive Ismail, was a man of ambitious ideas. He pushed Egypt's borders southwards, he built roads and public buildings and spent a great deal of money on personal luxuries. Where did the money come from? He taxed his people as heavily as they could bear; he sent expeditions southwards to plunder the Sudan for ivory and slaves; he borrowed large sums from European financiers. By 1875 he was in serious financial difficulties and offered his Suez Canal Co. shares for sale. Disraeli, the British Prime Minister, stepped in quickly and bought them for his government. The French were alarmed. They believed Disraeli aimed to control the canal for strategic and political reasons.

Still the Khedive could not balance his budget. Alarmed at the financial situation and the threat to the canal posed by the unrest in the country, Europeans who had invested money in Egypt urged their governments to intervene. Political pressure was brought to bear on the Sultan of Turkey (Egypt was a part of the Turkish Empire) who, in turn, forced Ismail to accept a committee of European financiers to try to solve Egypt's problems. Ismail did not like this and in 1879 he dissolved this committee. Now the French and British 'got tough'. They forced the Sultan to depose Ismail in favour of his son Tawfiq. Tawfiq was no more than a puppet ruler controlled by the Europeans and it was not long before affronted Egyptian nationalists rose in a revolt led by Urabi Pasha. France and Britain decided to quell the revolt but at the last moment the French withdrew and it was a British army which sailed to Egypt to crush Urabi's revolt at the battle of Tel-el-Kebir (1882). The British government hoped to withdrawn its army quickly but soon discovered that the presence of British troops was the only means of preserving peace and Tawfiq's government. Again the French were furious and accused Britain of having, in effect, colonised Egypt.

Meanwhile international rivalry was building up in the Congo basin. King Leopold II of Belgium had been inspired by the reports of H. M. Stanley and other early explorers of the region. He wanted to gain personal control of this vast area of Central Africa but cloaked his ambitions by forming an 'international' company to explore and exploit the region. H. M. Stanley became the main agent of Leopold's company and spent most of the period 1879–84 exploring, setting up trading posts and obtaining treaties from rulers along the river. In 1882 the French became suspicious of Leopold's intentions and concerned for the safety of their trading interests on the Gabon coast. They sent Count Savorgnan de Brazza to the Congo and he made a treaty with Makoko, one of the Bateke chiefs, which he claimed gave France possession of a large area to the north of the lower Congo. Now it was Portugal's turn to become alarmed. She saw in all this activity a threat to her interests in Angola. She now claimed to control the mouth of the Congo, which gave her control over the commercial activities of Leopold and the French. To strengthen her hand she sought Britain's help and a treaty was drawn up whereby Britain guaranteed Portuguese control of the Congo mouth. Once more the French were angry. They sought Bismarck's help in bringing pressure to bear on Britain.

Bismarck was delighted to see the other European nations squabbling among themselves, especially in distant Africa, in which he had not the slightest interest. But he did not want these squabbles to become too serious and lead to conflict in Europe. He therefore proposed a conference to meet in the German capital, Berlin, which would settle existing disagreements and establish the principles on which any further colonisation of Africa would be based. Bismarck knew that it would be difficult for him to dominate the coming conference if he had no colonial interests himself and so he reversed his discouraging attitude towards German imperialists. Now he actively encouraged them to set up German colonies in Africa. This led to German claims being made for Togoland, Cameroon, part of East Africa and South West Africa.

The harsh desert of Namaqualand and Damaraland yields sparse grazing on the plateau and seasonal grazing along the rivers. This area was the home of the nomadic Herero and related peoples. The expansion of Cape Colony had forced San, Khoikhoi and Boer groups into this land. In the inevitable clash with the local peoples a Khoikhoi leader called Afrikaner had been successful in bringing much of Namaqualand and Damaraland under his control in the early nineteenth century. In the 1840s German missionaries of the Rhenish Missionary Society began working among the Herero and it was largely as a result of the guns introduced by them that the Herero under the leadership of Kamaherero managed to turn the tables on the invaders. Peace was eventually established by the arbitration of the R.M.S. missionaries in 1870, but not long afterwards the land was invaded by Boer trekkers from the Transvaal. At this stage Kamaherero asked for British protection. After much discussion this was rejected by Britain although they did permit Walvis Bay (the only good harbour along the coast) and its hinterland to be annexed to the Cape in 1878. Combined with the usual British reluctance to shoulder new colonial burdens was the assumption that if ever they wanted to annex South West Africa they would always be able to do so.

In 1882 a German merchant, F. Lüderitz, established a trading post at Angra Pequeña on land bought from the local Namaqua chief. He was not the first German in the area. As well as the R.M.S. missionaries German traders had been actively involved in the export of ivory and ostrich feathers from South West Africa. The German government had on more than one occasion asked whether its nationals in South West Africa could count on British protection but had never received a satisfactory reply. The question was now asked again and still failed to receive a clear answer. In 1883 Lüderitz acquired more land and declared a German protectorate over it. The following year this protectorate was ratified in Berlin but a startled British government learned that it included, not just Angra Pequeña, but the whole of Namaqualand and Damaraland from the Orange River to the Angolan border. The British were appalled to find another power intruding into an area they had always believed they had some kind of option on. They feared that the Germans might make an alliance with the Boer states against them. In response to this threat they hastened to lay claim to Bechuanaland, thereby driving a wedge between German and Boer territory and keeping open the way to the north.

The Berlin Conference 1884-5

Meanwhile the Berlin Conference had begun. Briefly it did two things: it cleared up existing boundary disputes and it established the principles upon which further European claims to African territory were to be based. As far as South and Central Africa were concerned the conference confirmed British and German possessions; it rejected Portugal's claim to control the Congo mouth; it established the Congo Free State, under the control of Leopold II, as the administering authority in the Congo basin; and it stated that a vast area of Central Africa was to be a free trade area, open to the commerce and philanthropic exercise of all nations. Many boundaries were left vague and the principles laid down for future colonisation were as follows: an area could only be claimed if the claiming nation effectively controlled it and only if the other signatories to the Berlin Act agreed. No longer could colonial powers, like Britain, claim vague, unofficial protectorates. The Berlin Act made it necessary for any power wanting to claim part of Africa to actually send representatives there to 'grab' it. That is exactly what happened in the years after the Berlin Conference.

13. Partition and reaction
(1) The collapse of the great Bantu kingdoms

Before we consider in detail the scramble for South and Central Africa we must get an overall, bird's-eye view of the situation. Briefly, there were three thrusts into the interior. The British were pushing northwards through newly acquired Bechuanaland. Under the leader-

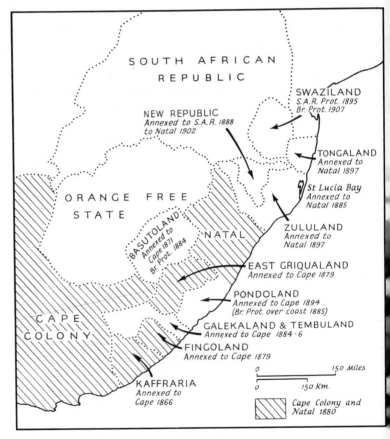

British annexations in south-east Africa.

ship of Rhodes and the British South Africa Co. they wanted to beat their rivals to regions which, they believed, would prove rich in minerals. They also wanted to complete the process of hemming in the Boer states. From the north the Belgian agents of the Congo Free State were making a bid for Katanga and the surrounding area. Largely in reaction to these moves the Portuguese and the Germans were trying to penetrate from east and west in order to link up their colonies on both sides of the continent. The Boers, fearing complete encirclement, attempted by force or diplomacy to obtain a link with the coast either to east or west.

Further British annexations in South Africa

Between 1884 and 1887 the south-east corner of Africa was 'tidied up'. By the latter date most of the Bantu communities of that area found themselves under British protection or annexed to the British colonies. Though most British governments still maintained the old reluctance over annexation they were spurred to rapid action by fear of German competition and Boer expansion to the coast.

After the Ninth Xhosa War Pondoland was the only African territory between Cape Colony and Natal to enjoy full independence. The Galeka and Tembu had been disarmed and made to submit to a measure of supervision in their internal affairs. Meanwhile European settlers continued to stray over the borders to claim farmland in these territories. A fresh crop of border incidents seemed to be maturing and a large group in the Cape parliament urged annexation but nothing was done until the events of 1884 lent a new urgency to the situation. German traders had appeared on the Pondoland coast and another Angra Pequeña incident seemed possible. The British now acted. Galekaland and Tembuland were annexed by Cape Colony in 1884 and a few months later the British government announced a protectorate over the Pondoland coast.

In Zululand the situation was, as ever, more complicated. In 1884 the mantle of the dead Cetshawayo fell upon his son Dinizulu, who attempted to reunite the kingdom. He sought help from some Boers who were living in Zululand. They agreed and got together a force of several hundred settlers, many from the British and Afrikaner states. The price of their assistance was 10,000 square kilometres of land on which to form an independent republic. After a series of quick victories Dinizulu's principal rival was forced into exile and Dinizulu was proclaimed king. But he was to be a vassal of the New Republic which was now established in northern Zululand. There could be little doubt that the Republic intended to drive a corridor to the 155 coast. Then the Germans appeared on the scene again. Towards the end of 1884 some German agents obtained from Dinizulu land around St Lucia Bay. This alarmed the government of Natal which sent urgent messages to London demanding the annexation of Zululand. The British government would have nothing of it but did agree to allow Natal to annex St Lucia Bay (1885). There were angry protests

Dinizulu.

from the New Republic, from the South African Republic and from Germany, but the British government refused to reverse the decision. Britain now controlled the only important harbours south of Lourenço Marques. Her south African interests and her route to India were safe.

But there were many people both in South Africa and Britain

who were unhappy about the growing New Republic. In 1886 talks began with the leaders of the New Republic. Britain agreed to the existence of the small state but its size was cut down considerably. As soon as that was settled the British lost no time in annexing Zululand to Natal (February 1887). Dinizulu, not surprisingly, objected to these arrangements. The new British Resident in Zululand exiled Dinizulu to the island of St Helena, 1,600 kilometres off the west coast of Africa. It was ten years before he was allowed to return to his people.

Meanwhile an attempt at direct control over Basutoland by Cape Colony had failed. In 1868 Moshweshwe's territory had been annexed as a British Crown Colony. Three years later the Cape government persuaded London to hand over the administration of Basutoland. This empowered the settlers to collect taxes from the Basuto and, in theory, to order the affairs of the colony in their own interests. In practice matters were not quite so simple. After the death of Moshweshwe the many divisions in Basuto society came to the surface. Trouble was started in 1879 by the blustering Sir H. B. Frere. He was determined to disarm all the peoples on the borders of Cape Colony. The attempt to remove the Basutos' arms aroused widespread resentment and created a division between those who complied with the order (one of whom was the new paramount chief Letsie) and those who did not. In an attempt to enforce the Cape government's decision, police were sent into Basutoland in 1880 and the War of Disarmament began.

Chaos now broke loose. To the old divisions within Basuto society were added the pro- and anti-Cape factions. Fighting took place in many regions. Refugees fled across the borders into neighbouring territories adding to their problems and also adding to growing tension between Boer and Briton. The Cape forces were quite unable to bring the situation under control and in 1884 admitted as much to London. As a result Britain once more assumed responsibility for Basutoland, which became a protectorate under the Crown. Northwards from Delagoa Bay the coast was in the hands of the Portuguese. In 1869 Portugal made a commercial treaty with the South African Republic which gave the Boers a trade outlet at Lourenço Marques, based on the assumption that the eastern coast as far south as 26° 30' S. belonged to the Portuguese. Britain contested this treaty and the argument was decided by arbitration, the judge being the President of France. In 1875 he decided in favour of Portugal, thus halting the realisation of British ambitions on the east coast and further aggravating the poor relations between the two European countries.

The Gaza, Shona and Nbedbele

In the interior, however, Portugal's position was still weak. The Shangana empire of Gaza blocked Portuguese penetration into the southern part of the region. Further north many of the *prazeros* had either been forced out by Shona, Gaza and Ndebele pressure or had become, in reality, African chieftains with no allegiance to Portugal. The Mozambique colony still occupied posts on the lower Zambezi but only by paying tribute to the local rulers. The Shona, themselves under pressure from the terrible Ndebele, prevented any Portuguese expansion to the south-west.

The situation began to change in the 1870s. The Gaza were faced with difficulties in the south and the north. In the south there was a continuing feud with the Swazi, which annually swallowed up large numbers of warriors. Also in the south the Portuguese were becoming more active. The growing importance of Delagoa Bay and of contact with the Boers urged the Portuguese to lay claim to the area of the lower Limpopo. In the north the threat came from Manuel Antonio de Souza (known as Gouveia), an Indian adventurer from the Portugese

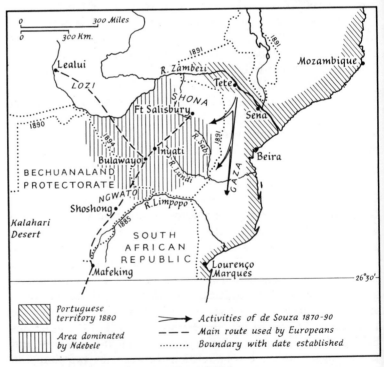

158   *European advance into East and Central Africa.*

colony of Goa. He established himself as a semi-independent authority in the Zambezi valley and by alliance and conquest gradually pushed southwards and westwards.

Faced with the contraction of his empire and the loss of tribute from former subject chiefs now 'liberated' by Gouveia, Mzila, the Gaza king, looked around for allies. He established friendly relations with the Ndebele and married his heir, Gungunyana, to one of Lobengula's daughters. He also made gestures of friendship towards the British. In 1870 and 1872 he sent messengers to Durban asking for trade, friendly relations and assistance in settling his dispute with the Swazi and the Portuguese.

Mzila watched his empire breaking up and the process continued after his death in 1885. Gouveia made himself master of all the northern part of the empire and in 1889 Gungunyana was forced to leave the Sabi highlands and establish a new capital near the Limpopo. By now the 'scramble' was on and Portuguese expeditions were sent into Gazaland to try to obtain treaties with Gungunyana. But Gungunyana had no intention of placing his land under Portuguese control and made fresh attempts to gain a measure of British protection. Still the answer from Durban was 'No'.

In 1890 a new factor entered the situation. Agents of the British South Africa Co., which had just begun operations in Matabeleland, came to Gungunyana offering a thousand rifles, twenty thousand rounds of ammunition and £500 a year in return for mining and prospecting rights in Gazaland. What the British South Africa Co. really wanted was complete encirclement of the Boer republics and an outlet to the sea. But the fate of Gazaland was settled in Europe, not Africa. The rival claims had led to strong nationalistic reactions in Britain and Portugal. Feelings ran very high in both countries and the politicians realised that a settlement would have to be reached. The Anglo-Portuguese treaty of 1891 (see below, p. 175) placed Gazaland almost entirely in the Portuguese sphere of influence.

A decision that had been made thousands of miles away in Europe was of no interest to Gungunyana. Once again he sent messengers to Natal and even to London to seek British protection. But the government in Durban was powerless in face of the 1891 agreement. So the Gaza resisted alone Portugal's attempts to make good her claims in the interior. So great was Gungunyana's reputation and so small were the Portuguese forces of occupation that for four years the white men made no serious attempt to confront the Gaza. Then, in 1894, some local chiefs, with Gungunyana's support, attacked the growing port of Lourenço Marques. They caused considerable damage and loss of life before being driven off by a relief force from Lisbon. 159

They fled to Gungunyana's territory for protection and were pursued by Portuguese troops led by Antonio Enes.

In November 1895 the invaders confronted the Gaza near their capital, Manjacaze. The Gaza were beaten in a quick battle and Manjacaze was burned down. Gungunyana escaped but was captured after another battle a few weeks later. He was exiled to the Canary Islands, where he died years later. The Gaza continued to resist; their chiefs had to be defeated one by one. Not until 1897 was the once mighty empire of Shoshangane finally destroyed.

But Gazaland was not the only area of resistance. In 1897 some of the *prazeros* and their allies around Sena had to be subdued. Barwe remained for many years a centre of trouble for the Portuguese. The local leaders were aided by refugee chiefs and *prazeros* fleeing from colonial armies. Not until 1902 was this last pocket of resistance cleared out by Portuguese forces.

Further west in Mashonaland fear of the Ndebele was still the dominant feature of political life. Several Shona chiefs made alliances with Gouveia in order to obtain guns. These guns were used for fighting among themselves but also for warding off the powerful Ndebele. As a result many Shona groups were able to throw off Ndebele suzerainty. With Ndebele and Gaza power weakened the Shona were, in the 1880s and 1890s, reasserting something of their old independence. When the Portuguese decided to extend the area of their effective occupation they took Gouveia into their service but when he tried to add Barwe lands to the Portuguese Empire some of his former Shona allies turned against him and killed him.

Activities of the B.S.A. Co.

Throughout the 1870s and 1880s Europeans had been pouring into Lobengula's territory in increasing numbers, most of them in search of important mineral deposits. After 1885 an important change came over European attitudes towards unconquered African territories. Competition between individuals and small companies was replaced by international rivalries. The powers who were interested in Matabeleland now felt a sense of urgency: they feared that if they did not stake their claim quickly someone else would. In 1887 a delegation from Pretoria signed a treaty with Lobengula on behalf of the Transvaal. This alarmed Cecil Rhodes and his supporters in Cape Colony who wanted any mineral wealth in Matabeleland to be for the British empire and who wished to prevent the expansion of the Boer states. Rhodes knew that the government in London, having recently been pushed into annexing Bechuanaland, would not be prepared to extend British authority over the Ndebele. But he did manage to persuade them to sign a treaty of friendship with Lobengula (the Moffat Treaty, 1888). This treaty brought Matabeleland within the British sphere of influence and committed Lobengula to accepting guidance from Cape Colony on matters of foreign relations.

The British government lacked both the will and the money to annexe Matabeleland but Cecil Rhodes had both. He planned to control as much of Central Africa as possible through a commercial company. In 1888 Rhodes sent representatives to Lobengula's court to gain mining concessions. After weeks of persuasion and bargaining Lobengula agreed to the Rudd concession in return for money and guns. He also received a promise that the concessionaires would help to keep other Europeans out of his territory. Rhodes now formed the British South Africa Co. to operate the Rudd concession.

For over five years Lobengula tried to prevent the white invasion of his country. He knew the Europeans had superior weapons and so he avoided an armed conflict as long as possible. He negotiated and bargained to preserve as much as he could of his people's land and way of life. Throughout those five years he behaved honourably and courteously towards the agents of the British South Africa Co., as even his enemies admitted. But the Company was bent on Lobengula's destruction and the exploitation of his land, either by peaceful or warlike means. It was vital for Lobengula to retain control of the Shona. Not only was his prestige at stake; raids into Mashonaland provided him with necessary cattle and slaves to augment his warrior bands.

In the middle of 1890 the first British South Africa Co. expedition set off for the concession lands. Lobengula had given permission for a small number of prospectors to look for minerals in Mashonaland. He was therefore alarmed to hear that the British South Africa Co.'s pioneer column consisted of 380 men, 200 of whom were armed police. Regretting his earlier decision, Lobengula sent messages to the advancing Europeans ordering them to stop. They ignored the order. Lobengula now refused to send the Company 200 young men whom he had agreed to supply to help with road-building. This did not worry the white men. They turned instead to Khama, the Ngwato chief. He had a long-standing dispute with Lobengula over some borderlands and was only too pleased to do anything which would embarrass or weaken his enemy. He supplied the British South Africa Co. with labourers. It took the pioneers three months carefully skirting Ndebele territory to reach the site of their future headquarters. They built a fort and named it after the British prime

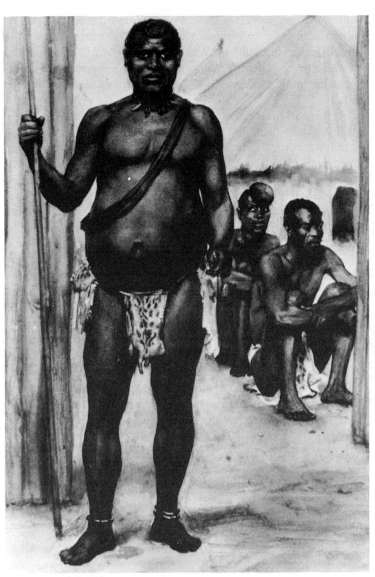

Lobengula, king of the Ndebele, 1889.

minister, Fort Salisbury. During all this time Lobengula made no move against them.

Before they had even established their new base the white men had arranged treaties of protection with some of the Shona chiefs. A few weeks later S. L. Jameson, Rhodes' personal representative in Central Africa, tried to extend Company rule eastwards over Manikaland.

Hoisting the flag at Fort Salisbury. On 13 September 1890 the British South Africa Co. pioneers hoisted the British flag in their new headquarters (modern Salisbury).

As we have already seen the Company was at the same time trying to obtain control of the Gaza Empire. For a while Lobengula did nothing, though he watched with alarm the growing power and authority of the white men. But inevitably the clashing interests of the Ndebele and the settlers led to unpleasant incidents and then to armed conflict.

By mid-1893 Jameson had decided to do battle with the Ndebele. He was urged on by many of the settlers, who, having found no gold in Mashonaland, wanted to look for minerals in Matabeleland. He prepared for the day of reckoning by bringing reinforcements into Mashonaland and by urging Rhodes to finance an invasion of Lobengula's territory. At the same time he deliberately provoked the Ndebele by acts of aggression and exaggerated demands for compensation. For his part Lobengula was patient, though angry. He sent protests to Cape Town and London, though few reached their destination. He tried to control his *indunas*, who were being severely provoked by the white men. He agreed to Jameson's increasingly unreasonable demands. For three months the situation worsened. The British government from distant London tried to restrain Jameson and his followers by forbidding any invasion of Lobengula's territory *unless the Ndebele attacked first*. Jameson's response to this was to do all in his power to provoke the Ndebele into an attack which would give him an excuse to enter Matabeleland in force.

By the end of September Jameson was ready for the offensive. He had attracted hundreds of volunteers to come from the Cape with promises of 6,000 acres of land and fifteen gold mining claims each. Three large forces were waiting at Fort Salisbury, Fort Victoria and Tuli. They were well equipped and even had some of the new Maxim machine guns. Eagerly they waited for the signal to advance. Seeking to justify his preparations Jameson sent untrue reports to Cape Town and London of Ndebele armies massing near the Company forts. The truth was that Lobengula had called his *impis* together in readiness for a *defensive* war. In early October he was still sending messengers south to protest his desire for peace (the messengers were shot at Tati).

A skirmish near Forth Victoria on 30 September at last gave Jameson a slender excuse for putting his plans into operation. On 4 October the invasion began. The three groups linked up and, as a single force of over 1,200 men, plunged into Matabeleland. Not until 24 October, when the white men were some 100 kilometres from Bulawayo, his capital, did Lobengula offer battle. So much for Jameson's claim that the Ndebele were a warlike tribe, intent on driving the British South Africa Co. out of Mashonaland! At this first battle at Shangani the Ndebele suffered a terrible defeat. On 1 November they regrouped at Imbembesi in a last attempt to save their capital, 27 kilometres away. The battle was soon over and the defeated Ndebele retired to Bulawayo. They burned the town to prevent it falling into enemy hands and retreated further.

From Bulawayo Jameson sent troops to find and capture Lobengula. The king, dispirited and ill with smallpox, had fled northwards accompanied by a small band of followers. Knowing that he was defeated Lobengula sent messengers with £1,000 in gold and an offer to surrender. Unfortunately the gold fell into the hands of two soldiers who kept it and suppressed the message. So Lobengula continued to retreat, followed by his enemies. But not for long: on about 22 January 1894 the last Ndebele king died. He was thus saved the final humiliation of being deposed and disgraced by his triumphant enemies.

But Lobengula's spirit lived on; the Ndebele did not accept British rule without further protest. For a while all seemed to be going well for the conquerors. The British government, unwilling to take responsibility for the administration of new colonial territory, placed Matabeleland under Company control. Farms and mining rights were given, as had been promised, to those who had helped in the invasion. The Ndebele were herded into two reserves along the Shangani and Gwaai rivers. Many worked on European farms and in the mines. They seemed to have completely lost their spirit and all was peaceful throughout Rhodesia, as the Company's territory was now called. But underneath, the Ndebele were still hostile towards the people who had taken their land and heaped indignities upon them. To add to their other problems a series of natural catastrophes brought very real suffering to the Ndebele between 1894 and 1896. Bad harvests, drought and a plague of locusts were followed by a severe outbreak of rinderpest which obliged the white administrators to destroy large numbers of Ndebele cattle to prevent the spread of the disease. Discontent grew and by April 1896 the Ndebele were ready to revolt.

The Shona, too, were growing restless. Many of them had welcomed the British South Africa Co. pioneers as powerful allies against the Ndebele and as traders from whom they could buy guns and manufactured goods. But the settlers affronted their Shona allies in many ways. They took land without permission. They punished Shona criminals without any reference to their chiefs. They seized men and women to work on their farms. They stopped Shona trade with the Portuguese and demanded higher prices for their own trade goods. Then, in 1894, they tried to levy a hut tax on all the people. Now the Shona chiefs clearly saw the white men for what they were, invaders demanding tribute from a people they claimed to have conquered.

But the Shona, unlike the Ndebele, had not been conquered. Individuals and groups resisted European pressures. They refused to provide labour. They refused to pay taxes. The Shona felt a sense of common grievance and they began to look for someone who could unite them. They found such leadership in Mkwati, a representative of the old Rozwi ruling dynasty, and the priests of the powerful Mlimo cult. These men urged the Shona, and the Ndebele, to rise against the white man, who was responsible for all the ills which had befallen the land.

The rising began on 20 March 1896 with an incident in which two Shona policemen were killed. Once blood had been shed the revolt spread rapidly. Within days about 140 white men, women and children, most of them on isolated farms, had been slaughtered. The rest hurried to the towns which were quickly fortified. By June almost the whole of Matabeleland and Mashonaland was up in arms. In their bitterness and anger the warriors killed white men and their helpers indiscriminately.

The early success of the rising was the result of surprise. In the long run it was bound to fail. It had no central leadership for, although its inspiration came from the priests of Mlimo, the fighting was directed by the chiefs. On the other side the Europeans, once alerted, were able to muster a large, trained and well equipped army to deal with the rising. Two thousand troops (professionals and volunteers) were soon on their way from white settlements in the

Cecil Rhodes in camp.

south while the British government despatched a relief force from London.

The Ndebele were the first to make peace. They had already had a taste of the Maxim gun and recognised it as a superior 'medicine' to anything the Mlimo priests had to offer. After only one decisive defeat at Umgusa River the surviving Ndebele forces retreated to the Matopo hills. From this stronghold they could have kept up a guerilla style of warfare for months, even years. There were two reasons why they did not do so. Firstly, the Ndebele leaders were divided among themselves. Secondly, Cecil Rhodes took the initiative and began peace negotiations.

Rhodes had every reason for wanting a speedy end to the campaign. His own political career had just crashed because of his implication in an attempted invasion of the Transvaal (see below, pp. 205–6). His influence in the affairs of southern Africa was, therefore, considerably reduced and he wanted desperately to reassert it. Also, the British South Africa Co. was under attack from Rhodes' opponents in Britain. Politicians who had always opposed colonial expansion could point to the Ndebele and Shona risings as proof that they were right. Colonial occupation, they said, obviously meant bloodshed and white aggression. Moreover Rhodes had claimed that the Company could rule Rhodesia without involving the home government in any expense. But what had happened? The Company had run into trouble and British troops had had to be sent to get it out of trouble. At no time did Rhodes' imperial schemes seem more threatened than in 1896.

He acted with characteristic directness and bravery. With a few companions he rode, unarmed, into the Matopo hills. When he had won the confidence of the Ndebele leaders talks began. In return for complete Ndebele disarmament Rhodes promised to disband the army in Rhodesia, leaving only a small, permanent police force, to give official recognition to most of the chiefs, to give government salaries to these chiefs and to provide seed so that the Ndebele could get on quickly with planting the new crops. By the middle of October 1896 peace had been restored to Matabeleland.

Meanwhile the struggle continued in Mashonaland. Here the power of religious leaders was greater. Spirit mediums and prophets provided medicine which was supposed to give warriors protection from enemy bullets. They promised that those who died in the cause of Shona freedom would be restored to life. They united the Shona peoples by recalling the glories of the Rozwi empire. They called down the wrath of the spirits against the white men and those who collaborated with them. They rejected Christianity, ordering the 167 massacre of missionaries and converts, and they reasserted traditional beliefs. They promised that with the expulsion of the white men a new age of peace and plenty would dawn. This teaching inspired many Shona to fight to the death. Mkwati and two mediums, Kakubi and Nehanda, were the preachers of this 'primary resistance' movement (as it has been called) and they successfully prolonged the conflict in Mashonaland for a year after the collapse of the Ndebele rising.

The Shona withdrew into hill strongholds from which they made sorties against small detachments of their enemy. The war was fought with great bitterness on both sides. The Shona pactised appalling atrocities on their victims. The whites used dynamite to blast their opponents to pieces in the caves and hilltops where they were hiding. One by one the Shona strongholds were overrun. By the middle of 1897 the people were becoming disillusioned with the power of their religious leaders. Mkwati was hacked to pieces by some of his own former followers. In December Kakubi was captured and Nehanda gave herself up to save her followers from further bloodshed. The leaders of the rising were tried, condemned and hanged, the last victims of a rising which had claimed the lives of over 600 whites and 6,000 Africans. The Shona did not come out of the conflict as well as the Ndebele. Certain of their grievances – forced labour and unjust punishment by local authorities – were redressed. But the Shona had to submit to taxation and white control. Above all they were no longer able to live where they wished in their own land but were moved into reserves.

Ngwato and Lozi reaction to the Europeans

The Ngwato were one of the most stable Tswana groups in the nineteenth century. They suffered severe reverses during the Mfecane and on one occasion were driven out of their homeland and had to flee across the Kalahari. Yet they always recovered. Their political system and their moral code seem to have been strengthened by their experiences. About 1829 they came under the control of the Ndebele. For several years they were forced to pay tribute to their overlords and to endure Ndebele raids on their cattle. Then, in about 1850, the Ngwato had become strong enough to throw off their vassalage. Their numbers increased. They learned better battle tactics from their enemies. They had wise and able leaders – leaders who had to be clever politicians because they had powerful enemies. The Ndebele were not the only threat. In 1868 Pretorius, the Transvaal president, tried to extend Boer rule over the Ngwato.

Chief Matsheng rejected Pretorius' demands but knew that his people stood little chance of maintaining their independence if those demands were backed by force. He needed allies and, like Moshweshwe, he turned to the government at the Cape and asked for British protection. The request was not granted but the crisis passed without outside aid becoming necessary. For some years Ngwato contacts with the white men had been developing. Matsheng had welcomed L.M.S. missionaries and since his territory lay athwart the main route to the interior, he gave hospitality to traders, prospectors and hunters on an increasing scale. Matsheng's successor, Khama, became a Christian and Ngwato relations with the British grew still closer.

In 1884 Ngwato territory was again threatened by the white man's politics. The Boers were trying to escape from the Cape's stranglehold over their economic affairs. Rhodes and his supporters wanted to keep open the road to the interior. The Germans suddenly annexed South West Africa (see above, pp. 152–3). Khama responded by asking for British protection. This time his request was granted and Ngwato became part of the Bechuanaland Protectorate (1885). British officials came to Shoshong but Khama's power and his people's way of life were little affected. What they did gain was security. The boundary with the Transvaal was clearly defined and there was little chance now of Boer invasion. Ndebele power was soon broken by the British South Africa Co. (with Ngwato help, as we have seen). Because British and Ngwato interests were in agreement Khama's people passed peacefully into the colonial period.

Having reluctantly acquired Bechuanaland the British government wanted to do their duty there as cheaply as possible. They sent as few officials as possible into the territory. Meanwhile Rhodes hoped that Bechuanaland would be handed over to the British South Africa Co. to administer. There was no clear boundary between the Protectorate and the Company's sphere of activity. Company agents were operating in Bechuanaland and the Company was financing a railway through Bechuanaland to Rhodesia. But Rhodes had his opponents in Cape Town and London who opposed any extension of the Company's activities. Their hand was strengthened by the Ndebele War of 1893. In the following year a clear boundary was drawn between Bechuanaland and Rhodesia.

By this time the long arm of British expansion had reached even further into the centre of Africa. Until the 1880s the Lozi had very little contact with white men from the south. Their commercial links were with their neighbours to the west and with the Portuguese on the coast of Angola. In 1871 a British trader, George Westbeech, reached Barotseland and impressed the Lozi with the guns he brought for they were superior to anything reaching Lozi territory from the west. The Lozi ruler needed guns for ivory hunting, and for defence against Ndebele raids. Westbeech was allowed to establish a base in Barotseland and became a trusted adviser of the king.

The Lozi rulers had serious problems which made them value greatly their powerful and influential friends. The greatest problem

Khama. This picture of Chief Khama of the Ngwato appeared in a book by a
European explorer, who remarked that the chief liked European clothes.

was internal discord. There were rivals for the throne and warring factions among the nobles. The growing number of guns available in Barotseland made the situation worse. Sepopa, who defeated the Kololo and restored the Lozi fortunes in 1864, was assassinated in 1876. His successor, Mwanawina, was driven into exile two years later by Lewanika. The new ruler had to be constantly on the watch for rebellion. At the same time he had to face new pressures from outside Barotseland. As well as the traditional Ndebele threat there were the Portuguese and British advances from the north-west and south respectively. After 1885 possible German penetration from South West Africa also had to be borne in mind.

In 1885 there was a rebellion in Barotseland. Lewanika was deposed and fled into exile. If he were to regain his throne he needed allies. Lobengula offered his support but Lewanika could not bring himself to trust the Ndebele king. Instead he sought the help of some Angolan traders. With their aid he launched a successful counter-attack. By the beginning of 1886 he was once again in full control of his kingdom but he realised more clearly than ever the need for powerful allies. He knew that Khama had gained British protection and he decided to seek this also. He allowed Francis Coillard, a missionary with the Paris Evangelical Mission, who had for some years been hoping to start work in Barotseland, to found a permanent station. Then he asked Coillard to take to Cape Town a message asking for British protection.

Coillard refused to become involved in Lewanika's plan for he knew that the king did not have the full support of his council. For over two years he held out while Lewanika tried to win over his advisers to the idea of British protection. At last, in January 1889, Coillard sent off the necessary letters to Cape Town.

Lewanika's appeal arrived just as Cecil Rhodes was forming his British South Africa Co. and the rich financier immediately saw it as an opportunity to paint another red area on the map of Africa. He bought the mining concessions that a Kimberley businessman, Henry Ware, had obtained from Lewanika and sent his own representative, Frank Lochner, to negotiate with the Lozi king. Lewanika was expecting an agent of the British queen and Lochner allowed him to believe that he had the full authority of the British government. He gained the active support of Khama and he bribed with presents Lewanika's opponents on the council. By these means Lochner managed to acquire for the British South Africa Co. a protectorate over what is now north-west Zambia (Lochner exaggerated the size of Lewanika's dominions and this resulted in boundary clashes with Portuguese, German, and Congo Free State authorities later – see below, pp. 185ff. The Lochner Treaty, signed in June 1890, gave Lewanika £2,000 a year and protection from outside enemies. In return the Company gained extensive mining rights and permission to develop education, trade and communications.

When he discovered that he had, to some extent, been tricked Lewanika sent messages to London. The British government, however, ratified the Lochner Treaty. In 1897 they sent an official British Resident as a permanent representative at Lealui. In the following year he negotiated a new treaty which clarified the situation. It cancelled the Company's commercial monopoly. It retained for Lewanika virtually complete authority in the Lozi homeland but extended the authority of the Company in other parts of the kingdom.

As Barotseland settled down to its new 'dual rule' certain changes occurred. By the Victoria Falls treaty of 1900 the Company gained the right to allocate land for European settlement in Tonga and Ila country. Nine years later this concession was extended to cover all Lewanika's dominions except Barotseland. Lewanika also had to change some of the social and economic traditions of his people. He gradually abolished slave trading and, in 1906, prohibited domestic slavery. He encouraged missionary work. He stopped some of the more unpleasant forms of execution. He tried to control the excessive consumption of alcohol. And he welcomed new agricultural techniques.

All these innovations caused some resentment among his people and Lewanika could only carry them out because he had the backing of the British. By collaboration Lewanika secured his own position and his country's at a time when resistance would have inevitably resulted in ultimate conquest.

14. Partition and reaction
(2) The conflict north of the Zambezi

In this chapter we shall be concerned with the colonial scramble in the north-eastern corner of our area, i.e. modern Mozambique, Malawi and eastern Zambia.

In 1885 Portugal seemed to be the only colonial power in a position to annex any of this area. In 1886–7 the northern and southern frontiers of Angola were fixed in treaties with France and Germany and the Rovuma River was named as an approximate boundary between Mozambique and German East Africa. In the south Mozambique was restricted by Cape Colony and the Boer republics. Beyond these limitations Portugal's potential for expansion was unrestricted. The southern boundary of the Congo Free State was undefined and the British South Africa Co.'s advance into Southern Rhodesia had not yet begun. The Bechuanaland Protectorate (proclaimed in 1885) did effectively close the interior as far north as 22° S but this still left a wide belt of 'unclaimed' territory between the two Portuguese colonies.

Portugal now set about linking Angola and Mozambique together. In her treaties of 1886 with France and Germany she had the following clause inserted: 'Portugal shall exercise the rights of sovereignty and civilisation in the territories which separate the Portuguese possessions of Angola and Mozambique, without prejudice to the rights which other powers may have acquired there.' As we have already seen, Portuguese forces began to try to make this claim a reality in the area of Mozambique south of the Zambezi. In this region Portuguese ambitions were finally checked by the British South Africa Co. Further north they were checked by the British South Africa Co. and by Christian missionaries.

Missionaries and traders in the Shiré Highlands and around Lake Malawi

By 1880 the lake was being regularly used as a highway to the interior   173 by British missionaries as well as a means of access to the small communities who lived around its shores. By 1880 also British commercial interests had followed the missionaries into the area. In 1878 the Livingstonia Central Africa Company Ltd (its name was later changed to the African Lakes Company) began operations. It ran steamers on the lake and on the Shiré and its aim was to demonstrate how commerce could go hand in hand with Christianity. The Company provided the missionaries with necessary supplies, thus helping them to work efficiently and to advance further. The Company also traded for ivory with the Africans, offering in exchange cloth and manufactured goods but *not* guns or liquor, hoping to encourage legitimate trade and break down the slave trade. In 1881 Company agents helped L.M.S. missionaries to build a track, known as the Stevenson Road, from Lake Malawi to Lake Tanganyika. By 1886 the missionaries and their African Lakes Co. allies were beginning to achieve some success in their 'civilising mission' but they knew very well what a long task lay ahead if the power of Arab and Yao slavers was to be completely broken and peace and progress brought to the small communities of the lake region. Many of them hoped that the British government would set up a protectorate and back their work with money, troops and technical aid. All they got was a British consul (1883).

Ever since the days of Livingstone's journeys in the 1860s and 1870s British missionaries and Portuguese officials had disliked and mistrusted each other. When the Portuguese decided to move into the area north of the Zambezi they deliberately began to make life difficult for the missionaries by restricting the movements of men and goods on the lower Zambezi. In 1887 they sent a party to make treaties with the chiefs in the Shiré valley and to the west of the lake. Alarmed, the missionaries sent urgent messages to London.

The British government was not very interested in the missionaries' problems. The area south of the Zambezi was, however, a different matter. Under pressure from Rhodes and his supporters the government was prepared to negotiate in order to keep this region open to British enterprise. For months talks went on between officials in London and Lisbon. During this time the missionary societies in Britain urgently pressed their case for a protectorate. This, coupled with the total refusal of the Portuguese to yield any territory, gradually changed the attitude of the British government.

Matters came to a head in 1889. A new British consul, Harry Johnston, was sent to Mozambique with instructions to make treaties with rulers in the Shiré Highlands. A Portuguese mission, led by Serpa Pinto, was already in the area with the same purpose. Pinto attacked a Kololo settlement, which had recently been placed under British protection by Johnston, and pulled down the British flag.

In Britain public opinion was outraged and Rhodes pledged his British South Africa Co. to finance the administration of any newly won British territory. The prime minister sent warships to patrol off Mozambique and Beira and demanded the withdrawal of Portuguese forces from the Shiré valley. His government ratified Johnston's treaties and the whole area along both sides of the upper Shiré became the British Central Africa Protectorate (September 1889). Unable to stand up to this bullying, the Portuguese government gave way.

Harry Johnston and the Nyasaland Protectorate

Johnston, who was also an agent of the British South Africa Co., now went on to make treaties with Kololo, Yao, Cewa and Tonga leaders. He made an agreement with the Arab slaver, Jumbe, and visited the notorious slaver Mlozi at Karonga. By the end of 1890 he had reached the Stevenson road and was trying to win over local chiefs so as to place his government in a strong bargaining position in their negotiations with Germany over the division of East Africa.

Meanwhile the Portuguese had suffered serious reverses further south and were undergoing a financial crisis in their own country. They were forced to come to terms with Britain. In the treaty, which was finally signed in 1891, they lost most of the area south of the Zambezi but managed to obtain a 'tongue' of land along the river as far as Zumbo. To the north of the Zambezi the Mozambique boundary was largely determined by the treaties Johnston had gained in the lake area. A large, undefined area to the west of Lake Malawi now lay in the British sphere of influence but the imperialists' 'Cape to Cairo' dreams were not realised. An Anglo-German treaty of July 1890 had drawn a line from Lake Malawi to Lake Tanganyika just north of the Stevenson Road. All territory to the north of that line now fell to Germany.

The British government now had to decide how and by whom their territories north of the Zambezi should be governed. As usual the government wanted to avoid setting up an expensive administration and were inclined to allow the British South Africa Co. to do the work. But the Company was for the time being fully occupied south of the Zambezi while on the lake the missionaries and the African Lakes Company, mistrusting Rhodes and his agents, rejected the idea of British South Africa Co. rule. The African Lakes Co. claimed the right to administer the treaty areas but it was quite unfit to do so. The preservation of law and order and the abolition of slave trading 175

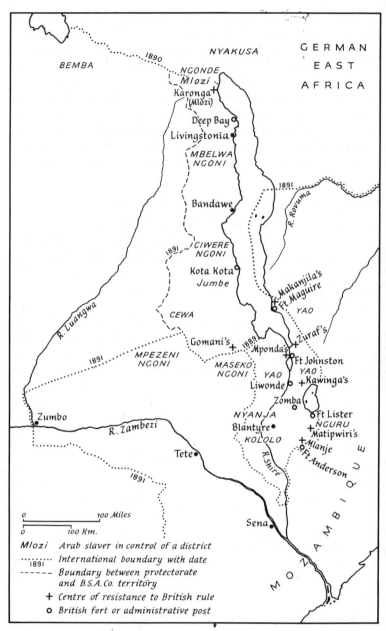

People and colonial boundaries in the L. Nyasa region.

would need far greater resources of money and manpower than the African Lakes Co. possessed.

In May 1891 the British government intervened. It declared a protectorate over the area covered by Johnston's treaties – soon to be known as Nyasaland. Johnston himself was appointed the first commissioner of the new protectorate. Johnston was also employed by the British South Africa Co. to extend British authority in the area to the west of the protectorate, which was now included in the Company's sphere of activity. While most of the small farming societies living to the south and west of the lake welcomed the protection of the white men, the leading Yao and Ngoni groups felt their ways of life were threatened by the Europeans.

The first major aim that Johnston set himself was the eradication of slave raiding in the Shiré Highlands. He arrived at Zomba in July 1891 with a small force of European and Indian soldiers and immediately set out to attack the powerful Yao chiefs. Chikumba was encountered and defeated near Mlanje, and a government post, Fort Anderson, was established to guard against future trouble. This became the pattern of Johnston's activity against the Yao. Mponda's capital at the southern end of the lake was destroyed and Fort Johnston was built nearby. Zuraf and Liwande were forced to sign treaties with Johnston and a government post was established at Liwande's capital.

Within five months many of the Yao leaders were cowed, at least for the moment, but the most powerful slave-dealing chief in the area, Makanjila, was undefeated. Makanjila had a large following and lived in impressive luxury in his capital on the east shore of the lake. In December 1891 Makanjila began raiding British allies and sent a force to attack Fort Johnston. The attack failed but the colonial power suffered another setback when Captain Maguire, leader of the British forces, and some of his men were killed while attempting to capture some of Makanjila's slave dhows. Johnston did not have enough men or equipment to dislodge the powerful chief. For the moment he had to admit defeat. But appeals for help to his superiors brought £10,000 from Rhodes and two gunboats from the British government.

With the boats and with fresh troops Johnston was able to launch another attack against Makanjila's capital at the end of 1893. The town was taken but Makanjila escaped into Mozambique. From there he led a series of raids into the Protectorate supported by other Yao chiefs who took the opportunity of renewing their resistance to the new regime. Meanwhile a new government post, Fort Maguire, was raised near Makanjila's. In 1894 Zuraf, Kawinga and Matipwiri rose in support of Makanjila. They were defeated one by one but it was not until the end of 1895 that the great Yao chief, bereft now of all support, retreated across the Mozambique border for the last time. 177

Fort Lister and Fort Anderson were built near the Mozambique border to watch the old southern slave route. The power of the Yao slaving chiefs was broken. So, too, was the Yao way of life. Now this people, who had for so long dominated a large area to the east and south of the lake, had to humble themselves before the white, learn his ways, pay his taxes, work on his farms and obey his laws. The transition was not easy for them.

At the northern end of Lake Malawi few people paid any attention to the white commissioner. Here real power was in the hands of Mlozi, the Arab slave trader. From his base at Karonga he controlled a thriving trade with the Bemba and the eastern Lunda. He dominated the Ngonde. And every year he despatched thousands of slaves towards

Mlozi, the last and most ruthless of the Arab slave raiders on Lake Nyasa.

the east coast. Johnston had won over Jumbe, the slaver of Kota Kota, and established a government post at Deep Bay, but these events had made little impression on Mlozi, who openly scoffed at the British commissioner in distant Zomba. He was encouraged in this attitude by German traders who, despite the declared hostility of their government to the slave trade, were supplying Mlozi with guns and ammunition.

As soon as victory in the south was assured Johnston hurried along the lake with as many men as could be spared from the Yao conflict. He arrived at Karonga in November 1895 and took Mlozi completely by surprise. After a few skirmishes the slaver was driven inside his stockade. Willingly the Ngonde co-operated with Johnston's men in the overthrow of their former master. After fierce fighting the capital was taken. Mlozi was speedily tried and executed. It was, perhaps, too merciful an end for a notorious criminal who had broken every law of humanity and been responsible for death and suffering on an enormous scale.

Shortly after this, Harry Johnston left Nyasaland. His place was taken by Alfred Sharpe, who had been his assistant for some time. It was Sharpe who had to deal with the last outbreaks of primary resistance. Since the declaration of the protectorate life had been becoming increasingly difficult for the Maseko Ngoni. Raiding was forbidden by the new rulers. White men travelled through or settled in the lands demanding that young Ngoni work for them as porters or farmhands. The Maseko leader Gomani found the situation intolerable. On the other side, white settlers and administrators complained that Gomani was 'unco-operative'. It was only a matter of time before a serious clash occurred. It happened in 1897, when Gomani went raiding into the Shiré Highlands. Sharpe sent an expedition against him. He was driven back to his capital. There, after a long battle, he was captured. Later he was tried and executed. The following year a similar series of events took place in the territory of the Mpezeni Ngoni, sparked off on this occasion by a sudden influx of gold prospectors into the area.

The spread of Portuguese control in Mozambique

Meanwhile, in Mozambique the occupying power was not experiencing such swift success. By 1891 the boundaries of Portuguese East Africa were more or less defined but that did not mean that the Portuguese exercised effective control within those boundaries. It took many years for the Portuguese to subdue their subjects north of the Zambezi.

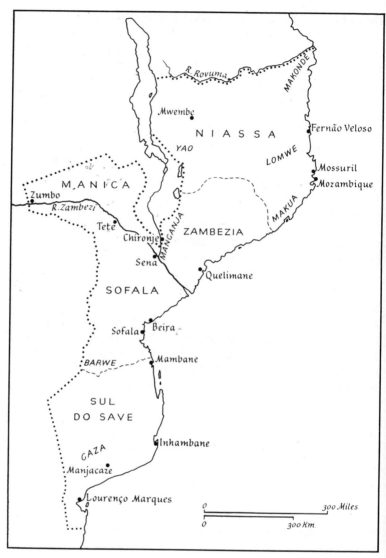

The expansion of Portuguese power in Mozambique.

The first area to resist Portuguese rule was the lower Shiré. As well as normal African objection to white domination there was resentment by the *prazeros* and their allies at the attempt to impose greater government control. There was also the feeling among some of the chiefs that they would rather be under British rule, like their neighbours across the Ruo River, than Portuguese. In 1884 the Massingire, a section of the Manganja, broke into revolt when Portuguese officials tried to arrest two of their chiefs. They overran trading stations and official posts on the Shiré, turned down the Zambezi and reached Mopea, only 130 kilometres from Quelimane, before being checked. In retaliation a mercenary army of 4,000 soldiers led by a wealthy Portuguese settler was sent into Massingire territory. This force put down the rising with the utmost savagery, laying waste a wide area of farmland.

When the army withdrew the Massingire largely resumed their independence, though officially their territory formed part of the Manica province of Mozambique. A military officer was appointed to Chironje in 1887 but lacked the staff to make his authority felt. In 1892 the Portuguese government admitted its inability to administer the area and handed it over to a private company. This proved successful along the Shiré valley but further inland other Manganja groups still resisted attempts at European control. Not until 1897 were these peoples subdued by the Zambezia Company with the help of a government expedition.

In Manica province the Ngoni were not brought under control until 1904. Not until then were the Portuguese able to think about the pacification of the rest of the Zambezia and Niassa provinces. The Makua were attacked by forces from Mossuril and Fernão Velosa in 1906. In 1910 the Arabs of Angoche Island were subdued. At about the same time the northern coastal peoples were brought under effective administration.

It was the Yao and their allies in north-west Niassa who were the last peoples of Mozambique to be subdued. Like the Yao groups in Nyasaland they were well organised and well supplied with guns which came to them along the trade route from Kilwa. For many years they successfully resisted efforts by the Niassa Company and the government to challenge their authority. In 1909–10 the Portuguese established posts along the Rovuma River (the boundary with German East Africa) in order to control the flow of arms. Then they moved against the Yao. In 1912 a government force reached Mwembe, the capital of the greatest Yao leader, Mataka V Cisonga. After fierce fighting the town was taken and Mataka fled across the Rovuma, never to return. With his flight the phase of primary resistance in Portuguese East Africa came to an end.

The Arabs west of Lake Tanganyika

Now we shift our attention north-westwards to see what was happening in the area which is today south-eastern Zaire. This area had been colonised in the years immediately prior to European penetration by Arab ivory and slave hunters. It was these Arabs who offered the stiffest resistance to the white men. The Berlin Act of 1885 had placed this area within the Congo Free State to be administered by King Leopold II of Belgium and his agents. In the following years these agents gradually penetrated the Congo basin, following the trail blazed by H. M. Stanley. Their main aim was to tap the vast ivory resources of the region and send boatloads of tusks westwards down

Makonde wood carving. The Makonde of north-eastern Mozambique and the neighbouring area of Tanzania are widely regarded as the finest carvers in eastern Africa. Their sculptures frequently display their feelings about the spirit world.

the Congo. This was obviously a threat to the livelihood of the Arabs whose wealth depended on the *eastward* flow of ivory to Zanzibar. In 1886 an agreement between Britain and Germany brought German East Africa into existence and German expeditions were launched inland from the east coast. So the Arabs' 'empire' was slowly being squeezed like a piece of wood between the jaws of a vice. What made matters worse for them was that the European powers were pledged, especially after the Brussels Conference of 1890, to the eradication of the slave trade.

By 1874 Tippu Tip, the most powerful of these Zanzibaris, had a degree of control over a vast area stretching eastwards and north-eastwards of Lake Tanganyika. He held this territory in the name of the sultan of Zanzibar but was, in effect, an independent ruler. His attitude towards Europeans was one of polite helpfulness. The few explorers and missionaries who reached his posts in the far interior were usually dependent on him for help, supplies and information; they certainly posed no threat to his power. In 1876 H. M. Stanley arrived at Kasongo, Tippu Tip's headquarters, and asked the notorious slaver's aid on his journey down the Congo. Tippu Tip accompanied Stanley for 500 kilometres and provided him with men for the rest of the journey. Had it not been for the Arabs' willingness to face dense forest, dangerous torrents, disease and inhospitable peoples Stanley's great journey of exploration would probably not have been completed. By 1883 Stanley was back as an agent of King Leopold. He established a post at Stanley Falls. The Arabs were informed that they must restrict their activities to the area upstream from the new post. Tippu Tip rejected this order and Leopold's agents were, for the time being, unable to enforce it. Indeed, in 1886 Stanley Falls was attacked and its garrisson killed by the Arabs.

But Tippu Tip knew the real power of the Europeans. In 1887 he agreed to become the governor of Stanley Falls in the pay of the Congo Free State. The Europeans gradually built up their strength. Expeditions travelled north-eastwards from Stanley Falls and far up the Lualaba. C.F.S. rule was imposed on many African rulers and there were frequent clashes with Arab slavers, most of whom lacked Tippu Tip's foresight and patience. But as long as Tippu Tip was present he was largely able to moderate the behaviour of his colleagues. He left in 1890.

Early in 1892 the major Arab leaders from Sef (Tippu Tip's son) at Stanley Falls to Rumaliza at Ujiji united in a rising against the Belgians. For eighteen months fierce fighting occurred over a wide area. Not until October 1893, when in a battle on the river Luama Sef was killed and Rumaliza forced to flee, was the power of the Arabs finally broken.

African and Arab rulers south of Lake Tanganyika

Further south Msiri and his Yeke reigned supreme between the Lualaba and the Luapula. As trade increased so did Msiri's slave-raiding activities. This and severe taxation angered his subjects. In 1886 the Sanga revolted. Msiri failed to crush the revolt which severely hampered his trade on the western routes. The following year a dispute with Nsimba, a powerful Arab trader, led to a war which threatened to close the eastern caravan routes. Msiri made peace with his enemy but it was becoming clear to his neighbours that the great chief's power was waning. This was also becoming clear to the growing number of Europeans who were visiting the Yeke kingdom. Missionaries reached Bunkeya in 1886 and when their reports about the country, and particularly its potential copper resources, reached Europe's capitals commercial concerns (including, as we shall see, the B.S.A. Co. and the C.F.S.) began to take an interest in Katanga.

The fortunes of the East Lunda kingdom revived briefly in the 1890s. Kaniembo Ntemena (Kazembe X) managed to regain much of his ancestral territory with the help of a Bemba army in 1890. In 1891, on the death of Msiri, the long war with the Yeke came to an end. Peace and stability returned to the ancient kingdom and refugees fleeing from slave raiders and European expansion poured in from all directions to place themselves under the Kazembe's protection. This was the situation until 1899, when the kingdom came under colonial rule.

Thousands of these fugitives had left the Zambian plateau which was still dominated by the Bemba. This large area was in a state of chaos. As well as raiding for slaves Bemba groups clashed with their neighbours and intervened in the political life of other states. Sometimes they worked with Arab traders and sometimes they fought against them. The approach of Europeans bent on the eradication of the slave trade made the Arabs and the Bemba, if anything, more vicious and aggressive. They fought hard to keep traditional trade routes open and as their livelihood was threatened they exacted more cattle and grain from their subject peoples.

European penetration into Katanga and eastern Zambia

By 1890 this area was encircled by Europeans. Missionaries were well established around Lakes Malawi and Tanganyika. The White Fathers had begun to penetrate Bemba territory and had been welcomed by some of the chiefs. Other Christian workers had visited Bunkeya and Plymouth Brethren missionaries had travelled through Angola

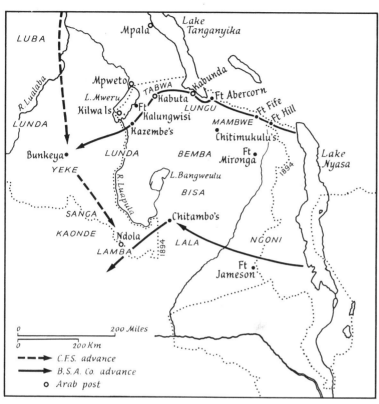

The colonial occupation of Katanga and North-Eastern Rhodesia.

to reach the Lake Mweru area. To the south Coillard and the Paris Missionary Society were well established in Lozi territory. But it was not the cautious infiltration of preachers which threatened the independence of African states. Imperialists, concession-seekers and commercial interests were now moving in on the area.

The British South Africa Co. and the Congo Free State were the principal rivals for control of this part of Central Africa, and particularly of Katanga. They hoped to find there rich deposits of copper which would make the long hard journey up from the Cape or along the Congo worthwhile. The treaty which Rhodes' representative, Frank Lochner, made with Lewanika in 1890 covered a large area north of Barotseland as far as the Congo–Zambezi watershed (an area over most of which Lewanika had no authority). Though events south of the Zambezi kept the B.S.A. Co. pioneers busy, Rhodes did make some attempts to make good his claim to the area further north.

One expedition led by Alfred Sharpe travelled along the Stevenson Road, skirted the southern end of Lake Tanganyika and marched 185 towards Lake Mweru. Sharpe persuaded a number of Mambwe and Lungu chiefs to sign treaties and grant concessions. Kazembe Kaniembo, who was just re-establishing his authority in the east Lunda kingdom, was happy to make a treaty with the B.S.A. Co. which he hoped would back him with men and guns. Sharpe reached Msiri's capital late in 1890 and had talks with the Yeke ruler. But Msiri would have nothing to do with the B.S.A. Co., even though, as Sharpe pointed out, King Leopold's agents would soon be invading Yeke territory from the north. A few months after Sharpe's departure the agents of the C.F.S. began to arrive. Again Msiri attempted to maintain his independence but A. Delcommune, leader of the C.F.S. mission, refused to take 'no' for an answer. He started to stir up trouble among some of the Yeke's dissatisfied subjects, the Sanga and Lamba. Relations between Msiri and the Europeans worsened. On 20 December, at a meeting between the Yeke leader and Captain Stairs, another C.F.S. agent, shooting started and Msiri was killed. This was the signal for widespread revolt throughout the kingdom and Msiri's successor, Mukundabantu, was forced to ally himself with the Europeans in order to regain control of his kingdom. For their part the C.F.S. authorities could now claim 'effective rule' in Katanga and neighbouring regions. This was recognised by the other European powers in 1894 when a boundary was drawn between the Free State and Rhodesia.

The British did not hurry to establish effective control in the area between the Luapula and the Nyasaland boundary. Events south of the Zambezi and around Lake Malawi kept them busy. Johnston established forts along the boundary with German East Africa and for a while a base was occupied on the shore of Lake Mweru. But Johnston could not administer this large territory from the Shiré valley and in 1894 Nyasaland was formally separated from what came to be known as North-Eastern Rhodesia. The B.S.A. Co. now had to appoint its own administration but they were not entirely free from government control. The commissioner of the Nyasaland Protectorate was to keep an eye on their activities and they were not allowed to keep Company troops in North-Eastern Rhodesia. The British government was determined to avoid a repetition of the Ndebele War.

As Company agents moved into their new territory they discovered the power of the Arabs everywhere collapsing. The Zanzibaris could not long survive when their routes to the coast were closed and their major trade centres destroyed. The Bemba were the main group the white administrators had to deal with. But the Bemba had passed the summit of their power. Bemba unity relied almost entirely on the ability of the reigning Chitimukulu to hold the loyalty of the various chieftancies. During the reign of Chitimukulu Sampa (1883–96) a rival chief, Mwamba, succeeding in drawing a great deal of support away from the paramount. One of the ways in which the rivalry of the two chiefs showed itself was in different attitudes towards the white men. Sampa tried to rally support by resistance to European encroachment. Mwamba, while suspicious of European aims, was openly more friendly towards them. Mwamba became the real power in the land in 1896 when Sampa was succeeded by a weak old man. Relations between the Bemba and the white men improved over the next two years.

It was in 1898–9 that the B.S.A. Co. established its control of the plateau – largely without bloodshed. When Mwamba lay dying (1898)

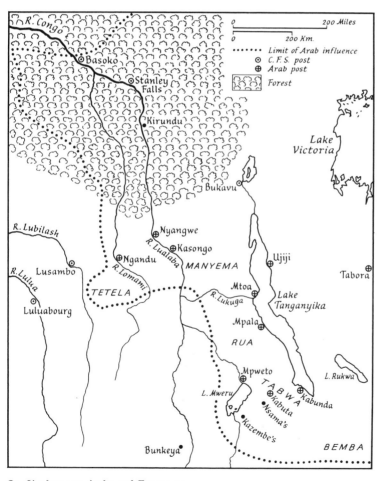

Conflict between Arabs and Europeans.

he sent for Bishop Dupont of the White Fathers' mission. The latter managed to gain control of the kingdom by persuading the leading men that Mwamba had named him as his successor. Within weeks Dupont 'abdicated' in favour of the B.S.A. Co., which peacefully took over Bembaland. The only opposition came from two chiefs in the north-west who were still carrying on a flourishing slave and ivory trade with the Arabs. They were easily defeated during the next few months.

The authority of the Congo Free State was not established so easily in the areas bordering North Eastern Rhodesia. The Free State covered an enormous area, much of it difficult to cross. The financial problems facing King Leopold and his agents were even greater than those which normally confronted pioneering colonial powers. The king kept the C.F.S. going with his own money but in 1890 and 1895 he had to obtain large loans from the Belgian government.* The C.F.S. agents were pushed hard by their superiors to pacify the country quickly and to start making it pay. This and their dislike for the humid climate of the Congo basin made them more than usually brutal in their dealings with the inhabitants of the region. It is not surprising therefore that there was a great deal of primary resistance.

In Luba territory there was almost continuous conflict from 1891 to 1917. When the C.F.S. agents arrived they found a succession dispute being waged by Kasongo Niembo and Kabongo. The newcomers gave their support to the former. Kabongo, looking for allies, found them in a group of Afro-Portuguese traders from Angola and also in a number of Tetela mutineers from the C.F.S. army. Warfare continued until 1905 when the C.F.S. forced their opponents to come to terms. The Luba kingdom was divided between the two rival claimants. Now it was Kasongo Niembo's turn to rebel. Believing that he had been let down by his white allies, he turned against them in 1907. It was another ten years before the colonial rulers could consider this part of the Congo 'pacified'.

When the C.F.S. pioneers arrived in the area of the upper Sankuru, Lulua and Lubilash rivers they found it in a state of turmoil. African slave traders – allies of the Arabs – were terrorising the Luba, Tetela and Songye inhabitants of the region. Advancing from the west the

---

*Until 1908 the Belgian government had nothing to do with the Free State. It belonged as a separate kingdom to Leopold II and was largely financed out of his personal fortune. Most Belgian politicians disliked the king's colonial adventures, particularly later when stories of C.F.S. brutality and harsh exploitation reached Europe. However, when the government made a loan to Leopold in 1895 it demanded the right to annex the Free State to Belgium in 1901. This right was exercised in 1908 (see below, pp. 258–9).

Europeans established a base at Luluaburg. There thousands of refugees flocked to place themselves under C.F.S. protection. The main slaving chiefs were Ngongo Leteta and Lumpungu. In 1890 a new C.F.S. base was established at Lusambo and from there attacks were launched on them. Ngongo Leteta and Lumpungu were wise enough not to fight to the bitter end. After a number of defeats they decided, in 1892, to change sides and helped in the establishment of C.F.S. authority in southern Congo. One interesting, and ultimately tragic, result of C.F.S. intervention in this area was the creation of the Lulua 'people'. These were the Luba refugees who fled to Luluaburg for protection. They were among the first peoples of the area to come into close contact with European civilisation (mission schools, new farming methods, etc.). Their way of life changed until they considered themselves different – and superior – to the rest of the Luba. Thus there developed a rift between the two groups and, in 1959, a terrible war was fought between these peoples of common origin.

15. Partition and reaction
(3) The Western Region

Portuguese expansion from the west

In 1884 the major European powers bargained among themselves for control of the Congo basin and other areas. The Portuguese lost control of the north bank of the River Congo and were only allowed

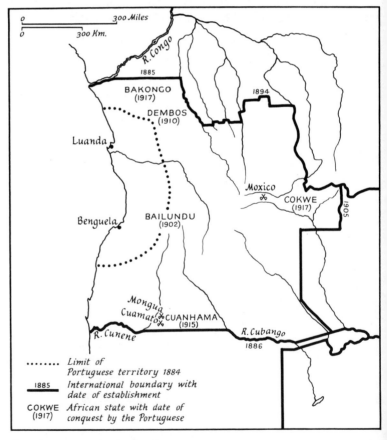

Portuguese expansion in Angola.

the south bank as far as Noqui. Further north Portugal did gain the tiny coastal province of Cabinda. In 1886 by a treaty signed with Germany, Portugal lost more claimed territory when Angola's boundary with German South West Africa was agreed.

Having been thwarted to the north and south the Portuguese made a great effort to push the eastern limits of Angola as far as possible and, in fact, to link up with their territory on the other side of the continent. The first major expedition in 1885 took them south-eastwards against the peoples living between the Cunene and Cubango Rivers. It took the Portuguese thirty years to 'pacify' the southern part of Angola. The Cuanhama, angered by European attempts to rule them and change their way of life, led the resistance and won many important victories against their would-be oppressors. In 1904, for example, they destroyed a force of 300 colonial troops encamped at Cuamoto. The Portuguese lacked the manpower to avenge such reverses speedily. They were also hampered by unofficial German activity in the form of gun-running to the Cuanhama across the border with South West Africa. In fact it was not until after the out-break of the First World War, when the Germans were occupied else-where, that the Portuguese were able to bring southern Angola under control. In 1915 the colonialists won an important victory at Mongua and then built forts throughout the area to prevent further risings.

Portugal was a small country economically very dependent on its colonies. They had to be made to pay for themselves. In Angola this meant the continuance and expansion of slavery, though it was given a new name – contract labour. This was, of course, fiercely resented by the people of Angola and there were several risings against the Portuguese.

In 1902 a revolt broke out in Bailundu among people long ac-customed to Portuguese occupation. It was led by the Bailundu chief, Mutu ya Kevela, but it soon spread to other peoples on the Bie plateau. Soon other Ovimbundu, upset by changes in the traditional trading patterns of central Angola, were involved. Over a wide area there were raids on government posts. Fearing a general uprising the Portuguese took harsh measures to suppress the revolt. Even so, order was only restored after eighteen months of bitter fighting in which thousands of Africans were killed.

Resistance was more successful in the north-west. Here the Dembos (the chiefs of the area) had earlier been subject to Portuguese control. But by 1880 they had thrown off foreign control and only allowed Europeans into their territory on their own terms. They had guns and their long association with the Portuguese had taught them much about European battle tactics. Over the years thousands of Africans 191 escaped from Portuguese-dominated areas and fled to the Dembos for protection. Not until 1907 did Portugal attempt to bring this part of Angola under effective control. Even then it took them three years.

We have already seen how Portugal's hopes of linking Mozambique and Angola in a continuous belt of territory were dashed by the B.S.A. Co. in the early 1890s. Though the borders of Mozambique were fixed at that time, the Angola–Rhodesia boundary was not. In 1891 it had been agreed that the dividing line should be the western limit of Lozi territory but the two powers could not agree where that was. The B.S.A. Co. argued that Lewanika received tribute from chiefs as far away as the Kwando River. The Portuguese countered by sending expeditions into Lovale territory. In 1903 the two powers agreed to submit their claims to an independent arbitrator. A committee under the chairmanship of the king of Italy (the peoples and rulers of the area concerned were, of course, not consulted) considered the matter and, in 1905, the eastern border of Angola was fixed where it is today.

The last part of Angola to be brought under control was the north-east. It was some years before the border with the Congo Free State was settled. The rival claims of the two colonial powers were eventually sorted out at a series of conferences held in 1891 and 1894.

A large part of the disputed territory was in a very confused state. The 1880s, as we have seen, witnessed an enormous expansion by the Cokwe who advanced south-westwards and north-eastwards from their homeland. The northward thrust carried them deep into Lunda and Luba territory and involved most of the peoples of the Congo watershed either as allies or adversaries. By 1898 the tide had begun to turn. The Lunda chiefs Mushini and Kawele stopped the Cokwe advance but no sooner had they reasserted their control than they found themselves in conflict with C.F.S. forces. There were a further ten years of conflict before Mushiri and Kawele were defeated and the Belgian's puppet king, Muteba III, was secure on his throne. Meanwhile the Cokwe had turned north-eastwards to invade the country of the Pende, the Lele and their neighbours across the River Kwilu. They were stopped, but not ousted from all their newly conquered land. Amidst the general disturbance other peoples, such as the Lwena, took the opportunity to launch wars of aggression. The Portuguese were in no hurry to pacify this troubled area and it was not until 1917 that they completed their subjugation of the Angolan Cokwe by defeating them in battle at Moxico.

The Congo Free State

192 'On about 20th May 1885, an act was signed by which the President

of the International Association of the Congo renounced in favour of King Leopold II the rights which had been conferred on it by treaty. This act, as can be imagined, was not made public.'* The act was not made public because the President of the International Association of the Congo and King Leopold II of Belgium were one and the same person. In 1885 Leopold thus became sovereign of the immense Congo Free State. There was no official connection between Belgium and the C.F.S.

Their activities in the eastern Congo and Katanga used up most of the Free State's men and energies. It was only slowly that other areas of the country were brought under control. The rivers were the obvious means of access to the interior and most of the Congo's main tributaries were explored. Posts were established in potentially important administrative or commercial positions and by 1890 over fifty of such posts had been set up. Luluabourg was the centre for what eventually became the Kasai Province.

African troops at the C.F.S. post at Vivi.

Many of the peoples of this region had never seen white men before. This, combined with the Cokwe troubles, probably accounted for the fact that Belgian occupation passed off largely peacefully. However, the C.F.S. agents did encounter resistance from the people of Kaniok and from the Yaka in 1895. In fact the Yaka gave their overlords sporadic trouble until 1906.

* M. Strauch in *Mouvement Géographique*, 28 June 1910. Quoted by G. Martelli in *Leopold to Lumumba* (Chapman and Hall, 1962), p. 115.

To help rule the country the C.F.S. raised an African army, known as the *Force Publique*. At first it was staffed by Africans from other parts of the continent but gradually local recruits were induced or forced into service and by 1905 the *Force Publique* had reached a strength of 16,000 men. These African soldiers were not always submissive to their new masters. There were mutinies at Luluabourg in 1895 and Boma in 1900. A group of Tetela mutineers avoided capture and punishment from 1897 to 1908.

The C.F.S. could not afford to bear the entire burden of administration. Leopold spent most of his own fortune and obtained large loans from the Belgian government. The answer was, as in other parts of Africa, to entrust certain areas to chartered companies. In 1892 the Congo was divided into two areas. About half of the territory was marked as *domaine privée*, that is it was reserved for development by the government. Other areas were left open to approved companies. Most of the Equateur, Leopoldville and Kasai provinces fell into the latter category. Katanga was not included in either category for the time being because of the immense communications problems involved in its development. For many years the principal exports of the Congo were ivory and rubber. The means used by agents of commercial companies and of the Free State were unequalled for their brutality even by the Portuguese (see chapter 19).

In theory the C.F.S. leaders recognised the authority of traditional rulers. A decree of 1891 had empowered senior officials to 'invest' chiefs with the symbols of office. By 1906 over 400 chiefs had been so invested. But in many more instances the C.F.S. put into positions of authority Africans whom they could trust and who had no connection with the people over whom they were set to rule. With their political leaders removed and their menfolk cruelly forced to support an alien economic system it is hardly surprising that there was little primary resistance in the Congo.

The German occupation of South West Africa

Germany's recognition of Adolf Lüderitz's annexation of Angra Pequeña in 1884 had been little more than a move in the game of European politics. The interior of South West Africa was mostly desert and semi-desert. Its occupation offered little hope of economic gain for Germany. However, for what it was worth the Berlin Act (1885) confirmed Germany's title to a long strip of the coast (more or less the whole coastline of modern South West Africa). There were some Germans who were prepared to invest money in the area in the hope that gold or diamonds might be discovered there.

In their attempts to lay claim to the hinterland the Germans came up against various Herero and Khoikhoi groups. In 1885 the German commissar, Heinrich Goering, made a treaty of protection with Maherero, the Herero paramount chief, and several lesser chiefs. But in 1888 Maherero, partly under the influence of agents from the Cape who did not want Britain's position in southern Africa challenged by the Germans, renounced the treaty. Only with the greatest difficulty did Goering manage to reverse the situation once more in 1890, shortly before Maherero's death. He did so by promising Maherero military help against his old enemy Hendrik Witbooi.

German expansion in South West Africa.

It was in 1890 also that the border between South West Africa and neighbouring British territories was agreed. In the Anglo-German convention of that year Germany was allowed not only a very generous hinterland in South West Africa but also a tongue of land (the Caprivi Strip) in the north-east, giving her access to the Zambezi.

But she still had to establish effective rule in her new territory. In Herero country she tried to achieve this by interference in local politics. Before Maherero died he appointed his son Nikodemus to 195 succeed him. Nikodemus was a strong and determined man – not the sort of man the Germans wanted to see as leader of a subject people. The colonialists therefore gave their support to a rival claimant, Nikodemus' brother, Samuel. Samuel was a weak character and a drunkard, prepared to promise anything to the Germans in return for their support. When in 1891 the German administrator, von François, declared Samuel to be paramount chief, he split the Herero into two groups.

Meanwhile von François had to deal with Witbooi. In 1892 he went to the chief's capital at Hornkranz to offer a treaty of protection. But Witbooi was very suspicious about 'protection'. When persuasion failed von François threatened to cut off Witbooi's supplies of guns and ammunition. Though the chief was worried he still refused to accept European domination. To strengthen his position he made peace with the Herero and appealed unsuccessfully to British agents for support.

Now von François decided to use force. On the night of 11–12 April 1893 he made a surprise attack on Hornkranz. In the massacre the village was burned down and 150 men, women and children were killed. Witbooi escaped with the rest of his followers to the Naukluft mountains, shocked and embittered by the Germans' cowardly raid.

Chiefs throughout the territory noted the German behaviour. The Hornkranz massacre made the job of pacification in South West Africa more difficult for the Germans. Sixteen months later Witbooi was attacked in his mountain retreat by a German force under the command of Theodor Leutwein. After a month of desperate fighting Witbooi was forced to surrender and accept German protection (September 1894).

In 1896 there was fresh conflict with the Hereros. The German government had decided to encourage white settlement in South West Africa. This meant that land would have to be found for the settlers. In 1895 Samuel Maherero was persuaded to agree a new boundary between Hereroland and land which would be available to whites. He also agreed that any cattle found on the wrong side of the boundary could be confiscated by the Germans. As we have seen many Herero groups did not accept Samuel's leadership and so refused to be bound by the new agreement. Early in 1896 the Germans seized thousands of cattle grazing on their side of the line. The Herero chiefs protested and Leutwein met them to discuss their grievances. Knowing that Nikodemus was the only one who was dangerous to the Germans, Leutwein used these discussions to provoke an argument with him. Nikodemus stood up to German threats and unfair demands and this

resulted in a war known as the War of the Boundary. In May 1896 the 'rebellious' Herero were defeated. Nikodemus was captured, tried and shot.

Worse horrors were still to come before South West Africa was pacified to the Germans' satisfaction. As more and more settlers arrived in the country a typical colonial border situation developed on the Herero frontier. The settlers despised and ill-treated the Africans. They abused African women. They cheated Africans out of land and cattle.

The colonial authorities made some attempt to guard the interests of the indigenous peoples but, in practice, they suffered abominably at the hands of the arrogant settlers. In 1897 a rinderpest epidemic struck the territory. Medicine was rushed from Europe to treat the cattle belonging to the *settlers*. Losses among the Germans' herds were few. About half the Herero cattle were wiped out in six months. In 1903 two new laws were put forward in the territory of the Bondelswarts Khoikhoi: 'Every coloured person must regard a white person as a superior being', and 'In a court the evidence of one white man can only be outweighed by the statements of seven coloured persons'. In the same year a German accused of murdering a Herero woman was acquitted in a colonial court. His guilt was so obvious that even the government was appalled by the verdict. The case was taken to a higher court which sentenced the murderer to a mere three years imprisonment. Incidents like these enraged the Africans who, at the same time, were gradually losing more and more land and cattle to the grasping settlers.

The first to rise against the foreigners were the Bondelswarts in October 1903. Leutwein hurried south from the colonial capital of Windhoek to deal with the situation. The absence of the German leader and most of the Windhoek garrison encouraged the Herero to launch a war they had been planning in secret for some time. Even Samuel Maherero, who had gained more than his people by collaboration with the colonialists, was now disillusioned with the Germans and authorised the uprising. In January 1904 the Herero raided Okahandja and killed a hundred and fifty settlers and traders. Soon there were outbreaks of violence throughout the central and northern areas of the colony. Even some Ovambo groups in the far north rose in revolt.

Leutwein had to make peace quickly with the Bondelswarts and hurry north to face the new challenge. Reinforcements were rushed out from Germany and major battles were fought at Onganjira and Owiumbo. Then Leutwein decided to stop fighting until he could fetch enough troops from Germany to be able really to crush the Herero once and for all. By the middle of 1904 the Germans had assembled an army of 6,500 professional soldiers as well as settler 197 volunteers and levies from African allies. They were equipped with modern rifles, field artillery and machine guns and were under the leadership of Lieutenant-General von Trotha, an experienced and ruthless officer.

The Herero in the meantime had assembled near Waterberg not far from the edge of the Kalahari desert. Von Trotha's forces met the Herero at Waterberg on 11 August. The battle was indecisive but Samuel, seeing the superior forces ranged against him, decided to escape eastwards with his people in the hope of receiving sanctuary in Bechuanaland. Some crossed the desert successfully but thousands died of thirst on the journey.

An African carving of the German Emperor, Kaiser Wilhelm II. The artist had noticed that the German leader had one arm shorter than the other.

Not content with having defeated his enemy von Trotha mounted a campaign of ruthless extermination. The fact that any Hereros survived at all is due partly to their skill in avoiding detection and partly to the reluctance of many German administrators and junior officers to carry out von Trotha's savage instructions. In 1905 the new governor revoked the extermination order and the Herero remnant returned to resettle their homeland.

The end of the Herero war was not the end of resistance. In October 1904 Hendrik Witbooi, now eighty years old, cast off his alliance with the Germans and led a new revolt. Several Khoikhoi groups, appalled at the German treatment of the Hereros and believing that they were next in line for extermination, joined him. Guerilla fighting went on for over a year in the difficult, mountainous terrain of Namaqualand. In October 1905 the remarkable Hendrik Witbooi died as a result of wounds received in a skirmish. This was a blow to his supporters, many of whom surrendered. A number of chiefs, however, continued their resistance and it was not until the end of 1906 that the last 'rebel' leader, Johannes Christian of the Bondelswarts, surrendered.

The pacification of South West Africa had been expensive for Germany. As well as the considerable financial burden which the wars had placed on the German treasury there had been considerable loss of life. Over 1,600 German soldiers and hundreds of settlers had been killed. The Germans had lost tens of thousands of their African subjects. This led to a serious labour shortage. Thousands of cattle died, with serious consequence for the beginnings of farming in the colony. It was not a good start for the colonial period in this part of Africa.

16.   The British and the Boers – The Final Reckoning

Kruger and the Transvaal

The Pretoria and London conventions had left the South African Republic (Transvaal) independent but poor. The two Boer republics were largely encircled by British and Portuguese territory and the annexation of Bechuanaland and Rhodesia made this encirclement complete. The Transvaal had no links with the coast and was dependent for supplies on neighbouring territories (principally Natal and Cape Colony). This was a situation which the governments in Cape Town, Durban and London were anxious to maintain. Two events made it difficult to control the northern Boer state: Paul Kruger became president of the Transvaal in 1883, and gold was discovered at Witwatersrand in 1886.

Paul Kruger ranks second only to Cecil Rhodes among the dominant white politicians in nineteenth-century southern Africa. He was in every way an extremist: in his religious views; in his Afrikaner nationalism; in his hatred of the British; in his determination to get his own way; and above all in his conviction that he was right and everyone who opposed him was wrong. He was in every way a typical Boer. He had little formal education. He led a simple life. He believed completely in the Bible and allowed nothing else to influence him. He loved 'freedom', which meant for him liberty to exploit the land and peoples of Africa without restraint by the British. He was rugged, strong and brave. Like Rhodes, he was loved, respected or hated but never ignored. What Kruger wanted above all was to create a Transvaal which was truly independent and which had its own outlet to the sea.

This could never have been achieved by Kruger's strength of personality alone. What made it possible was the new wealth which the discovery of gold brought to the Transvaal. The reef (i.e. vein of gold-bearing rock) discovered beneath the hills of the Witwatersrand proved to be extremely rich in gold. Although it was not realised for some years, the Witwatersrand reef was the finest goldfield in the world. But it was the sort of rock which could only be worked with

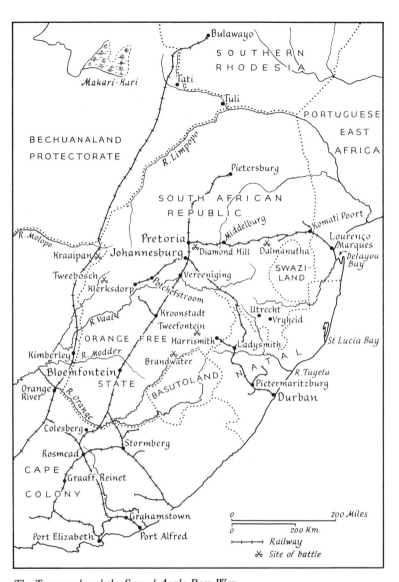

The Transvaal and the Second Anglo-Boer War.

up-to-date mining techniques and expensive machinery. The Boers therefore had to allow foreign companies to operate in their country. The foreigners – 'Uitlanders' as the Boers called them – flocked in. Johannesburg grew in ten years from a small mining camp to a town of 100,000 inhabitants.

As population, industry and trade grew, direct access to the coast

(a) Johannesburg 1888.

became even more important for the Transvaal. However, the British colonies were even more determined to prevent such access. They wanted to share in the Transvaal's wealth and they feared that the Boer state might become not only the richest but the most powerful state in southern Africa. There were other factors in the Transvaal's favour. For one thing, Rhodes and his supporters in the Cape government could not be too 'tough' with the Boer states for fear of antagonising the large Cape Dutch population. For another, Portugal and

(b) Johannesburg 1971.

Germany, who had previously had little interest in the Afrikaner nations, now took a new interest in the Transvaal. They were prepared to give Kruger financial help to build a railway to the coast and to give him diplomatic support in his quarrels with the British. This, then, was the background to the Transvaal's struggle to obtain a link with the east coast which we must now consider in detail. As we have seen Britain checked every move made by the Boers to control a stretch of the east coast.

Zululand, Tongaland and Delagoa Bay

If he could not have direct access to the sea Kruger was determined to have a railway link. This was urgently required not only by the Transvaalers, but by the rapidly growing mining community at Johannesburg. In 1887 an American company began work on a railway from Delagoa Bay to the border of the Republic. This began a 'scramble' to provide a rail link with Johannesburg. Natal businessmen urged the importance of extending the Durban–Ladysmith line into the Transvaal. Cape leaders discussed the possibility of running a railway through the Orange Free State or of building a branch of the Kimberley line to Johannesburg. Meanwhile Cecil Rhodes made repeated efforts to buy up the Delagoa railway company and to gain control of the area of southern Mozambique through which it ran. Kruger knew that motives of economic and political domination lay behind all these moves. 'Every railway that approaches me I look upon as an enemy, on whatever side it comes. I must have my Delagoa Bay line first, and then the other lines may come.'

Swaziland

In 1881 and again in 1884 the British and Transvaal governments formally acknowledged the independence of the Swazi kingdom. But the Boers coveted Swaziland's rich pastures and Kruger wanted to annex the kingdom in order to push his boundary closer to the coast. He had not abandoned the hope of gaining Kosi Bay. The king, Mbandzeni, had allowed a number of Boer settlers into his territory and the usual frontier problems had already begun. The situation was made even worse by the activities of British prospectors working mining concessions. In 1887 Mbandzeni tried to solve the problem by appointing an Englishman as 'Resident Adviser and Agent' but this official had little real power and soon Swaziland was a battle ground of rival British and Boer fractions.

When Mbandzeni died in 1890 and was succeeded by a minor

further chaos threatened. British and Transvaal officials travelled to Swaziland to help the leaders work out a constitution which would bring peace to the country. By the first Swaziland Convention the independence of the kingdom was confirmed and a government was established representing the Swazi and the two immigrant groups. It made little difference: political chaos, inter-racial strife and territorial disputes continued.

In 1891 Britain and Portugal agreed their Central African boundaries and the encirclement of the Transvaal was complete. In the same year lack of money forced Kruger to agree to an extension to Johannesburg of the railway line from Cape Town. The first train on this line reached the gold mining centre in September 1892. Shortly after this Kruger was very nearly defeated in a presidential election. In 1893 the second Swaziland Convention took place. It permitted the Transvaal not to annex Swaziland, but to declare a protectorate over it. It also held out the possibility of a railway link to Kosi Bay. This arrangement was blocked by the queen regent of Swaziland. She utterly rejected any suggestion of a takeover by the Transvaal. Instead she applied for British protection.

Britain did not want another protectorate. On the other hand the unsatisfactory situation in Swaziland could not be allowed to continue. In 1894 the British yielded to Kruger's repeated demands and allowed him to declare a protectorate over the Swazi kingdom. But Kruger's satisfaction did not last long. A few months later Britain annexed Tongaland and the Transvaal's last chance of direct access to the sea was gone. In the same year the Delagoa Bay line was completed and the Durban line also reached Johannesburg. As for the Swazis they had to endure five years of harsh Boer rule. For 'protection' in Boer language meant exploiting the land and people of Swaziland and destroying their political institutions.

The Uitlanders

During these years a worse problem was developing in the Transvaal – a problem which led eventually to what is called the second Anglo-Boer War or, more simply, the Boer War. The problem was the relationship between the Afrikaners of the Transvaal led by Kruger and the Uitlanders supported from outside the country by Rhodes.

Most of the Uitlanders were British and they had all gone to the South African Republic to profit in one way or another from the development of the gold mining industry. The Transvaal government needed Uitlander skills and money but hated the Uitlanders themselves. Their official attitude towards the foreigners was harsh:

This is our country, and if you come here to seek wealth, it must be entirely on our terms. They are that you shall have no votes and no rights, and we shall so tax you, both directly on the mine profits and indirectly by enormous duties on imported mine-requisites, that a large part of what you get will pass to us.

The Uitlanders, naturally, resented being treated as second class citizens. There were extremists who shared Rhodes' view that the Afrikaner states must eventually come under British rule probably as part of a united South Africa. If the Transvaal became the richest state in South Africa and if British people were allowed no say in the government and development of the country the desired union might never come. Worse still, South Africa might become united under Boer leadership.

The non-Afrikaners in the Transvaal had many genuine grievances. One was language. Official and most legal business was carried out in the Boers' language, High Dutch. Most schools also used this language. Many of the English-speaking schools were closed down by the government so most Uitlander children had little chance of gaining a formal education. Another evil was the corruption in government circles. Boer politicians, who were supposed to have such high, biblical principles, took bribes, gave contracts to their friends and relatives, granted monopolies in essential goods, stole Uitlander property and passed new laws to benefit small sections of the community. Taxation was a serious cause of discontent. Heavy import duties were levied on essential mining gear. Profits were taxed at a high rate. Exorbitant fares were charged on Boer controlled stretches of railway line. Some Uitlanders calculated that over ninety per cent of the government's revenue came from taxation on the small foreign community. Probably the main source of ill-feeling was the Transvaal voting regulations. In 1890 the government decided that no Uitlander could have the vote until he had lived in the republic for fourteen years, had had Transvaal nationality for twelve years and had passed the age of forty. No non-Afrikaner could take part in presidential elections. In fact, the Uitlanders had no constitutional means of airing their grievances or influencing the government. It is not surprising that they turned to unconstitutional and even violent means.

The Jameson Raid

It was against this background that Cecil Rhodes planned the biggest political gamble of his career. He smuggled arms and ammunition into the Transvaal and agreed to support a rising in Johannesburg with an invasion by a small B.S.A. Co. force. The force – from Matabeleland – was to be led by Dr Jameson.

The secret was never very well kept in Johannesburg. Towards the end of 1895 the Boers realised that trouble was brewing. The police prepared for action and the politicians suddenly began to make concessions. They agreed to reduce some import duties, to increase subsidies for English-speaking schools, and to reconsider the whole issue of voting rights. This was enough to undermine the revolutionaries. They had never been very united and they decided to postpone the Johannesburg rising indefinitely. Rhodes realised that the opportunity had passed. The only man who refused to admit defeat was Jameson.

He was waiting at Pitsani on the Bechuanaland–Transvaal border with 470 mounted men. On 29 December he decided to wait no longer.

British troops in the Battle of Colenso during the Second Anglo-Boer War.

He believed that once they knew of his invasion the faint-hearted Uitlanders would rise in his support. On his own initiative he ordered the invasion to begin. Chamberlain, Rhodes, the Uitlander leaders and the British High Commissioner in the Transvaal all sent messages to Jameson urging him to stop the raid. He ignored them all. The 'invasion' was soon over. Some of the Uitlanders came out in support of Jameson but the High Commissioner soon recalled them. On 2 January the B.S.A. Co. party was defeated in a skirmish at Doornkop and forced to surrender.

Although Jameson and the others who took part in the rising escaped with fines and light prison sentences, the results of this fiasco were serious. Rhodes was forced to resign as prime minister of Cape Colony. The Transvaal grew closer to Germany when the emperor, Kaiser Wilhelm II, sent a telegram to Kruger congratulating him on repulsing the 'armed hordes which broke into your country'. Germany also sent troops to Delagoa Bay to be at Kruger's disposal should he need them. This, of course, angered the British government and people. To the north the Ndebele and Shona took advantage of the depleted garrisons to rise against Company rule. But the most serious consequence of the raid was the worsening of relationships between the Boers and the British. In Cape Colony the raid had angered the Cape Dutch and widened the gulf between the two white communities. The idea of a united South Africa was dropped. The Orange Free State and the Transvaal drew closer together. And in the South African Republic Kruger now had total support for his anti-Uitlander policies. He was re-elected as president for the fourth time in 1898. So bitter were the feelings between Boer and Briton now that war was probably inevitable.

The second Anglo-Boer War

The Transvaal began to spend large sums of money on weapons and military equipment. Most of it came from Germany and was imported along the Delagoa Bay railway. The government introduced new laws dealing with immigration, press censorship, the right to expel aliens and control of open-air meetings.

British extremists formed the South African League and began to campaign against the Transvaal government. In December 1898 a Transvaal policeman shot and killed Tom Edgar, an Englishman suspected of murder. Many Uitlanders believed that Edgar had been gunned down in cold blood and expected to see the policeman tried for murder. He was not; he was tried on the lesser charge of manslaughter – and acquitted. Not only was he acquitted; the judge complimented him on his devotion to duty. The Uitlanders were furious. The South African League organised a protest and drew up a petition which soon had over 20,000 signatures.

The petition was to the British queen and it requested that her government would protect the rights of her citizens in the South African Republic. The appeal reached London in March 1899 and presented the British government with an unpleasant choice – to desert British subjects in their hour of need or to risk war with the Transvaal. Britain's leaders tried to avoid this choice. Months of futile negotiations followed. Fresh troops were sent to Cape Colony and detachments already in South Africa were moved towards the borders of the Republic. The Transvaal government threatened war if the troop movements were not cancelled. The British rejected the ultimatum. On 27 September the Free State assured their Transvaaler brethren of their support and on 11 October 1899 the second Anglo-Boer War began.

The British army was one of the finest in the world. The Boers were a rabble of undisciplined farmers. Few people thought the war would last more than a few weeks. It went on for two and a half years. It cost the lives of over 21,000 British soldiers and over 30,000 Afrikaner men, women and children. The main reason for the prolongation of the conflict was the Boers' skilful tactics. They were desperate men fighting for what they believed was their country. They knew that country well; the British generals did not. The Boers were natural hunters and therefore fine marksmen. It was natural for them to adopt a guerilla type of warfare, fighting in small bands, moving swiftly, attacking small detachments of the enemy, always able to rely on the womenfolk in their scattered homesteads for food and supplies.

This method of fighting had its drawbacks. It left initiative and authority with the unit commanders. There was no overall strategy. Thus the Transvaalers failed to make the most of their numerical superiority in the early stages of the war. They invaded neighbouring territories and laid siege to Ladysmith, Kimberley and Mafeking. The startled British leaders sent reinforcements to South Africa. They fought their way northwards with difficulty, suffering heavy losses. Instead of inflicting decisive defeats on the British at this stage the Boers persisted in their siege of the three border towns. The invading forces were thus able to push slowly into Afrikaner territory. By the end of February Kimberley and Ladysmith had been relieved and, in a battle at Paardeberg, the Free State had been knocked out of the war. On 17 May the siege of Mafeking was raised. On 28 May the southern Boer state was annexed as the Orange River Colony and a week later British forces had occupied Johannesburg and Pretoria. Kruger fled into Mozambique.

The British leaders believed that all they had to do now was dictate the peace terms. They were wrong; the real war was only just beginning. All over the occupied Boer states guerilla bands began to operate. Early in 1901 the British commander, Lord Kitchener, worked out a new strategy to deal with the new situation. He built block houses and defensive lines of barbed wire to make it impossible for the Boer horsemen to travel freely over the country. To starve the guerillas into submission he destroyed all farmsteads suspected of supporting them. Houses and crops were burned, stock was confiscated and the women and children were put into special camps.

Kitchener's policy was successful from a military point of view but it was politically disastrous. The destruction of Boer homes caused widespread resentment and quite failed to force the guerillas into a speedy surrender. But it was the 'concentration camps' which resulted in international protest. Many of the camps were over-crowded and unhealthy. Disease spread so rapidly that in about eighteen months 26,000 women and children died in the camps.

Meanwhile the Boers fought on, encouraged by Kruger from his safe retreat. But Kitchener's tactics made prolonged resistance impossible. At last a meeting was arranged between the leaders of the two Boer states at Klerksdorp in April 1902. They recommended a larger conference attended by elected delegates empowered to act on behalf of the Afrikaner people. This conference, attended by sixty Boer representatives, assembled a few weeks later at Vereeniging. At first the majority of delegates were in favour of continuing the war. They believed the Cape Dutch would rise in their support. When they realised that there was no hope of this they gave way. The treaty of Vereeniging which ended the war was signed on 31 May 1902.

The British were generous in their peace terms. The Boer states were to remain British colonies. The Transvaal lost its south-eastern corner (the former New Republic) to Natal. The Boers had to surrender their arms and swear allegiance to the king of England. English was to be the official language throughout the Union. Swaziland became a British protectorate. In return the British made the following concessions: The colonies were to have eventual self-government. There was to be no question of voting rights for Africans before self-government was achieved. High Dutch might be used in schools and law courts. No Boer fighters were to be put on trial for their wartime activities. The British government would pay three million pounds to the Boers for the rebuilding and restocking of farms and would make interest-free loans available to individuals for two years.

17. The period of colonial rule
(1) The British Sphere

South Africa

Three themes have dominated the history of South Africa in the twentieth century – the fate of the majority, African population; economic development; and power politics among the ruling white minority.

During the troubles described in the last chapter the position of the African peoples had continued to deteriorate. The political power of their traditional rulers had been broken. Their homelands continued to diminish as white farmers and officials appropriated land for other purposes. But the population did not decrease and many men had to leave home to find work on European farms or in the fast-growing towns and cities. This meant not only that they had to learn strange new languages, ideas and techniques, but also that they became 'detribalised' – severed from their social and historical roots.

The situation was worse in the more densely populated Natal and Boer states. Cape Colony (or Cape Province as it became in 1910) incorporated little Bantu land. Its African population consisted largely of Khoikhoi and Cape Coloured (people of mixed racial origin deriving from Khoikhoi, San, immigrant slave and European elements) peoples. Because of these regional differences and the distinct Boer and British racial attitudes three different approaches to the 'native problem' evolved. In the Cape a liberal attitude prevailed. Africans could gain education of a European type and own land. Those who owned or leased land over a certain value were free to vote on a common roll with Europeans. In Natal, with its long history of frontier conflict, most British political leaders favoured a policy of separation. They tried to keep Africans in reserves and tribal trust lands. Within these areas the Africans were to follow a path of separate political development and they were not to leave these areas without passes. In the Afrikaner states the rulers unflinchingly maintained their absurd, antiquated notion of racial supremacy. They rejected any idea of political rights for black men. Africans were doomed, in their view, to permanent inferiority and servitude.

At the peace of Vereeniging no safeguards had been established for the political standing and development of the African majority in the Afrikaner territories. When those territories were granted self-government in 1906–7, once again nothing was done about African political rights. In 1910, when the four South African territories came together in a political union, the Cape representatives completely failed to have liberal ideas embodied in the new constitution. The four provinces carried their own prejudices with them into the new Union and this led, as we shall see, to a long period of political instability (see below, pp. 219ff).

But some Africans were now beginning to take a part in politics themselves. Most of these men were not traditional leaders but Africans who had received an education at the mission schools and who now wanted to use their advantages in the service of their fellows. The first champion of African rights was John Tengo Jabavu. As early as 1884 he had begun to publish a liberal newspaper – *Imvo zaba Ntsundu* – in the Xhosa language and in English. In 1902 another newspaper – *Ilanga Iase Natal* – began to appear in Durban. Its producer was an African clergyman, the Reverend John Dube. In the same year the first African political group appeared. This was the African People's Organization, founded at Cape Town by Dr. Abdullah Abdurahman.

The people of Natal were becoming increasingly restless at the loss of their lands, at labour laws and pass laws, at unfair treatment in the courts. The government introduction of a poll tax in 1906 came as the last straw. A small rising occurred, which was swiftly and ruthlessly crushed. The leaders were tried and condemned to death by a white court. Appalled with the harshness of the verdict, the British government tried, unsuccessfully, to stop the executions. When the Durban government ordered the hangings to be carried out despite African opinion and the opinion of liberals inside and outside South Africa, a more serious revolt flared up in Zululand. The Natal whites were only able to suppress this rising with the aid of troops from Transvaal and the Cape. Afterwards the Natal authorities arrested the king, Dinizulu, who had not, in fact, stirred his people to revolt. At his trial Dinizulu was defended by William Schreiner, an experienced and respected Cape liberal politician. It made no difference: Dinizulu was condemned to four years' imprisonment. He never resumed the throne and with him Shaka's dynasty came to an end.

The South African Native National Conference was formed in 1909 and sent Jabavu and Walter Rubusana to London to represent African opinion over the formation of the Union. When the new constitution came into force Rubusana and Abdurahman gained seats on the Cape Province council.

A more radical body was formed in 1912. This was the African National Congress, which aimed to act throughout the Union to protect African interests. Its first secretary-general was Solomon Plaatje, a Tswana journalist, and he became the mouthpiece of the Congress in attacking much of the legislation which the Union government produced. At this point a split occurred in the ranks of African politicians. Jabavu formed the South African Races Congress to make a rival bid for black support. The S.A.R.C. was less extreme than the A.N.C. and worked closely with white liberals. It lost a great deal of support when it backed the Natives Land Act in 1913 and it did not survive Jabavu's death in 1921.

The Natives Land Act was one of the first attempts by the Union government to deal with 'native' problems. Because of land pressure and the greater wealth obtainable outside the reserves, Africans were renting farmland, squatting on European farms and even buying land. This spread of black population into 'white' areas disturbed the 'master race'. The result was the Natives Land Act which forbade Europeans and Africans from buying land in each other's areas and restricted the rights of squatters and tenants. The A.N.C. and other opponents of the Act did manage to stop it being implemented in Cape Province, where it would have interfered with ability of Africans to gain the franchise but elsewhere, and particularly in the Orange Free State, it was enforced with typical Boer brutality.

It was the situation in the mining towns which really brought the racial issue to a head. Many unskilled and semi-skilled jobs in the mines were done by Africans. This was cheap labour and the mine owners welcomed it. Then a new class of 'poor whites' began to appear. These were men who had to seek industrial jobs because they could not make a living elsewhere. These men resented jobs being given to Africans and were ready to support Afrikaner racial policies in order to push the black men out of the mines.

The European workers had the advantage of being able to organise themselves into trade unions in order to bring pressure to bear on employers and government. The Africans were forbidden by the Masters' and Servants' Act of 1842 to take industrial action. Thus, in 1911 the poor whites were able to secure restrictions on the employment of African labour. The position was further clarified two years later in the Native Labour Regulation Act.

Some Africans felt that they, too, would benefit from the strength and solidarity provided by a trade union. Many Africans served during

the First World War (1914–18) and felt that the white man now owed them a better deal. In 1917 Clements Kadalie, a Nyasalander, founded the Industrial and Commercial Workers Union (I.C.U.). This was more than a trade union; it brought together non-Europeans from all over the Union and supported their demands for justice both inside and outside industry.

The next two or three years saw several demonstrations, strikes and outbreaks of violence by Africans in the industrial areas. Some were organised by the I.C.U., whose membership was rapidly growing, but others were the work of small unions and organisations and the strike of 71,000 mineworkers on the Rand in 1920 had no organised leadership at all. Africans were learning how protests can be made and pressures brought to bear in a democratic context. This was very unwelcome to Afrikaners and what we might call other Afrikaner-minded whites. The Europeans were afraid of the vast black majority among whom they lived. After a number of unpleasant incidents the government, in 1920, set up a Native Affairs Commission as a permanent advisory body to the prime minister and promised regular consultations between government and acknowledged African leaders.

A South African gold mine.

But the situation was growing steadily worse. Despite government promises, no land had been added to the African reserves. Half of the black population lived in towns and agricultural areas. More educated leaders were emerging from their ranks. They were becoming bolder in their demands and better organised in the pursuance of their aims. The situation was complicated by white political groups who manipulated the African organisations for their own purposes. For instance the Industrial Workers of Africa was formed in 1917 with the backing of European socialists. On top of this came the economic depressions of the 1920s and 1930s. As profits dropped unemployment rose. Mine owners were under considerable economic pressure to employ cheaper African labour.

J. Hertzog, who became prime minister in 1924, decided separation was the answer to South Africa's racial problems. One of his first pieces of legislation (1926) was the Mines and Works Amendment Act. It openly introduced the colour bar into industry by excluding Africans and Asians from skilled jobs in the mines and a variety of semi-skilled occupations. Despite the widespread unpopularity of this measure Hertzog indicated that he intended to carry through more segregationist legislation. One result was that the I.C.U. grew in strength to 50,000 and became the undisputed mouthpiece of African radicalism. It moved its headquarters to Johannesburg and began to make a real impact on the population of the northern industrial areas. The police planted spies in the organisation and European communists tried to gain control of it for their own ends. When Clements Kadalie purged the communists from the I.C.U. they began to organise trade unions on the Rand and by 1928 the largely communist Non-European Trade Union Federation could boast a membership of 10,000. The communists now gained in strength while the I.C.U. declined. In a drastic situation more and more Africans turned to the extreme solutions put forward by the Moscow-backed left-wingers. The financial affairs of the I.C.U. fell into chaos and in 1929 Kadalie resigned.

1929 was also a year of parliamentary elections. Faced with increasing African and communist activity the Afrikaner-minded politicians were able to play on the electorate's fears. This election is still remembered as the 'Black Peril' election, which indicates the sort of alarm white extremists were spreading. During the election there were race riots in many areas. The return of Hertzog paved the way for further segregationist policies. The prime minister and his supporters knew that they must act quickly if they were to realise their dream of a white South Africa. The biggest obstacle was the traditional liberalism of the Cape. There the number of qualified African voters was growing steadily and it was obvious that they would ultimately outnumber the European voters. In 1931 the government changed the electoral laws, giving the vote to white women and removing the property qualification for white men. This meant that African voters were now safely outnumbered.

The government could still not afford to ignore African and white liberal opinion but it was now powerful enough to push through most of its race measures and to turn South Africa into a country virtually dominated by Afrikaner philosophy. The Natives' Urban Areas Amendment Act (1930) further restricted the movement of Africans to the towns. The Native Service Contract Act (1932) ordered that Africans in rural areas of Natal and Transvaal must return to their reserves or become labour tenants on European farms where they were forced to work for the farmers. Most significant of all was the Natives Representation Act of 1936. This further reduced Africans' political power in Cape Province by removing them from the common roll. They were now to vote in three all-black constituencies and were to be represented in parliament by three Europeans (there were 153 members in the assembly). In its final form the Natives Representation Act had been much modified from the original, more extreme draft that Hertzog had proposed. Even so it was opposed by African leaders, white liberals and almost all the churches of South Africa. One politician prophesied about the Act and its effect on the African voters:

> Now what is the political future for those people? This Bill says to these Natives 'There is no room for you. You must be driven back on your own people.' But we drive them back in hostility and disgruntlement, and do not let us forget this, that all this Bill is doing for these educated Natives is to make them the leaders of their own people, in disaffection and revolt.

But the Africans did not revolt. Though they were badgered by the police and the law courts; though tens of thousands of them were imprisoned every year for failure to pay poll tax or for not carrying passes; though they were brutally treated by white employers; though hundreds of thousands of them lived in appalling shanty-town slums on the edges of the cities – they did not revolt. Such riots as occurred were usually sparked off by gangs of white thugs or over zealous policemen, as at Vereeniging in 1937 when three policemen were killed and many Africans wounded.

On the other side of the coin it must be said that many South Africans were better off than their counterparts in other parts of the continent. They lived in a prosperous country and some of them, at least, had a share of that prosperity. Few black men were as well off as the South African industrial workers. They had educational opportunities and possibilities of limited advancement. This could not be said of people living under, for instance, Portuguese or Belgian rule. Few Africans were free men in 1939. Those living under Hertzog's regime were no worse off than those living under other colonial regimes.

Asians

The Afrikaner-minded people of South Africa had decided that anyone with a white skin was born to be a master, was capable of being educated to a high standard and had a superior culture. People whose skin were of a different colour were in every way inferior. This meant not only pure-bred Africans but also Cape Coloured people and Asians. Up to 1939 Cape Coloured people were considered to be politically and socially on a par with white men. They were protected by the traditional liberalism of the province in which most of them lived. Asians were not so fortunate.

Indians began to travel to Natal in the 1860s to work on the sugar plantations. Most of them stayed on to settle and raise families. Later more prosperous Indians arrived and established businesses. By 1890 the European rulers were becoming alarmed. Not only was the Asian population growing but Indians were accumulating land and commercial interests. The government began to restrict Asian rights and tried to control immigration. The vote was taken away from them. It became almost impossible for them to obtain trading licences. When immigration continued white mobs rioted at Durban docks to prevent Asians landing. Eventually it was the government of British India which took a decisive stand. In 1904 they refused to allow emigration to the Transvaal gold mines (the O.F.S. had already placed a ban on Asian immigration) and in 1911 they prohibited Indians from travelling to Natal.

When Indian labour was refused to the Transvaal mine-owners they turned to another part of Asia. They recruited unskilled workers from China. Their reason was the need to get the gold mines working at maximum capacity after the war. Recruiting among the Bantu peoples was going badly and so the employers had to look elsewhere. The Chinese arrived and were treated as slaves. They were poorly paid. They were herded into overcrowded camps which they were not allowed to leave during the little leisure time that they had. Disease, vice and violence prospered in the camps. There was an outcry of protest in Britain and throughout the British Empire. But it was not until 1910 that British government enquiries resulted in the end of Chinese labour and the repatriation of all the surviving workers.

The Boers of the Transvaal were even harsher in their attitude towards Indians than were the leaders of Natal, even though they had a much smaller problem. Although the Indians had come into the country as free British subjects they, like the Africans, were subjected to every kind of racial discrimination. They were forbidden to own land. They had to live in their own quarters. They were kept out of bars, theatres and other public places. They had to register with the police and suffer the indignity of having their thumbprints taken. The Indians found a champion in the person of a young lawyer who had come from the mother country in 1893. This was Mohandas Karamchand Gandhi, later to win fame as the architect of Indian independence. He organised large bands of Indians in passive resistance to the governments of Natal and Transvaal. Although many of his followers were imprisoned Gandhi did succeed in winning minor concessions for Indian people of South Africa. When he left during the First World War the South African Indian Congress and the Transvaal Indian Congress continued his work. Partly as a result of their activities the Transvaal Asiatic Land Tenure Amendment Act was passed in 1936. It eased restrictions on Indian ownership of land and businesses but it was still based on the assumption that brown-skinned people were second class people.

Economic development

During the period 1900–39 South Africa became by far the richest part of the continent. Cattle and sheep farming remained the most important aspect of the agricultural life of the Union and by the end of the period wool had become one of the country's most important exports. By 1900 fast steamships had begun to connect South African ports with Europe. One of the results of this was the development of fruit growing around the Cape and on the Natal coast.

But it was industrial development which made the biggest difference to South Africa's economy. By the beginning of the century the country already had a complex railway system. With its rich mineral deposits South Africa was now ready for an industrial revolution. The mineral belt which produces gold and diamonds also contains deposits of coal, iron ore, chrome, copper, manganese and other minerals. Most of these deposits had begun to be exploited by 1939. Coal was mined at Newcastle and close to the Rand. This coal was vital to the gold industry and also led to Durban's becoming an important refuelling port for ships. In 1928 the South African Iron and Steel Corporation was established and six years later opened the country's first major steel works at Pretoria. With coal, iron, steel and railways the way was open for massive and varied industrial development. All kinds of secondary industries – chemicals, textiles, engineering, canning, etc. – came into being. Johannesburg, Newcastle, Port Elizabeth, Durban and Cape Town became the centres of large industrial areas. The African peoples gradually changed their economic and social traditions and accepted the white man's values. They had little chance to do otherwise. They needed money to pay taxes and to buy manufactured goods introduced by the Europeans. By the 1930s men were coming to the South African industrial areas not only from all over the Union but also from Rhodesia, Bechuanaland, Basutoland, Swaziland and Nyasaland. While there they lived in special compounds provided by the employers.

As the world's largest producer of gold South Africa inevitably played an important part in international commerce. This had disadvantages during the early part of this century. Between 1914 and 1918 most of the leading economic nations were at war. Trade, of course, declined during the conflict but after the war, when everyone was anxious to set business and industry going again, there was a boom. South African farmers and industrialists hurried to share in this boom by producing as much as possible for exports. Then in 1921 there came a world slump. Banks failed, prices fell, factories closed and businesses went bankrupt. This hit the South African economy hard. It was then that the real foundations of industrial development were laid. The government decided that it was bad for the country's prosperity to depend only on exports of gold, diamonds and wool. It encouraged the formation of new industries by such measures as protective tariffs to discourage competition from foreign imports.

For a while all went well. Then, in 1929, the Great Depression hit the world. This was the worst commercial slump there had ever been. International trade collapsed and many countries went off the gold standard (i.e. they stopped keeping stocks of gold to give their currencies a fixed value). So, not only were South Africa's agricultural and industrial exports badly hit, but the demand for her principle product – gold – also declined. Again the government had to take strong action. Farmers and some industries were subsidised. Duties were placed on trade with non-gold standard countries. It was a difficult time but South Africa survived it more easily than most states. The reason was her gold. In a time when the value of money was dropping (or in the case of countries like Germany, collapsing) many governments and financiers rushed to buy gold, the one commodity which kept its value. In fact, increased demand drove up the price of gold from 85 shillings per ounce to 140 shillings per ounce in the mid-thirties. Foreign investors were eager to buy shares in South African mines and industries and, by 1935, the Union had recovered from the depression.

White power politics

The issue which dominated the political life of the country during these years was whether South Africa would be an Afrikaner or a British nation. Afrikaner politicians spoke of a united republic, independent of Britain and founded on strict racial segregation. British leaders largely followed Rhodes' idea of a united South Africa based on British liberal, democratic traditions, which should be an integral and proud part of the British Empire. Moderates realised some form of compromise would be essential.

It was largely because moderate counsels prevailed that political union came so quickly. In 1903 a customs union was established which enabled goods to pass quite freely from one state to another. In 1906 and 1907 Transvaal and the Orange Free State were granted self-government. In 1908 talks about possible union began between the four governments. L. Botha and J. C. Smuts, the Transvaal leaders, were largely responsible for leading the convention to agreement. The main feature of the new constitution – confirmed by the British parliament in the South Africa Act (1909) – were as follows: The head of state would be a governor general appointed in London. Parliament was to consist of an elected Assembly and a part-elected part-nominated Senate. Government would be by a prime minister and cabinet responsible to the House of Assembly.

The most difficult problem to overcome was that of franchise. Afrikaners were not prepared to recognise the Cape Coloured voters. Cape leaders were not prepared to change their tradition of multi-racial common roll voting. The delegates reached a compromise. Assembly seats were allocated to the provinces in proportion to the adult European men in their population but actual voting in each province would be in accordance with established tradition.

The formation of the Union of South Africa on 31 May 1910 brought new political parties into being. Botha formed the South African Party (S.A.P.), which largely reflected Afrikaner attitudes. It was opposed by the largely-British Unionist Party (U.P.). From the beginning the S.A.P. proved too liberal for some sections of Boer opinion. In 1914, J. M. B. Hertzog, a Free State political leader, broke away to form the National Party (N.P.), the aims of which were

South Africa celebrates the creation of the Union, 1910.

Afrikaner domination and the severance of South Africa's close links with Britain.

At this point the Union became involved in the First World War. The British government asked Botha's aid against Germany's African colonies. Botha agreed. Many Boers bitterly resented this involvement in Britain's war. Some revolted and a few even joined the German forces in South West Africa. This protest was brushed aside. Botha, himself, led the successful invasion of German South West Africa and then Smuts took a contingent to East Africa, where he assumed command of the imperial forces in German East Africa (Tanganyika). Troops also left the Union to fight in Europe. This willing and successful participation brought South Africa prestige and the gratitude of the victorious European powers. But this did not mean that they were prepared to hand over South West Africa as part of the spoils of war. Botha wanted to add the ex-German territory to the Union. The League of Nations (an international organisation similar to the modern United Nations) thought otherwise; it permitted South Africa to administer the neighbouring state as a mandated territory (i.e. they were responsible as trustees to the League of Nations for the administration of South West Africa until such time as the League might decide that South West Africa was ready for self-government).

220

After Botha's death in 1920 Smuts became prime minister. He had to face growing political problems. Hertzog was gaining ground with Afrikaner extremism. He wanted a republican constitution for South Africa and secession from the empire. But it was the economic difficulties of 1920–1 which gave him his chance. The poor whites in the industrial areas were largely represented by the new Labour party. Their main problem was the threat of being put out of work by cheaper African labour. They, therefore, favoured a racial policy in employment and this gave them a common cause with Hertzog's Nationalists. In the general election of 1920 the S.A.P. won 41 seats, the Nationalists 44 seats, the U.P. 25 seats and Labour 21 seats. In the new Assembly the N.P. and Labour stood together while the U.P. supported the S.A.P. This produced a stalemate and made the work of government impossible. Another election was held the following year. This time the S.A.P. and the U.P. merged. In the voting all men of moderate opinion seem to have rallied to the new S.A.P. in order to defeat the forces of Afrikaner extremism. The result was: S.A.P., 79; N.P., 45; Labour, 9.

But Smuts was unable to deal with the mounting industrial unrest. On the Rand there were frequent demonstrations. White trade unions grew stronger. Communist agitation increased. Negotiations with the discontented workers failed. Strikes and violence became commonplace. By 1923 the situation had become so bad that the government had to use force to restore law and order. This, of course, made Smuts unpopular and when he called a general election in 1924 he was defeated by an alliance between the N.P. and the Labour Party.

South African forces in the First World War.

The Pact government was formed and Hertzog became prime minister, determined to turn South Africa firmly in the direction of Afrikanerdom.

Hertzog's government put through the first really segregationalist legislation, as we have seen. It put Afrikaans fully on a par with English as an official language. More and more Afrikaners began to enter the civil service. In 1926 Hertzog gained more independence for his country within the British Empire.

But Hertzog still found that attempts to push through extreme measures led to opposition from moderates in all parties in the Assembly. Some segregation bills had to be dropped. The attempt to drop the ceremonial use of the British national anthem and the Union Jack led to near riots. The Nationalists still managed to gain an overall majority in the election of 1929 but Hertzog continued to lose support, and in 1933 he had to agree to Smuts' suggestion to form a coalition of the two main parties. The following year they merged completely to form the United Party. This was largely a victory for the Nationalists, for the policies of the new party were those of the old N.P. with some modifications.

The centenary of the Great Trek in 1938 aroused great emotions among the Boer people and led to a fresh determination to turn South Africa into a truly Boer state. But in September 1939 Hertzog failed to pursuade the Assembly not to support Britain in the Second World War. He was defeated by 80 votes to 67. He resigned, Smuts returned to power and war was declared on Hitler's Germany. South Africa was still not ready for an Afrikaner takeover.

Southern Rhodesia, economic development

The B.S.A. Co. was primarily interested in mining. It had organised the settlement of land between the Zambezi and Limpopo in the belief that rich mineral deposits comparable to those of Katanga and the Rand would be found there. Prospectors were soon swarming all over Mashonaland where they knew there was gold, and several mines were opened. Production gradually increased but by the outbreak of the First World War it was obvious no rich seams of gold were going to be discovered.

However, there was still the hope that other minerals might be found which would make up for the disappointment over gold. Coal was discovered at Wankie in the 1890s and this eventually proved to be a very rich field. In the early years of this century chrome deposits were found at Selukwe and asbestos at Shabani. The successful exploitation of these resources depended almost entirely on the development of an extensive transport system. In 1899 Salisbury was linked to the coast by means of a railway line to Beira. Meanwhile the Bechuanaland line from Mafeking had reached Bulawayo (1897) and was extended to Wankie (1903) and to Livingstone, on the Zambezi (1904). Salisbury and Bulawayo were linked by rail in 1902. Road developments had to wait until the 1920s. It was not until after the First World War that cars and lorries began to appear in Southern Rhodesia. In 1927 the government agreed to sponsor out of public funds the building of tarmac roads. The new roads proved particularly valuable for the transport of farm produce and during the Depression road-building works helped to lessen the burden of unemployment. In 1933 the Rhodesia and Nyasaland Airways was founded.

Farming became and was to remain the mainstay of Southern Rhodesia's economy. European farmers went in for large-scale production of maize, tobacco and beef. By 1914 these products were being exported, mainly to neighbouring countries. During the war, when farming was disrupted in East Africa, Rhodesian exports to Kenya and Tanganyika increased considerably. There was a steady stream of immigrants into the country. Most of them took up farming and many of them did not survive the hard early years. The majority, however, by courage, experimentation and application of modern techniques made a success of their new life.

As time went by the government was able to give increasing help to the farmers. Experimental stations were set up to test plant strains and animal breeds. Marketing boards were established (for maize and dairy products in 1931; for tobacco in 1936) to help the farmers sell their products and gain a fair price for them. Government encouragement led to new crops being grown – wheat, potatoes, barley, groundnuts, tea and fruit.

At first the Africans had no desire to become involved in the white man's world. They kept to their traditional patterns of agriculture. But the settlers wanted labour, they wanted land and they needed to exercise control over African farmers in order to stop the spread of stock and crop diseases.

Force and taxation were used to obtain black labour. In 1902 a poll tax of £1 on every adult made and 10 sh. on every wife after the first was introduced. This meant that men had to go in search of seasonal labour in the towns or on European farms. But some employers resorted to their own brutal methods of obtaining labourers and forcing them to work for low wages. Africans soon discovered that they could sell their services. Not only did Rhodesian mine owners and farmers need labourers; the mines of the neighbouring Transvaal were desperately short of workers. Economic pressures therefore forced white employers to provide somewhat better pay and conditions.

But migrant, seasonal labour led directly to something the Africans came to hate – the pass laws. For failure to carry a pass or for not having it properly stamped an African could find himself arrested and imprisoned. Offences under the Masters' and Servants' Ordinance (1902) were also punishable at law.

Many Africans maintained an independent life as farmers. The B.S.A. Co. had from the beginning set aside some areas as reserves where the people could pursue their traditional way of life. Other land was held by the Company* to be either sold (to buyers of any race) for farming or allocated as reserve land; but the African population was growing so rapidly that it soon overspilled the reserves and since few Africans could afford to buy land much of the unallocated land was passing into European hands. The results were a declining standard of living for the rural Africans and an increased flow of Africans to the towns – which the Europeans found uncomfortable. The Land Apportionment Act of 1931 attempted to deal with this problem. Part of the unassigned land was re-designated as native purchase areas. Here Africans could buy land on favourable terms. On the other hand they were forbidden to acquire land in European areas.

As a result both of African initiative and of government action the standard of farming in the reserves and in the purchase areas gradually improved. African farmers learned European techniques. They improved their herds and the productivity of their land. Some of the chiefs reorganised the allocation of land in the reserves so that each owner could consolidate his holdings instead of having to farm scattered allotments. The government provided expert advisers, cattle dips, water supplies, etc. Soon many African farmers had surpluses for sale which they were able to dispose of through the marketing boards.

The peoples of Rhodesia – black and white – also began to benefit from improved social services. Hospitals, clinics and medical services were provided. Immunisation and regulations concerning water supplies, sanitation and food preparation helped to cut down the incidence of disease. Official and voluntary organisations educated groups of Africans in hygiene and first aid. Swamps were drained to combat malaria. Most of the country's education was in the hands of mission schools but these did receive small grants from the government. Most

---

*It was held by the Company until 1918 but then, after a dispute with the British government, it was decided that the B.S.A. Co. had no rights over unallocated land which then became Crown property.

of these schools gave only primary education though some centres offered training for semi-skilled occupations. There was almost no chance for an African boy or girl to pursue an academic secondary school course. In 1927 a Native Education Department was set up to encourage African education and to ensure reasonable standards in schools.

Settler politics

Southern Rhodesia was the only area of Africa where company rule survived into the colonial period. Until 1923 this colony remained under the control of the British South Africa Co. Despite protests

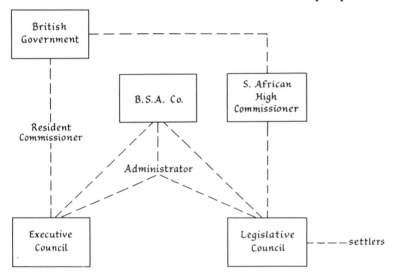

White control of Southern Rhodesia – the 1898 constitution.

from missionaries and philanthropists the British government refused to take Southern Rhodesia over as a directly-ruled colony. Certain limitations were placed on the B.S.A. Co.'s authority by an Order-in-Council of 1898 which set up a new constitution for the colony. This made the Company Administrator the principal official. He presided over the Executive and Legislative Councils. But the British government exercised some control through a Resident Commissioner who also had a seat on the Executive Council. Furthermore laws passed by the Legislative Council had to have the approval of the South African High Commissioner. The Company nominated the other members of the Executive Council and was represented on the official side of the Legislative Council. British settlers were from the 225 beginning allowed to elect members of the Legislative Council and by 1907 there was a majority of elected members on this council. Africans were excluded from voting by a property qualification which restricted the franchise to people owning a house worth at least £75. This figure was raised whenever Africans seemed likely to qualify. The settlers confidently expected that they would eventually gain self-government, probably as a province of South Africa.

But there were some who did not want closer links with the south. They saw how strong Afrikaner nationalism was growing and they feared that union with South Africa would simply lead to Rhodesia being swamped by Boers. They formed the Responsible Government Association under the leadership of Charles Coghlan, a Bulawayo lawyer. The R.G.A. was opposed by the Union Party, led by Herbert Longden.

The B.S.A. Co. found the work of administration difficult and expensive and were frustrated by the 'interference' of the British government. Matters came to a head in 1918, when a British court decided that all unassigned land in Southern Rhodesia belonged to the Crown. The Company had considered this land to be one of its assets and the directors let it be known that they wished to give up their administrative responsibilities. Most settlers welcomed this decision. They had felt for a long time that B.S.A. Co. representatives were more interested in making a profit out of Southern Rhodesia than in the good of the country.

The Company, the British government and the Union Party all favoured integration with South Africa. The South African prime minister, Smuts, worked hard to win Southern Rhodesia for the Union. But most of the settlers were now behind Coghlan and the R.G.A., which won twelve of the thirteen elected seats in the Legislative Council election of 1920. Throughout 1921 and 1922 the two sides campaigned inside and outside Rhodesia. At last the British government decided to let the settlers decide in a referendum whether they wanted to join South Africa or not. The result of the referendum in October 1922 was 5,989 in favour of union with South Africa, and 8,774 against. A year later a new constitution came into force. The British government took over full responsibility for the colony but the white electorate had a considerable degree of self-government. The B.S.A. Co. kept its commercial interests in the country.

The new constitution provided for a Governor and an elected parliament of thirty members. The government had authority over all internal matters except legislation concerning Africans, which had to be approved in London. There were two parties represented in the new parliament. Coghlan's R.G.P. now renamed itself the Rhodesia

Party and was opposed by the Independants. The Rhodesia Party won a large majority and remained in power under the country's first two prime ministers, Coghlan and H. U. Moffat. The economic difficulties resulting from the Great Depression brought political changes in the early 1930s. At length G. Huggins brought together dissatisfied members of other parties, including the Labour Party, and formed the United Party, which won the election of 1934.

Under Huggins' leadership Rhodesia gradually recovered from the Depression. Most of the new economic and social reforms already referred to were introduced by Huggins' administration between 1934 and 1939. The United Party (U.P.) also introduced the idea of parallel development. This was slightly different from the South African concept of separate development in that it foresaw a time when Africans would share in the government of the country, but white Rhodesians regarded that day as very far off. In fact, the African was a second class citizen in the land of his fathers.

African politics

The Shona and Ndebele had learned in the 1890s the futility of armed resistance to the white men. In the early years of colonial rule these communities turned in on themselves, asking only to be left alone as much as possible to follow their traditional way of life. Only gradually, as young Africans began to benefit from education at mission schools, did a new phase of African political activity begin to appear. Many Africans served in the First World War and felt that their white rulers owed them something for their support. It was after the war that a movement led by the Ndebele chief, Nyamanda, came to prominence. He was angered by Company confiscation of Ndebele land. When the Crown assumed responsibility for unassigned land in 1918 Nyamanda asked the British government to make Matabeleland a protectorate. He had the support of some experienced black politicians from South Africa, but in London no attention was paid to his requests.

The first attempt to create a nationwide African movement came in 1923. It was the work of Abraham Twala, who had come from South Africa. He formed the Rhodesia Bantu Voters Association to unite the few Africans who had the vote. The R.B.V.A. gave its support to the Rhodesia Party in return for concessions regarding African education and land purchase rights. But the Association had no effective bargaining power: there were so few African voters that white politicians saw no need to take the R.B.V.A. seriously. A few other similar African political groups were formed but suffered from 227 the same weaknesses. They appealed only to the very small minority of educated Africans. Most of them were led by outsiders because there was a shortage of politically mature Rhodesians. They made very little impact on the mass of the African people.

The land issue was always the greatest concern of the Africans and the various associations took every opportunity to bring their grievances to the attention of the government. When the British government set up a commission to look into land allocation in 1925, the associations prepared hundreds of Africans to give evidence. The result was not what African leaders had hoped. The commission recommended small additions to the reserves and the complete segregation of the races. This led to a meeting of representatives of all the associations in 1929 at which the government's land policy (and also the education and local government policies) was firmly rejected. It was all of no avail; the Land Apportionment Act became law. Yet the voice of educated African opinion was not silenced; it grew gradually louder as more young men received secondary schooling. In 1934 the Southern Rhodesia African National Congress was founded. Its most active leader was Thompson Samkange, a Shona Methodist minister. It gathered a larger membership than the older associations and for many years it made African opinion heard.

An important event in the story of African nationalism in Rhodesia was the spread of Industrial and Commercial Workers' Union activity into the colony. In 1927 Robert Sambo was sent from South Africa to form branches in Southern Rhodesia. Branches were started among the workers of Salisbury and Bulawayo. The government became alarmed. They deported Sambo and tried to stamp out the I.C.U. They failed; the movement gathered strength among urban workers. I.C.U. leaders urged more radical policies on their supporters and their interests extended beyond industrial activity. Neither Congress nor the I.C.U. achieved much in the way of forcing the government to change its policies but they did give valuable training to African politicians of the future.

Less constructive was the breakaway church movement. As in other parts of the continent this movement was born of anger over white domination in church and state, and frustration that nothing could be done to dislodge the Europeans. The independent church movement became quite strong in Mashonaland in the 1930s where sects like the Watchtower Church and the Church of the White Bird were formed.

Nyasaland

228   In 1907 a new constitution was drawn up for the Nyasaland Protecto-

rate. This provided for a Governor as head of state under the Crown, assisted by an Executive Council of five officials (including the Governor) and a Legislative Council which was, in fact, the members of the Executive Council plus three unofficial members nominated by the Governor. One of these unofficial members was always a missionary whose task was to represent African interests. The affairs of Nyasaland were never complicated by the activities of a large community of racialist settlers seeking their own ends.

In governing the protectorate the authorities relied as far as possible on traditional African rulers. District Commissioners were in charge of local government and from 1921 the country was divided into three provinces each under the control of a Provincial Commissioner. The D.C.s relied largely on local chiefs for the collection of taxes, administration of justice and provision of labourers for public works. It was largely up to the D.C.s to decide what arrangements they came to with local rulers but often the chiefs were paid by the government for their co-operation. Yet the chiefs were not just 'stooges' of the colonial régime. Some would not co-operate with the new masters. For instance, in 1907 some chiefs in the Fort Johnston area, under the influence of a prophetess, Nyangu, refused to collect taxes and the authorities were forced to organise the work themselves. The chiefs often found themselves faced by a dilemma: if they co-operated fully with the Europeans they would become unpopular with their own people but if they resisted the new rulers their authority would not be recognised. There were instances of people revolting against chiefs who collected taxes and also of chiefs who were deposed by the government for refusing to do so.

A new system was introduced in 1912. The District Administration (Native) Ordinance of that year created a new class of African officials. Villages were grouped together under the control of a Village Headman. Several of these headmen formed a section under the control of a Principal Headman and a number of sections added up to a district which was supervised by a British District Resident, who was regarded as a chief. These new African officials performed most of the day-to-day tasks of local government. The system was devised for the convenience of the colonial power and did not have its roots in traditional styles of government. However, most of the Principal Headmen appointed by the government were, in fact, chiefs. This system was applied throughout Nyasaland except the Shiré highlands, where the existence of white settlers complicated matters.

By the 1920s British colonial policy was beginning to change. F. D. Lugard, an ex-colonial administrator, had recommended in his book *The Dual Mandate in Tropical Africa* the principle of indirect rule (rule through African authorities) and the idea that colonies should be developed for the benefit of both black and white races. This had some effect in Nyasaland. In 1929 some judicial powers were handed back to the chiefs. In 1933 a Native Authority and Courts Ordinance replaced the Principal Headmen with Native Authorities, whose powers were wider. They had power to levy taxes and to devote part of the proceeds to local development projects. African courts were set up to administer traditional law. But there was, in practice, little hand-over of power from the D.C.s to the African officials and by 1939 progressive Africans were growing increasingly dissatisfied with what they considered as a mockery of the principle of indirect rule.

The fact that there were few white settlers in Nyasaland was to the ultimate advantage of the country but it reflected another fact – that the economic development of the colony was very slow. There were no important mineral deposits, and plantation farming in the Shiré highlands got off to a slow start. Although coffee was grown commercially early in the 1890s, the importance of the crop declined a few years later after a bad attack of disease in 1904. Thereafter tobacco became the most important crop but international prices varied greatly from year to year and this discouraged large-scale European investment. In 1921 there was a serious slump in world tobacco prices and a number of European-owned farms closed down. By this time tea was becoming an important plantation crop. It had been introduced in 1903 but was not produced commercially until after the First World War, when it became the most important crop in the eastern highlands. The farmers were again badly affected by the Great Depression and it was not until the mid 1930s that Nyasaland's agriculture began to recover. By 1939 the protectorate was able to export farm produce to the value of £1.5 million.

African farming always played an important part in the economic life of the protectorate. To pay taxes and to improve their standard of living smallholders produced cash crops such as fire-cured tobacco and cotton. They were contributing significantly to Nyasaland's exports by 1939. Others, while pursuing a traditional, subsistence type of farming, produced surpluses of maize, rice and groundnuts for sale locally.

Throughout the period Nyasaland remained very poor in comparison with its Rhodesian neighbours. Its economy could only be balanced by grants-in-aid from Britain. Lack of finance prevented the government building roads, railways and other public facilities as rapidly as it would have wished. Railway building began in 1907 but it was 1914 before Blantyre, the commercial centre of the high-

The Zambezi bridge from Sena to Dona Anna.

lands, was linked to the Zambezi. In 1922 the Portuguese linked Sena by rail to Beira on the coast. This made it possible for export goods to be transported from Blantyre but they had to be conveyed across the Zambezi by ferry. For years a Zambezi bridge was planned but the financial difficulties of the 1920s and 1930s prevented work beginning on the project until 1933. The bridge was, for those years, an enormous undertaking. It was the longest railway bridge in the world – over 3,700 metres in length. It was opened in March 1935. In the same year the Nyasaland railway was extended northwards to the lake at Chipoka and on to Salima. Only then could fish and other goods produced in the lake area be conveyed to the railhead and thence to other parts of the protectorate, to Beira and to other parts of the world.

African politics

Nyasaland's Africans played a very important part in the rise of nationalism. There were two main reasons for this. First, the absence of a large settler community meant that African political aspirations 231 were not ruthlessly stamped out as they were elsewhere. Secondly, the activities of the Livingstonia Mission produced a large number of educated men capable of expressing their grievances and leading their people in challenging the authorities. Two kinds of African nationalism emerged, one in northern Nyasaland and the other in the Shiré Highlands. We shall think about each in turn.

In the north the movement took the form of a religious breakaway movement. The Livingstonia missionaries had enjoyed remarkable success among the Tonga and other peoples of the area. Many Africans were converted to Christianity and more attended the mission schools. Part of the reason for this success must be attributed to the prestige which close association with the white teachers brought. Those who were baptised and even more those who were educated at mission schools formed a black élite and were much respected by their fellows. But there were problems connected with church membership which showed themselves from an early date. One was the firm stand taken by the missionaries against polygamy, dancing, beer drinking, coming-of-age ceremonies and other local customs. Baptism was only given to those who renounced all these things. This led to frustration, for hundreds of men and women who were kept waiting for baptism, and to humiliation for others, who after baptism slipped back into the old ways and were disciplined by the church. As time went by more and more people were dissatisfied because they could not express their faith in ways that they understood.

Another problem was caused by the reluctance of the missionaries to appoint ministers and church officials from among the educated Africans. For instance Yesaya Zerenji Mwase, the first Tonga minister, completed his theological training in 1902 but was not ordained until 1914. It is not surprising that some of these men became the leaders of breakaway churches.

The first separatist churches were formed among the Tonga in the 1890s but it was the Watchtower movement, begun in 1908, which was the real start of religious independence in Nyasaland. This movement was begun by Eliot Kamwana, a Tonga who went to South Africa where he became a member of the Jehovah's Witnesses sect. He returned in 1908 and began preaching in his own country. But his beliefs developed along very individual lines and he was rejected by the Jehovah's Witnesses' leaders. Kamwana now formed a sect called the Watchtower Churches of Christ. He had an immediate and astonishing success and soon the new sect had tens of thousands of members. Although Kamwana's movement was a religious one there was a political side. Kamwana attracted supporters by teaching that the world would come to an end in 1914 and that an African state would then come into being led by true believers. The government found Kamwana's activities dangerous and he was deported towards the end of 1909. But the Watchtower movement continued to grow. Another religious leader of the period was Charles Domingo. Like Kamwana, he had been a member of the Livingstonia Mission but he left to join the Seventh Day Baptists, another Christian sect. He had most of his preaching successes among the northern Ngoni where he founded a number of churches and schools. He was even more outspoken than Kamwana in his criticism of the colonial regime. He accused the government, the missionaries and the businessmen of all seeking to dominate Africa and attacked specific colonial policies.

In the south, protest took on a much more political nature, although the most famous nationalist was, in fact, an ordained minister. This was John Chilembwe, a Yao from Chiradzulu. He went to the United States for higher education and returned in 1900 to become a minister in his home area. He worked hard for his people but did not attempt to turn them against the government. Rather, he urged them to improve themselves so that they would gain positions of influence. But land grievances and the failure of the administration to deal with a serious famine in 1913 stung him into opposition. Then came the First World War and Chilembwe was very angry to see Africans being recruited for the army: 'Let the rich men, bankers, titled men, store-keepers, farmers and landlords go to war and get shot. Instead the poor Africans who have nothing in this present world, who in death leave only a long line of widows and orphans in utter want and dire distress are invited to die for a cause which is not theirs.' At the beginning of 1915 Chilembwe was engaged in a dispute with A. L. Bruce, a European landowner who was treating his African workers and tenants badly. Bruce tried to silence Chilembwe by burning down some of the latter's churches. This only stung Chilembwe and his supporters into violence. They attacked one of the estates and killed three European agents. The rising lasted for two weeks but because it was spontaneous it was not well-organised and government forces soon brought it under control and Chilembwe was shot while trying to escape.

African political activity did not die with Chilembwe. It continued largely through two organisations: the Native Authorities whom we have already mentioned, and Native Associations. To consider the Native Authorities first; while some of their members were merely obedient agents of the government others were progressive. They tried to use the little influence they had to urge new policies on the colonial rulers. They demanded government secondary schools, compulsory education and a greater share in local and central government.

John Chilembwe.

The Native Associations were groups of educated Africans who met to discuss African problems and sought to gain redress. The first to be formed was the North Nyasa Native Association which was convened in 1912. Others followed and by 1930 they existed in most parts of the protectorate. These associations championed the cause of individuals who, they believed, were badly treated by officials or employers. They also pressed the government to change its policies on land holding, education, forced labour and other matters deeply affecting African life. The associations were content to bring pressure to bear on the government from outside rather than trying to gain representation on the Legislative Council. They did not amalgamate to take united action although those in the Northern Province did form the Representative Committee of Northern Province Native Associations in 1924. This may be regarded as the forerunner of African political parties in Nyasaland.

Land and population

Nyasaland's greatest problem was its large population relative to its size. As we saw in earlier chapters, the area around Lake Nyasa attracted many different peoples who settled and fought with each other for land. With the enforced peace of the colonial era population grew and with it pressure on land. The situation was made worse by the large alienations of land (about 14% in the 1890s) for European use by the early administrators. Although the European population remained very small (about 2,000 in 1939) white people held a disproportionately large amount of land. The situation was eased by the Native Trust Land Order-in-Council of 1936. The government bought the large B.S.A. Co. estates in northern Nyasaland and declared them, together with most of the rest of the protectorate, Native Trust Land. By this Order ninety per cent of Nyasaland was reserved exclusively for African use. But there was still serious overcrowding, particularly in the Shiré Highlands. The problem was partly solved by migrant labour. Young men and heads of families spent long periods each year working in the mines and factories of South Africa and the Rhodesias.

Northern Rhodesia

Northern Rhodesia came into existence in 1911 when the two B.S.A. Co.-administered territories of North-eastern and North-western Rhodesia were brought together. The colony continued to be ruled by the Company until 1924 under a simple constitution. A council of Company officials under the chairmanship of an Administrator formed the government. The British government which was represented by a Resident Commissioner had ultimate control. There was only a small settler population so there was little pressure in the

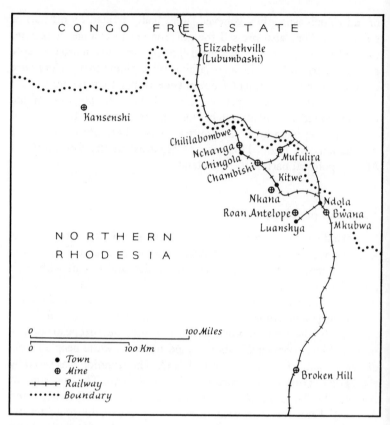

Northern Rhodesia mines.

early years for white representation in the legislature. In 1917, as a result of their support for Britain during the First World War, the settlers gained a constitutional change. An Advisory Council was set up which included five elected settler members. Local government was in the hands of District Commissioners who were largely free to decide their own relationship with traditional rulers. Generally speaking the chiefs remained in control of justice save in matters of serious crime and land dispute. They were also expected to assist in the levying of taxes and the transmitting of government decisions.

After the First World War conflict between the settlers and the B.S.A. Co. grew, the settlers, as in Southern Rhodesia, complaining that the Company was not sufficiently concerned about the development of the colony. The British government commission (the Buxton Commission) which considered the position of the Company in Southern Rhodesia also examined the situation north of the Zambezi (1921).

As a result the B.S.A. Co. was relieved of its administrative duties in 1924. Northern Rhodesia became a protectorate under the control of a Governor assisted by Executive and Legislative Councils. The Legislative Council consisted of nine official members and five unofficial members elected by the settlers.

Surface plant at Chambishi copper mine with the open pit in the background.

This period also produced a new attitude towards local government and traditional African authorities. In 1929 the Native Authorities Ordinance and Native Courts Ordinance were introduced. In each area a Native Authority (usually a local chief) was designated to rule under the supervision of the D.C. He also presided over the Native Court, which had wide judicial powers. In 1936 the powers of these African administrators were increased to include the collection of taxes and the spending of money on local projects.

237

Economic development

Although the neighbouring Katanga copper-field was known about, it was not until 1924 that the Zambian deposits were discovered. The most promising mineral deposits found in the early days of Company rule were the lead and zinc ores at Broken Hill (1902). Within two years mining began. Also in 1902 copper ore was discovered in the Ndola area and claims were staked at Bwana Mkubwa, Roan Antelope and Chambishi. In 1910 further finds of copper ore were made at Nkana and Mufulira. The ore in these sites was oxide ore. It was not easy to work and the percentage of pure metal which could be extracted from it was low. So, for several years the only mines in operation were Bwana Mkubwa and Kansenshi (the centre of a long-established copper industry operated by the Kaonde). In 1924 the B.S.A. Co., now free of the financial burden of administration, carried out fresh prospecting on the Katanga border. This led to the discovery of deeper strata of copper sulphide ores. These deposits turned out to be rich in metal and almost inexhaustible. New techniques enabled the ore to be extracted and worked without difficulty, and the demand created by the new motor car industries of Europe and America resulted in high prices for copper. Between 1927 and 1930 there was a copper boom. New mines were opened, enormous amounts of foreign capital were invested and the number of Africans employed on the Copperbelt rose from 8,000 to 23,000. Then came the Great Depression. Prices suddenly dropped, mines closed and thousands of Rhodesians were thrown out of work. But the world needed copper and Rhodesian copper was better and cheaper than that of most of her rivals. For these reasons Northern Rhodesia recovered more quickly from the Great Depression than most other African countries. From 1935 the development of the Copperbelt picked up and by 1939 copper exports were earning Northern Rhodesia £10 million a year.

The growth of the mining industry largely determined railway building and the pattern of European settlement. The railway reached Northern Rhodesia in 1904 when an extension of the Rhodesia Railways' Wankie line in the south was brought across the Zambezi at Livingstone. The line was immediately extended to Broken Hill (1905) and by 1909 it had reached the Copperbelt. The following year an extension was built across the Congo border to Elizabethville (modern Lubumbashi). This northern stretch was eventually linked (1931) with Angola's Benguela railway and Northern Rhodesia thus had two outlets to the coast. In order not to lose trade Rhodesia Railways made an agreement with the copper-miners whereby the latter agreed to ship all their copper southwards and buy all their coal from Wankie in return for low freight rates. Most European settlers made their home close to the railway line or on the Copperbelt, though a few farms were established around Abercorn and Fort Jameson. Despite the efforts of the government to encourage settlement the European population, which was about 3,500 in 1920, only grew very slowly. In 1935 the administrative capital was moved from Livingstone to Lusaka, a more convenient centre for the country's white population.

Agriculture and land

The government encouraged European farming so that the growing towns and mining areas could be supplied with food and so that the country's economy would not be entirely dependent on minerals. The small number of farmers who came, mostly, from the south reared cattle and grew maize. The areas selected for European settlement were for the most part areas where the African population was very sparse and in the early years it was not necessary to create reserves. But this was not so around Fort Jameson where the government wished to attract Europeans into 500 square kilometres of land taken from the Ngoni. In 1907 a reserve was set up for the Ngoni. It was soon overcrowded and there was considerable suffering among the Ngoni. In 1913 the reserve area was increased.

In other areas also the policies of the colonial government created difficulties for the people. The Bemba lived in scattered chieftaincies over a wide area of the north-east region. This was inconvenient to the government who forced them into larger settlements where their agricultural activities could be supervised and where it was easier to collect taxes. For many years the Bemba resisted this and the authorities found it very difficult to enforce government policy. Lozi patterns of traditional farming were also affected. They were forced in 1906 to give up domestic slavery and tribute labour. This caused the collapse of their agricultural system and they did not recover for many years. All African communities were affected by the introduction of taxation. A hut tax was introduced in 1901 and had spread to all parts of the colony within a decade. Some people who lived near European settlements were able to earn the necessary money by taking up cash crop farming. The majority had to send their young men to work. Some went to the Copperbelt, others to the mining and industrial centres of other southern African colonies. The situation was made worse in some of the reserve areas because the government refused to make neighbouring land available for African use. Large areas of potential farmland were kept empty because the politicians believed that the rate 239 of European immigration would rise. Largely for the same reason little effort was made to teach Africans modern farming methods. In short, the only agricultural policy the colonial government had was based on the false hope that the settler farms would ultimately provide the greater part of the protectorate's produce. When this did not happen the politicians had no alternative plan. As a result the country had to depend on imports; soil erosion and crop diseases went largely unchecked; Africans were prevented from practising shifting agriculture but not taught any alternative; the productive capacity of men and land was being wasted.

African politics

Considering the hardships experienced by thousands of Africans as a result of colonial policies it is, perhaps, surprising that before 1939 there was little organised protest from Northern Rhodesia's black majority. There are many reasons for this. The population was widely scattered. Most white settlement was concentrated into a narrow strip of territory. The more powerful chiefs, such as Lewanika of the Lozi, had come to terms with the new administration. For many years African mineworkers (who might have become a politically-conscious group) stayed in the towns only for short periods before returning to their homes and showed little interest in agitating for social or political change. Above all educational development in Northern Rhodesia was extremely slow (by the time of independence in 1964 there were only 100 graduates and 1,200 holders of School Certificates in the country).

In the western part of the country Lewanika maintained an unusual degree of control. By the Victoria Falls treaty of 1900 the king's position and his government remained largely unchanged. The chiefs had to collect taxes but were allowed to retain part of the money collected as salary. Lewanika had to agree to part of his territory being alienated for European settlement but it is doubtful whether the Lozi really had effective control of the area in question before the colonial era. Lewanika was determined that his people should benefit as much as possible from co-operation with the white man. He devised schemes for growing fruit and vegetables for sale in Livingstone and he forced the B.S.A. Co., as early as 1906, to open the Barotse National School, which remained the only state-owned school for a quarter of a century.

On the Copperbelt the African workers were slow to organise themselves. The migrant, seasonal labour suited everyone. The mine owners liked the system because they did not have to pay high wages nor did they need to provide family housing for the workers. The white employees liked the system because it gave little opportunity to the Africans to learn skilled jobs and so to challenge their position. In 1936 the white miners formed a union and one of the first tasks it set itself was obtaining from the employers an agreement that Africans would not be allowed to do skilled jobs. There was a considerable gap between African and European wages. During the Depression the pay of black workers was reduced but it was not automatically increased as the copper industry began to recover. By the mid-thirties the attitude of the Africans was changing. Many of them were now staying longer on the Copperbelt and bringing their families to live with them. They began to complain about living conditions and wages. In 1935 rumours of a tax increase were enough to bring the workers at Nkana, Roan Antelope and Mufulira out on strike. This again only resulted in riots, the deaths of seven Africans and a fruitless government enquiry into conditions on the Copperbelt. But the black workers had begun to make their demands known. In 1940 there was another strike at the Nkana and Mufulira mines. This time the workers were asking for an end to colour discrimination in matters of job allocation and improved wages. This time seventeen strikers were killed by troops sent to control the situation and the Colonial Office in London was forced to enquire into the matter.

The royal barge of the Lozi king.

In other areas political developments similar to those in Nyasaland took place. In 1923 the Mwenzo Association was formed in the northeast. It was similar to the North Nyasa Native Association and was started by men such as David Kaunda, father of independent Zambia's first president, who had been educated by Livingstonia missionaries. Unfortunately, it only represented the tiny educated minority of North-eastern Rhodesia and it was dissolved in 1928. Two years later a number of welfare associations were founded in towns along the 241 railway. These also existed to give expression to the opinions of educated Africans. From time to time the associations made protests about central or local government policies but, like the Mwenzo Association, they lacked real influence. An attempt in 1933 to form a United African Welfare Association of Northern Rhodesia came to nothing.

Basutoland, Bechuanaland and Swaziland

The last countries to be discussed in this chapter are Basutoland, Bechuanaland and Swaziland – the High Commission Territories. These were the countries in southern Africa which, though surrounded by settler-dominated colonies, were under the direct protection and control of the British government. All three territories had chosen direct British rule and rejected incorporation into neighbouring states.

Britain, as usual wishing to spend as little as possible on colonial administration, sent the minimum number of officials to the High Commission Territories and, as far as possible, pursued a policy of indirect rule. In Basutoland the senior official was a Resident Commissioner who ruled largely through the king and his advisers. The other two territories had a Commissioner who also used the existing government as a framework for their administration. In Swaziland the chiefs formed a Swazi National Council which met with the Commissioner once a year. In 1921 European residents in Swaziland succeeded in having an Advisory Council formed. The members of this council were elected by the white population.

Throughout the twentieth century the history of these territories has been dominated by their relations with their more powerful neighbours. Large numbers of men work in the mines and industries of South Africa and Southern Rhodesia. They are reliant for important commodities on the lines of communication, most of which run through South Africa. They sell surplus farm produce to their neighbours. They belonged to a customs union set up in 1910. For many years South Africa wanted to annex the Territories. When the union of the Boer and British states was under discussion in 1909 many of the leading politicians assumed that control of Basutoland, Bechuanaland and Swaziland would pass to the Union government. But leaders in the Territories resisted this and any decision to transfer control was deferred. The South Africa Act (1910) provided for the eventual take-over of the three territories by the Union only under strict conditions concerning non-violation of land and political rights. Frequently South Africa's leaders pressed Britain for a decision on the transfer of the Territories. They even tried to arrange the annexation of land without the transfer of power. For instance, Smuts wanted to negotiate the cession of part of Swaziland in 1921.

As time went by South African demands were more insistent. The politicians claimed matters such as crop and stock disease, famine and insect control were difficult to handle because different authorities were involved. Cattle movements into and out of Bechuanaland had already been restricted because of the fear of spreading disease. Settlers in Bechuanaland also asked for the protectorate to be incorporated in the Union. Matters came to a head in 1933 when the acting High Commissioner deposed Tshekedi Khama, the acting Chief of the Ngwato. This seemed like a signal for the exercise of direct control in all three territories, even though Khama was soon reinstated. But at the same time these events were taking place Hertzog was formulating a racial policy in South Africa which alarmed African leaders and white liberals. The British government was less inclined than ever to hand over responsibility for the Territories and the leaders of Basutoland, Swaziland and Bechuanaland certainly would not tolerate the idea. From London Sir A. Pim was sent to examine the situation in the Territories and report back to the government.

Pim's report did not make pleasant reading. It showed the ministers in distant England that Swaziland, Basutoland and Bechuanaland were suffering the results of thirty years of neglect. Since the three states had come under British rule scarcely any money had been spent on land improvement, education, roads, or technical assistance. As a result serious problems now faced many areas; soil erosion, lack of water, disease, famine and a general lack of development were widespread. The British government at last began to make funds available (1935) and also widened its policy of indirect rule.

18. The period of colonial rule
(2) The Portuguese sphere

Portugal's attitude towards her colonies

> Our country's interest urgently demands the development of our colonies. Only through these colonies will Portugal be able to take the place she deserves in the concert of nations; only on their preservation and prosperity does her future greatness depend. Speech of das Pares in 1879.*

Those words, spoken by a Portuguese minister of state in 1879, go a long way towards explaining the attitude adopted by Portugal towards her African possessions. Portugal has always been an *extremist* among colonial powers. Britain, France, Germany and other nations have exploited their colonies. They have prospered from trade with African territories. But they have never been *dependent* on that trade. Because their colonies were not vital to them, other colonial powers have undertaken the education and social improvement of their African subjects. They have fostered political growth (though not always African political growth) in their territories. None of this is true of the Portuguese colonial record in Africa.

Portugal is a small, poor country. The mainstay of the economy is peasant agriculture. There is little industry worth mentioning, for Portugal has had no industrial revolution. Such commercial activities as did exist were run almost entirely by foreign financiers. Not only is this country economically backward; it is politically backward also. The people have always lived under a dictatorship – whether the dictator was a king (the monarchy survived until 1910) or a president. Moreover, during the period when her colonial administration was really being established in Africa, Portugal's home politics were in a state of chaos. Between the years 1903 and 1926, there were eight presidents, forty-eight governments and twenty revolutions.

It is not surprising that such a country, economically poor and having no democratic tradition, should have made every effort to exploit its African territories and subjects, without any consideration for the African peoples themselves. But this is only the overall picture.

* Quoted in J. Duffy, *Portugal in Africa* (Harvard, 1962) p. 107.

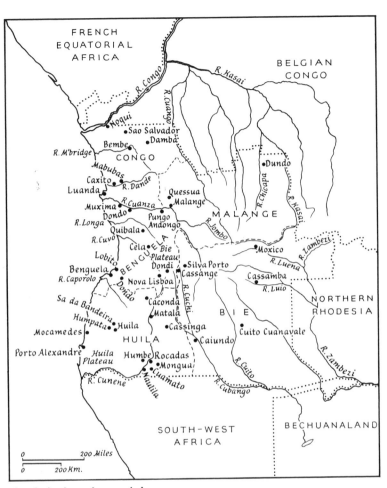

Angola in the early twentieth century.

You should not think that all the governor-generals and administrators of Angola and Mozambique were harsh tyrants. Some, in fact, urged more moderate policies on the government in Lisbon. But the economic and political situation proved too strong for the would-be reformers.

We can discern two stages in the establishment of colonial administration in Mozambique and Angola after the initial period of occupation and pacification: 1911–19 saw attempts to re-establish the administration on more liberal lines; 1920–30 were the years of political crisis in Portugal when colonial rulers assumed more power, but the results were disastrous and eventually Prime Minister Salazar re-imposed centralisation. Let us look at these stages in turn.

Away from the coasts and the main inland towns, Portuguese   245

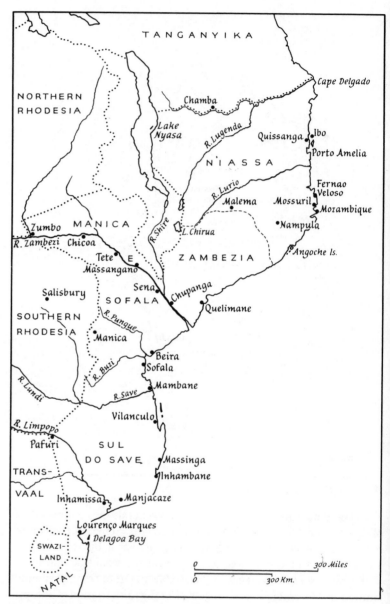

Mozambique in the early twentieth century.

control of the land and people was precarious. Resistance to European rule was to continue, as we shall see, right through to the present day and in many outlying areas colonial rule depended on the military commanders who were completely responsible for their districts (*capitanias-mores*). Some areas, which were less 'troublesome' were termed 'civil districts' (*circunscerioes civis*). Whether military or civil administrators, these agents had complete authority over the local population and were almost entirely unsupervised. 'The administrator and his divisional assistants, the chiefs of posts, were virtually white chiefs ... Some administrators were incorruptible and others were not, but the dishonest or abusive administrator, isolated in the bush of Mozambique or Angola, possessed infinite opportunity for harm in these early days of the system.'*

Administrative systems

Not all of Portuguese Africa lay under the capricious hand of these civil or military administrators. Within the colonial framework different administrative systems operated side by side. In Mozambique Quelimane district remained under *prazo* administration while the Niassa and Mozambique Companies governed most of the northern region. The commercial and agricultural agents were allowed full authority under the governor-general because it was vital for Portugal that the colony should be exploited and developed – no matter who did the exploiting and developing. There was therefore no question of company or estate agents being hampered by government administrators anxious to look after the interests of the local people (as happened in other colonies). All the white men co-operated to 'make Mozambique pay'. This was reflected in the larger towns where the local administrators were assisted by a council of Portuguese residents.

In Angola the situation was simpler. The governor ruled directly over the whole colony, most of which still lay under the control of military administrators. After 1911 an attempt was made to convert *capitanias-mores* into *circunscrioes civis*.

There were many weaknesses in this system of administration. No regard was paid to the welfare of the African peoples of Angola and Mozambique. As long as the colonies were ruled firmly from Lisbon they could not develop as different individual territories. Colonial administrators were often hampered by rival factions among the Europeans. One high commissioner (the title was changed from governor-general in 1920) of Mozambique complained, 'Intriguing politicians, those in the colony and those at home, can easily create for the governor or high commissioner insurmountable difficulties, which keep him from realising any useful work in his administration.'*

* J. Duffy, *Portuguese Africa* (Harvard, 1959), pp. 248–9.
* Quoted in J. Duffy, *Portuguese Africa*, p. 251.

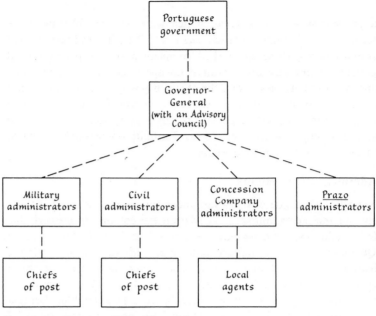

Portuguese administration in Mozambique.

'Liberalisation' 1911–19

These defects became more and more obvious as the first decade of the century drew to a close. Critics of the system clamoured for reform: 'In our archaic process of colonial administration we began from a false point of view, that it was necessary to impose a military regime' wrote one Portuguese politician.* Another said, 'Military governors follow a pattern of colonial occupation characterised by violence, heroics and great expense. Almost all our colonial statesmen ... favour a preponderance of military personnel ... it is necessary to reduce expenses with an occupation more commercial and educational than military and destructive.'†

By 1907 Mozambique was considered 'pacefied' and by 1911 Angola, too, was ready to move to the next phase of colonial administration. Military administration gave way to civil and the authorities began to think seriously of African problems. This change was the basic ingredient of the Colonial Reform Act of 1907. The man who did more than anything else to try to change the prevailing attitude towards the peoples of Angola and Mozambique was Norton de Matos, gover-

---

* J. P. do Nascimento and A. A. de Mattos, *A colonisacao de Angola* (Lisbon, 1912), pp. 7–8.
† Carneiro de Moura, *A administracao colonial portuguesa* (Lisbon, 1910), pp. 259–60.

nor-general of Angola. His motto was 'the first concern of the colonial administration is the African'. He ordered that the indigenous people were to be considered and treated as Portuguese citizens. They must not be exploited by the state or by farmers or private companies. They were to be encouraged to work for themselves and to gain education.

Many of these ideas were embodied in new colonial laws passed in Lisbon in 1914. They gave the governor-generals more power. In Portugal an Office of Native Affairs was set up to make final decisions on African problems. This office immediately laid down the lines on which the black people in the colonies were to be 'civilised' and 'assimilated'. Schools, medical posts and hospitals were to be set up. Agriculture was to be encouraged by the provision of seed and technical assistance. Africans were to be divided into two categories – *assimilados* (this meant those who could be considered as full Portuguese subjects because they had learned the language and ways of their colonial masters and dropped the 'uncivilised' tribal customs) and the others who were still on the road to civilisation and needed corrective laws.

These laws, though far from ideal, were an improvement on anything that had gone before, but they were doomed to failure. There were three reasons for this. First, there was the opposition of the white population in Angola and Mozambique. While the government believed the salvation of the colonies to lie in Europeanising the Africans, estate-owners and commercial agents had one idea and one only: '. . . what we have to do in order to educate and civilize the *indigena* is to develop in a practical way his aptitudes for manual labour and take advantage of him for the exploitation of the province.'* Such men did all they could to hamper the liberalising work of officials.

The second reason for the failure of the reform movement was the poor quality of the administrative agents sent out to Africa by the metropolitan government. They were usually untrained, underpaid and carried so much responsibility that they were unable or unwilling to master their jobs, let alone pursue a clear policy. Complaints were made of administrators who overtaxed the Africans in their districts, took bribes for providing labourers, withheld pay from Africans working in the Rand mines and used African girls' schools to provide a supply of concubines for themselves and their friends. It was useless for Norton de Matos and other high-minded governor-generals to pass enlightened laws as long as their implementation relied on such corrupt or ineffective agents.

* Mousinho de Albuquerque, *Moçambique* (Lisbon, 1934), II, pp. 138–9.

The third reason was the continuing political and economic upheaval in Portugal. The First World War (1914–18) did not involve Portugal directly but it did place fresh strains on her economy. What the colonies needed if the new liberal policies were to stand any chance of success was a period of peace and stability. For twenty years after 1914 they shared with the rest of the world a period of economic and political chaos.

Autonomy and decline

In 1920 the Portuguese government enacted a series of laws which gave Angola and Mozambique self-government in financial affairs and allowed the governor-generals (now re-named high commissioners) considerable freedom. It was what men like Norton de Matos had wanted for years – the freedom to develop each territory in its own way. The ministers in Lisbon sat back to watch the speedy development of their colonial territories. What happened was that by 1926 both territories were nearly bankrupt. Heavy loans had to be provided by Portugal to keep colonial administration going. Why was this?

Lourenço Marques. Though the Portuguese territories were economically weak, the colonial rulers prided themselves on the growth of towns like Lourenço Marques, largely rebuilt in the early twentieth century.

Angola and Mozambique are not rich in resources and much time and money was needed to make them pay. But the 1920s were years of economic depression throughout the world and few people were prepared to invest money in Central Africa. From 1926 onwards the Portuguese colonies gradually lost more and more of their freedom and by the Colonial Act of 1930 they once more came under firm centralised control.

All these changes of administration and declarations of policy do not disguise the fact that every Portuguese in Africa, whether administrator, farmer or missionary, looked down on the people of the country. The Africans were considered either as 'stupid savages' or as 'children' who might, one day in the far distant future, attain the status of civilised men. They were certainly not regarded as people who had a society and civilisation of their own.

Contract labour

Nothing indicates this more clearly than the contract labour system.

> All natives of Portuguese overseas provinces are subject to the obligation, moral and legal, of attempting to obtain through work the means that they lack to subsist and to better their social condition. They have full liberty to choose their work, but if they do not work public authority may force them to do so. [Labour Regulation, 1899]

This was the basis of the official attitude towards African labour. The end result of this attitude was slavery. Slavery and slave trading had been abolished by international agreements in the nineteenth century but in the first decade of the twentieth it became clear to the world that they had been resumed by the Portuguese under the name of the contract labour system.

One of the jobs of the chiefs of post was to provide workers for European employers. With the authority of the law of 1899 (a law whose harsh provisions were often exceeded by the authorities) they rounded up Africans, taking them away from their own plots of land to serve under a white taskmaster. The contract labourers were paid a small wage by the Europeans and were occasionally allowed to return home but they had few other rights. They were whipped, underfed, badly housed and treated with utter contempt.

The worst example of this modern slavery was the provision of workers for the cocoa plantations on the Portuguese West African islands of Principe and São Tomé. In cocoa the Portuguese at last found a commodity that was in great demand and which they could sell easily. They therefore wanted to develop their island plantations 251 to the full. This involved the transportation of tens of thousands of 'contract workers' (*contratados*) to Principe and São Tomé every year. Most of them were obtained in the Belgian Congo frontier district of Angola. The long march from there to the coast was an almost exact replica of the terrible slave caravans of the mid-nineteenth century. Hundreds of Africans died on the way from exhaustion or brutality. Families were divided. Village communities were broken up. The sea journey from the west coast was a degrading experience as the following account shows.

> After we had stopped at Luanda and taken on forty-two more slaves, making our full complement 272 men and women, not counting the numerous babies, we called at Ambriz, and there a singular abomination occurred. For in the early morning one of the slaves, seeing the district of which he was a native not far away, slid off the fo'c'sle, where the slaves were crowded together, and tried to swim for freedom. The sea was full of sharks, and I could only hope that they would devour him; for a boat was dropped at once from the ship, and in ten minutes it had overtaken the swimmer.
>
> Leaning over the side, the two black men and the white officer battered his head with their oars and sticks till he was quiet, and then dragged him into the boat, laying a piece of sailcloth over his nakedness that the feelings of the ladies on board might not be shocked. Dripping and trembling, he was taken below by the doctor and the Government agent, who accompanied every consignment of slaves, and there he was chained fast to a post. 'Boa chicote!' shouted the first-class passengers: 'Flog him! Flog him!'*

The *contratados*, though supposedly hired for a fixed term, were never allowed to leave the plantations. Only after several European nations had protested against the inhuman traffic and some British and German firms had stopped buying cocoa from São Tomé and Principe did the Portuguese government enforce some moderation of the system. But, far away from foreign gaze, in the mines and on the farms of Portugal's mainland territories, inhuman conduct towards African workers has continued down to the present day.

Economic development

Much of Portuguese Africa's economic development in these years came as a result of the development of neighbouring territories. In the 1920s the Benguela Railway was built largely with British and Belgian capital as an extra link between the mineral-rich Katanga and the coast (see above, p. 238). This led to the further development

*W. H. Nevinsen, *More Changes, More Chances* (New York, 1926), p. 75.

Contratados *being shipped to São Tomé.*

of Benguela and the growth of plantation agriculture on the central plateau. On the other side of the continent Beira and Lourenço Marques similarly grew as a result of railway lines built in the 1890s as outlets for Southern Rhodesia and the Transvaal. In 1922 a rail link was completed between Nyasaland and Beira (see above, p. 231). The only important industrial venture begun in Portuguese territory was diamond mining in the region of northern Angola bordering the richer deposits of the Belgian Congo. The mining concession was given to the Diamang Company which built its own headquarters town of Dundo and soon became all-powerful in the area. Diamonds and tolls on transit goods provided most of the colony's revenue in the inter-war years. Agricultural production in both colonies came from scattered plantations of coffee (the only important export crop), cotton, sisal, maize, sugar and palms.

Naturally, the African peoples of Mozambique and Angola did not calmly accept loss of land, freedom and dignity. In both territories opposition to the white man and his rule continued from the time of 'pacification', though the Portuguese were usually able to suppress expressions of discontent.

African reaction to Portuguese rule

As in other colonial territories, African resistance leaders had realised   253 the futility of armed revolt by about 1915. But unlike many other territories, armed resistance did not lead rapidly to political activity. Elsewhere, Africans were taking advantage of European-run schools to gain knowledge and skills which they could use to work for better conditions and, eventually, independence. In the Portuguese territories, African education was almost non-existent and what schools did exist were for the most part badly run.

Nevertheless African political groups did begin to appear in Angola in the 1920s. In 1923 the Liga Africana was formed. It was a government-approved body and pledged itself to present African grievances to the colonial power 'without making any appeal to violence and without leaving constitutional limits'. It drew support not only from Angola, but from all Portuguese territories. It was never very effective since it was always under the thumb of the Europeans. In 1929 the Liga Nacional Africana was formed and was later followed by the African Guild. The activities of both of these groups were similar to those of the Liga Africana. They posed little threat to the government. Whenever any of these societies did show signs of becoming an African nationalist movement, the Portuguese, who were kept informed by agents within the societies, acted swiftly. Many smaller, local organisations – some of them semi-religious – sprang up in the years before the Second World War and were rapidly suppressed.

As we saw earlier, Portugal's hold on Mozambique in the last decade of the nineteenth century was more precarious than its control of Angola. Most of the early resistance movements there (in Gazaland, in the Zambezi valley and on the coast and islands around Mozambique) belong to the period of colonial conquest and have already been dealt with. In two areas armed resistance went on longer. In the north-west the Yao chief, Mataka, fought off every attempt by the Niassa Company to extend its authority into his territory. Only in 1912, when the government sent a large expedition against him, was he forced to flee into German East Africa. The last serious attempt at armed resistance came as late as 1917, when chiefs in Barue held out against government troops for several months.

The Liga Africana was represented in Mozambique and, with the African Guild, was the only African association allowed to exist. Local potentially nationalist groups were kept firmly under control. However, as the economy of the colony began to recover in the late 1930s, another problem appeared. This was the growth of towns. As Africans moved to the industrial and commercial centres in search of work, so there sprang up terrible African slums known as shanty-towns. These places became centres of political unrest. A few African journals and magazines were published and, though their contents were censored by the government, articles expressing the real feelings of most Africans sometimes appeared in print. A quotation from one such article, from *O brado africano* – 'The African Cry' – in 1932, provides a fitting close for this section.

We are fed to the teeth.
Fed up with supporting you, with suffering the terrible consequences of your follies, your demands, with the ... misuse of your authority ...
We are no longer willing to make greater and greater useless sacrifices ...
Enough ...
We want to be treated as you treat yourselves ...
We want bread, we want light ...
We don't want to pay for services which are of no use to us ... for institutions whose benefits we never feel.
We no longer want to suffer the bottomless pit of your excellent colonial administration!
We want of you a more humane policy ...
We don't want ... laws founded on the difference of colour ...
The gangrene you spread will infect us and later we will not have the strength to act. Now we do ...
Enough, gentlemen. Change your ways. There still is time.*

* Quoted in J. Duffy, *Portuguese Africa*, pp. 305–6.

19. The period of colonial rule
(3) The Belgian and German spheres

The Belgian Congo

The history of the Congo in the colonial era falls into two periods. Up to 15 November 1908 the area was an independent sovereignty ruled by King Leopold II of Belgium and known as the Congo Free State. On that day responsibility was assumed by the government of Belgium and the colony was renamed the Belgian Congo.

Politics, administration and economics in the Congo Free State

The Free State provides the worst example of maladministration and exploitation in the whole colonial history of Africa. There were three main reasons for the brutal exploitation for which the Congo Free State became notorious. They were the size of the country, the nature of the administrative system and Leopold's economic policy.

Leopold wanted either directly through his own agents or indirectly through concessionaire companies (the C.F.S. levied taxes on the companies and also held shares in many of them) to make as much money as possible from trade with the Congo. All land not actually occupied by African houses or fields was declared 'vacant' and was therefore open to foreign exploitation. This policy took no account of the fact that the Congo peoples regarded large tracts of forest and grassland as theirs for hunting, gathering and farming. Africans were also forced to work for the white men. C.F.S. agents were empowered to extract a 'labour tax'. The companies were supposed to pay for African labour but in practice they copied the officials in adopting force. The agents employed by the C.F.S. and the companies were often drawn from the worst elements of European society. Conditions in the Congo were bad for these men and pay was poor. They were expected to augment their salaries by bonuses paid to them for the collection of rubber and ivory. It was left to them to use whatever methods they considered appropriate to force labour from the Africans under their control.

256　　　The full story of Congo atrocities will never be known but it is clear that the crimes committed against the peoples of the region included whipping, beating, maiming, murder and the burning of villages.

Laws existed to protect the Congolese from ill-treatment and exploitation but there were no courts in the interior to hear complaints and the chiefs to whom appeal could be made were usually overawed by C.F.S. or company officials who, in effect, meted out the only 'justice' seen in these areas.

There were many Christian missions operating in the colony

In the Rubber Coils. This contemporary British cartoon shows what some observers thought of the activities of King Leopold II and his agents in the Congo.

staffed by men from several countries. Some of them were afraid to speak out against the C.F.S. officials for fear of being excluded from the Congo. But in 1890 the Aborigines Protection Society in London heard a report based on information gathered by the Congo Balolo Mission and from then on no year went past without protests being made by British, American, Swedish and other missionaries.

The volume of criticism mounted. Protests were made to Leopold himself and to foreign governments who were urged to bring pressure to bear on the Belgian king. But little was achieved. In 1896 Leopold did set up a Commission for the Protection of the Natives, consisting of six missionaries. It satisfied some critics but it had no powers and could do little for the Africans.

It was E. D. Morel and Sir Roger Casement who eventually succeeded in changing the situation by forcing the British government to take official action. Morel was a journalist with a great interest in Africa. For some years he had been exposing the Congo situation in articles and speeches. He argued that the treatment of Africans in the Congo and the exclusion of non-Belgian traders were both violations of the Berlin Act of 1885. In 1903, the British government, acting on information received from Morel and his friends, consulted with the other signatories of the Berlin Act and at the same time asked Sir Roger Casement to carry out his own investigations on the spot. Casement took little time to compile his report. He had once served in the International Congo Association and had spent many years in diplomatic service in Africa. He opposed the policies of the C.F.S. and condemned them in his report. He showed that those policies had been responsible not only for brutality and exploitation but also for a large-scale depopulation in the Congo. He also contacted Morel with the object of starting the Congo Reform Association (founded in 1904).

When Casement's report was published it aroused considerable public interest. The activities of the Congo Reform Association kept that interest alive in Europe and the United States. King Leopold was angry but he had to bow to world opinion. He set up his own commission of enquiry, which confirmed Casement's findings (the report published in 1906). Leopold promised reforms but the opponents of the C.F.S. were not satisfied. Some of them were already suggesting that Belgium should take over administration of the Congo with a constitution guaranteeing African rights. Many in Belgium were coming to the conclusion that the king should not retain control of the Congo. But Leopold held on for two more years – years marked by long arguments with his own government. He gave way at last, approving on 18 October 1908 the Treaty of Cession transferring all C.F.S. territory and assets to Belgium. The treaty became effective on 15 November. Just over a year later King Leopold II died.

Politics and administration in the Belgian Congo

The new administration was placed in the hands of a Colonial Minister who was assisted by a small committee of experts. These men gradually introduced reforms. Officials received better pay and no longer had to be commercial as well as administrative agents. An important weakness remained in the administrative system in that it was still too centralised. Important decisions were still made in Boma (the capital until 1929) or even Brussels and the men on the spot were left little opportunity to develop their own initiative. Government monopoly of rubber, ivory and other natural products came to an end. Forced labour was stopped and replaced by a money tax which was less burdensome. A new judicial system was introduced. Belgium continued to make a great deal of money out of the Congo but much of it was now ploughed back into the colony. Modern towns appeared. Roads and railways were constructed. Hospitals and schools were built and the Congo could soon boast a more widespread system of primary education than any other African colony. As mining and industry developed Africans were attracted to the towns. The Belgian authorities tried to discourage seasonal migrant labour by providing facilities in the towns which would encourage the workers to settle with their families. The activities of Christian missions were encouraged and their numbers increased dramatically.

By the 1930s the Belgian Congo was the envy of other colonial powers. The Belgians seemed to have achieved a benevolent paternalism. Only in Katanga and along the lower Congo were there large European populations which adopted the inevitable 'settler mentality'. Throughout most of this vast territory the traditional patterns of life had been little affected except for the material benefits which the white man had brought.

But there were flaws in the system. There was a lack of secondary education. The rulers felt that the 'native' should not be educated above his station. He should only learn manual and technical skills and enough other accomplishments to make him useful in his local society. Most of the teaching given was in local vernacular languages. The Belgians saw no need to develop any national ideas among the Africans. There was no political development. It would have been difficult enough in any case for the Congo's fourteen million Africans scattered throughout such a vast territory to have developed any nationalist aspirations but such aspirations as did appear were either stamped out or channelled into local politics.

As in other colonies where African attempts at political expression were frustrated many people took up with separatist religious movements. In 1921 the Kimbanguist movement began. It was started in the lower Congo region by Simon Kimbangu who preached from April to September 1921. He was then imprisoned by the authorities and in prison he remained until his death in 1951. Kimbangu made such an impression in five brief months that small groups of disciples kept his teaching alive, despite persecution, until 1956 when the ban on their activities was lifted. Kimbanguism gained support particularly from the Kongo (Bakongo) people who, though divided by colonial boundaries, were striving to maintain their cultural identity. They found comfort in the prophecies of Kimbangu and his disciples. Later Kimbanguism was to have close links with Abako, the Kongo cultural and political association (see below, pp. 279f).

The Watchtower movement also spread into the Congo. Teachers from Nyasaland and Northern Rhodesia arrived in 1923. The movement, which came to be known as Kitawala in the Congo, spread rapidly in Katanga. By 1939 it had thousands of members both in urban and rural areas. Its popularity is not surprising. Only at Kitawala meetings could Africans listen to preaching like this:

> ... the Bible makes no distinction between whites and blacks ... it is only here in the Congo that the government considers the natives as slaves. We are fed up with this and the new God of the Kitawalist doctrine is here to help us....

Economic development

The most remarkable aspect of the history of the Belgian Congo was its economic development. The main source of the colony's wealth was Katangan copper. In 1892 C.F.S. agents confirmed that there were, in the area until recently dominated by Msiri, important deposits of malachite ore which could be easily worked. Further prospecting revealed three main copper-bearing regions – East Lufira, Kambore and Kolweze. Furthermore, the agents discovered other valuable minerals; there was gold at Ruwe and tin at Busanga. But for many years these fields simply could not be worked because there were no adequate means of transporting the metals out of Katanga. The driving force behind the survey of Katanga was Robert (later Sir Robert) Williams. He had been one of Rhodes' agents but when he realised that richer mineral deposits lay on the C.F.S. side of the boundary with Northern Rhodesia he obtained prospecting rights

An early Congo river steamer.

from Leopold. In 1899 he formed a company called Tanganyika Concessions Ltd to exploit the astonishing resources of Katanga which his agents discovered. Williams was determined not to allow the communications problem to stand in his way. He obtained permission from Leopold and the Portuguese government to build a railway from Benguela on the west coast to Katanga. The thousand-mile long railway was begun in 1903 (see above, p. 238).

In 1906 King Leopold formed the Union Minière du Haut-Katanga in which Tanganyika Concessions Ltd held forty per cent of the shares. It was the Union Minière which developed the mineral fields of Katanga. Work began in 1907. It was expensive and slow because machinery had to be brought by river and overland. In 1909 Elizabethville was founded and became the centre of the Union's activities. In 1910 the Rhodesia Railway reached Elizabethville providing, at last, a route for Katanga's exports. White men began to flock in from Europe and southern Africa to work in the mines. So important had the area become that the Belgian government created a special administration for Katanga, placing it under the control of a governor responsible directly to Brussels and not Boma.

Development was still slow. It was difficult to obtain fuel for the furnaces. Then it was discovered that coal from Wankie could be used. Another problem was the scarcity of African labour, the Congolese not being anxious to offer their services. This problem was overcome by using workers from neighbouring countries. By the end of the First World War the Congo was producing over 27,000 tons of copper a year as well as tin and gold. By this time cobalt and uranium had also been discovered and diamonds were being mined in South Kasai.

After the First World War the development of mining was rapid. In 1931 the Benguela Railway at last reached Elizabethville, giving Katanga another outlet for its goods. Although the mine owners were badly hit by the Depression, the commodities they supplied were so much in demand throughout the world that, by 1935, they were able to put their difficulties behind them and continue their expansion. By 1939 the Congo's exports were valued at 2,250,000,000 francs, most of which were made up of minerals (tungsten, silver and zinc had by now also been discovered in the fabulous Katanga).

Rubber production experienced a great boom in the early years of the twentieth century. This was largely because of the world need for car and bicycle tyres. Most of the rubber produced was wild rubber. By 1906 annual production had reached 6,000 tons, valued at 47,000,000 francs. Then the world rubber boom came to an end. Prices dropped and so did production. Between 1914 and 1918 Congolese rubber was again in demand to help Belgium and her allies in the First World War but after 1918 rubber never regained its earlier importance in the Congo's economy.

Most of the Congo's agricultural produce was grown on European-owned plantations. In the western part of the country there were large palm plantations which provided Belgium with oil for soap and lubricants. Coffee was grown in northern Katanga and in an area bordering the western shore of Lake Tanganyika. Cotton, sisal, cocoa, sugar and tobacco were other important cash crops. Most Africans continued to practise subsistence farming. However, the government was doing something to help the peasant farmer. In 1933 the National Institute for Agronomic Study in the Congo was set up to make modern farming techniques and practical aid available to the African community of the Congo.

In a country the size of the Congo almost a half of which is made up of dense forest good communications are vital to development. The land itself provided some means of transport in the form of the River Congo and its many tributaries. In the early days of the Free State, water transport was of the utmost importance and steamers were soon operating on many rivers. The Congo and Lualaba were navigable for over a thousand kilometres above Leopoldville as far as Stanleyville. The lower stretches of the Kasai, Kwilu and Sankuru gave some access to Kasai province. But the river system had many unnavigable stretches. The most important of these 'gaps' in the early years was the stretch of the Lower Congo between Stanley Pool and the sea. Here the way was blocked by a series of cataracts. The entire Congo system was useless as a commercial highway if this obstacle could not be overcome. In 1889 a company called the *Chemin de Fer du Congo* was set up to build a railway from Matadi, at the mouth of the river, to Leopoldville. This line was completed in 1898. In 1906 and 1910, two unnavigable stretches of the Lualaba were by-passed by lengths of track and thus the extreme eastern regions of the colony were linked to the west coast.

But by this time Katanga was becoming the commercial centre of the Congo, and attention was turned to ways of linking the mining area with the coast. The extension of the Rhodesia Railway to Eliza-bethville in 1910, as we have seen, enabled the Katanga mines to begin production but the Belgian leaders were not happy about being dependent upon another country for the means of exporting its main product. In 1906 Leopold II founded the *Compagnie du Chemin de Fer du Bas-Congo* for the purpose of building a railway from Elizabeth-ville, via Kamina and Luluabourg to Port Francqui on the River Kasai. From Port Francqui goods could be carried by river to Leo-poldville. The building of the line was a considerable engineering feat and was not completed until 1928. At the same time the Benguela Railway was being built. This was an even more impressive piece of engineering, which not only gave Katanga another link to the sea but also did a great deal for the development of Portuguese Angola.

South West Africa

The task which faced the German rulers after the African risings of the early years of the century (see above, pp. 195ff) was one of reconstruction. The government decided to base the economic future of the colony on a double foundation – concession companies, which would largely be responsible for exploiting the country's mineral wealth, and settler farmers.

Economic development 1905–14

After the risings the colonial government confiscated over 26 million hectares of African land. In 1905 Crown Land accounted for well over half the total workable land of the colony and the government was in a position to encourage European settlement. Land was sold cheaply and between 1905 and 1913 the number of settler farmers almost trebled to just under 1,600. Most of them took land in the 263 north around Windhoek, Amaruru, Grootfontein and Okahandja, but as railways were built more settlement areas appeared.

There were three major reasons for the slow influx of settlers: shortage of cattle, shortage of water and inadequate transport. The government had just begun to solve these problems when the First World War broke out. Most of the farmland was suitable only for cattle rearing. The start of cattle farming was slow but government action to preserve African herds and the importation of breeding stock gradually improved the situation. The settlers also reared sheep and goats. By 1914 stock farming in South West Africa had begun to flourish.

Finding water was a more expensive task and one requiring direct government action. In 1907 the government set up a Water Department which organised the drilling of boreholes wherever they were needed. Although over 1,600 boreholes had been sunk by 1914 less than a thousand of them were usable.

As elsewhere in colonial Africa railways were essential to development. In 1897 work began on the line from Swakopmund to Windhoek, which was completed in 1902. Northern extensions from this line reached Tsumeb in 1906 and Grootfontein in 1908. In 1912 Windhoek was linked to Keetmanshoop, which already had a rail link with the coast at Lüderitz. Railways were vital to the import and

264 *Beach mining for diamonds in South West Africa.*

export of livestock and the completion of most of these lines led immediately to an influx of new settlers.

In 1903 almost a third of the colony's land was in the hands of concession companies. They were supposed to be developing the mineral potential of South West Africa but had not yet made any significant discoveries. In fact they were being severly criticised for speculating in land by selling plots to settlers at high prices. As a result the activities of the companies were restricted by the German government. In 1908 diamonds were discovered near Lüderitz. There was an immediate rush of fortune-seekers to the diamond field but the government granted a monopoly to one of the companies. Though this brought a storm of protest from settlers which led to the resignation of the governor and the colonial secretary, the decision was not reversed. Production increased steadily in the years of German rule, exports rising from 51,000 marks in 1908 to 59,000,000 marks in 1913. The area covered by diamond-working also spread further south and north as fresh discoveries were made along the coast.

The Ovambo had mined copper at Tsumeb for generations and European commercial mining was begun there in 1908. Lead was discovered in the same area. By 1913 the annual value of copper exports was 8,000,000 marks. The colony's total production for export earned 70,000,000 marks in that year, most of this coming from diamonds, copper, cattle, hides, wool and ostrich feathers.

African life

Germany, like Belgium regarded colonies as areas of land to be exploited for the benefit of the fatherland. This and their experiences during the risings resulted in a harsh attitude towards the Africans. In 1907 by special decrees Africans were forbidden to buy land, riding animals and large quantities of livestock. They had to carry passes and their movements were severely restricted. European employers had almost unlimited rights over their African workers, who were little better than slaves. The courts were dominated by the white men and it was virtually impossible for Africans to gain redress for any wrongs done to them.

The First World War and the mandate

All the British and German African colonies were involved to a greater or lesser extent in the First World War. The South African government decided to support Britain and to invade the neighbouring German territory. There was an immediate protest from Boer nationalists. In the Transvaal and the Orange Free State troops mutinied, politicians interfered with army recruitment and extremists contacted the German military leaders with a view to gaining assistance for the overthrow of the pro-British government. Botha and Smuts put the rebellion down after three months of sporadic fighting, which had to be carried out as carefully as possible in order to avoid a degree of bloodshed and ill-feeling which might have precipitated a new Anglo-Boer war. By April 1915 all was ready for the invasion of South West Africa. 60,000 troops advanced into the colony in five columns to face a German army of 9,000. The defenders surrendered on 9 July at Khorab. The victors took as few prisoners as possible and tried to ensure the normal running of the country. Martial law was declared and South West Africa was placed under the control of an Administrator.

After the war delegates from the victorious nations met in Paris to settle the peace. They agreed that Germany's colonies should be taken away but that these lands and their peoples should not merely become 'prizes' to be squabbled over. Rather the interests of the peoples of these lands and their development should be the main concern in arriving at a settlement of their future destiny. It was suggested that each of these colonies should be placed under the supervision of certain nations which were given a 'mandate' to hold the colonies 'in trust' for the peoples of those colonies. This is how the Covenant of the League of Nations worded it:

> To those territories and colonies which, as a consequence of the late war have ceased to be under the sovereignty of states which formerly governed them, and which are inhabited by peoples not yet able to stand by themselves under the strenuous conditions of the modern world, there should be applied the principle that the well-being and development of such peoples form a sacred trust of civilization. . . . The best method of giving practical effect to this principle is that the tutelage of such peoples should be entrusted to advanced nations who by reason of their resources, their experience or their geographical position can best undertake this responsibility . . .

The mandate for South West Africa was given to the Union government. It is worth noting that the lofty ideals of the League of Nations found little echo in South Africa. Smuts, while accepting the mandate, was contemptuous of the principle behind it. Africa, he said 'is inhabited by barbarians, who not only cannot possibly govern themselves, but to whom it would be impracticable to apply any ideas of political self-determination in the European sense'.

The mandate came into effect in 1920 and for a while the country continued to be ruled by an Administrator. He was assisted by an Advisory Council. A commission appointed by the Union government decided that a new constitution similar to those of the other states of the Union should come into force in South West Africa when the number of adult male British settlers in the country had reached 10,000. This change occurred in 1925. The German settlers had been allowed to stay and, in 1924, had been granted British citizenship. Farmers had flocked in from the Cape to buy cheap land and the magical number of 10,000 was soon reached.

The new constitution provided for an Executive Committee and a Legislative Assembly in addition to the Advisory Council. Twelve of the eighteen members of the Assembly were to be elected by the settlers. There was, of course, no question of African representation. It was thought adequate for one member of the Advisory Council to be appointed for his knowledge of 'native affairs'.

White political opinion soon split into two groups represented by the United National South West Party (usually known as the Union Party) and the Deutscher Bond (or German Party). The former favoured full integration into South Africa while the latter worked for the colony's independence and even its restoration to Germany. In 1933 Germany came under the dictatorship of Adolf Hitler, who promised to regain all Germany's colonies, so the Deutscher Bond's aim was not just an empty dream. In 1934 the Assembly voted for the abolition of the existing 'unworkable' constitution and the absorption of South West Africa into the Union as a fifth province. This was vigorously opposed by the German Party so the Union government set up a commission to examine the situation. It decided that the existing constitution was unsuitable and recommended the territory's absorption into the Union 'subject to the mandate'. But, in fact, no change occurred. The political atmosphere both inside and outside South Africa was so tense in the years leading up to the Second World War that it was considered unwise to risk fresh clashes.

White settlement and land problems

The granting of the mandate was a great boon to the Union government. They now had land to offer to the many South Africans who were clamouring for it, and a means of rewarding soldiers who had fought in the 1914–18 war. By the end of 1923, 730 farm plots totalling almost 5,000,000 hectares had been allocated to new

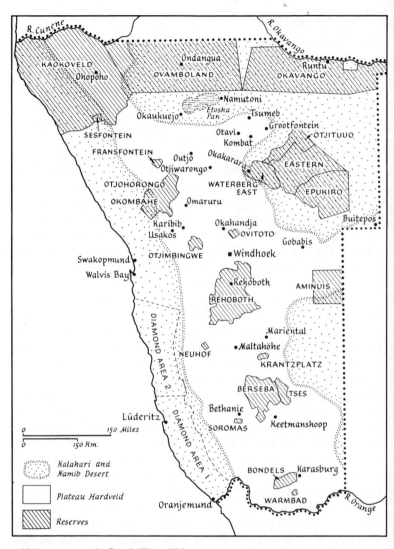

African reserves in South West Africa.

settlers. By 1939 there were over 3,300 European farms totalling 25,300,000 hectares. Some of this land had gone, against the wishes of the Legislative Assembly, to 301 Boer families who entered the territory in 1928. They were the remnants of Boer groups who had migrated to Angola in the last quarter of the nineteenth century and now sought repatriation to their 'homeland'. They were provided with farms and loans for the purchase of stock, etc.

268 The increase of white settlement naturally created a land problem

involving the African inhabitants of the territory. The new administration adopted the South African solution of racial separation. A number of reserves were marked in which the African peoples might own land and rear herds. According to an official report of 1922 'grazing is good, water is sufficient' in these reserves. A glance at the map will show how accurate that report was. Most of the reserves were in desert or semi-desert areas. As usual the indigenous people of the country were allowed to retain only the land which white settlers did not want.

'Native' legislation was introduced to bring South West Africa into line with the rest of South Africa. This included pass laws, a Masters and Servants Proclamation governing the relations between employers and employed, restriction on African movements in towns and white settlement areas, and measures designed to 'encourage' Africans to seek employment by Europeans. So the Africans were scarcely better off than they had been under German rule. So much for the 'sacred trust' supposedly embodied in the mandate.

African reaction

We have seen how repressive colonial régimes, when they take undisguised racialism as their creed and use superior technology, not to improve the lot of colonial peoples but to keep them in subjection, can crush the spirit of the people they rule. The situation was much the same in South West Africa. The white rulers believed or professed to believe that rapid development would be bad for the 'natives'; they should be allowed to progress 'at their own pace'. Bolstered by this philosophy the administration had no guilty conscience about spending as little public money as possible on African development. Educational and medical work were left almost entirely to missionaries. If we take education as an example we find that of the total sum available about ten per cent was usually spent on African primary education. For instance, in 1935 the government spent £95,000 on educating the children of the 36,000 Europeans in the colony and £12,000 on educating the sons of 235,000 Africans. The government's 'native' policy was frequently criticised by the League of Nations Permanent Mandate Commission, which obtained annual reports on all mandated territories, but the politicians concerned showed almost as much contempt for the League as they did for Africans. From their point of view the policy of avoiding rapid development had the satisfactory results of keeping up a supply of low-paid labour and preventing the emergence of educated African leaders.

But not all the people of South West Africa were crushed by 269 government policy. The first people to rise against their masters were the Bondelswarts Khoikhoi who had played a prominent part in earlier revolts. Having suffered greatly at the hands of the Germans, they supported and helped the Union forces in 1915. They expected some reward for this assistance and asked for permission to return to their old homeland and for the return of their leaders, Jacobus Christian and Abraham Morris, who had escaped to South Africa when pursued by the Germans. Both these requests were turned down by the new rulers. In addition the Bondelswarts were taxed heavily to force them to work on settler farms. When they did so they were frequently ill-treated and underpaid by the farmers. Complaining to the authorities brought no redress.

In April 1922 Abraham Morris returned, without permission, to his people. They refused, when ordered to do so, to give him up. Instead they retired to a hill called Curuchas, took up a defensive position and prepared to shoot it out with their white oppressors. With about two hundred guns between them they never stood a chance. The authorities used bombs and machine guns to crush the revolt. The result was over 550 Bondelswarts killed, wounded or taken prisoner. Both the Union government and the Mandate Commission made enquiries into the Bondelswarts rising. As a result some of the people's grievances were dealt with. Jacobus Christian was restored as their leader, mission stations and schools were encouraged, taxes were reduced and labour relations were improved.

Three years later the Rehobothers rose in revolt. This community (or, rather, a large section of it) was demanding nothing less than complete independence. In pursuit of this end they chose their own leaders, in defiance of other elected leaders who were approved by the government. They appealed to the Union government and to the League of Nations. Having failed in their appeals the Rehobothers prepared for armed resistance. This time the administration acted with greater wisdom. Before the revolutionaries had time to organise themselves (April 1925) the government sent a large, well-armed force to the trouble spot. This succeeded in impressing on the Rehobothers the futility of resistance.

Economic development

The economic development of the territory was affected by the world depression of 1920–1 and the much worse Great Depression of 1929–31. In addition South West Africa was hit by a disastrous spell of drought from 1929 to 1934. After the First World War the new
270 government prohibited the export of livestock to allow farmers to

build up their herds and flocks. By 1935, despite the drought, stock numbers had trebled and the territory was exporting 129,000 cattle and 120,000 sheep and goats every year. In 1920 the German diamond companies were bought out by Consolidated Diamond Mines Ltd. Fields north of Lüderitz discovered in the 1920s proved to be rich in stones of the highest quality. By 1939 diamond exports were worth about £1,000,000 per annum. The copper mines continued to be worked by the German company which had first started them. Before the outbreak of the Second World War copper exports were earning South West Africa about £400,000 a year. The years when South West Africa was under the League of Nations mandate were years of precarious economic balance. Until 1930 the territory was just able to balance its budget. From then until 1934 the country was in debt. From 1935 onwards there was a gradual recovery. But the black majority in South West Africa had little cause to rejoice at the country's recovering fortunes. For increased national prosperity made very little difference indeed to them.

20. Independence

(1) The Congo

During and after the Second World War (1939–45) African nationalist movements grew stronger and the demand for independence more insistent. In this last section of the book we shall be examining the rise of nationalism in South and Central Africa. We shall see how in some countries the movement came to fruition in the establishment of democratically elected governments free of foreign control while in others the demand for majority rule was stifled.

The Second World War and its results

In the Second World War there was no fighting in the southern half of Africa but the war did have profound effects on this part of the continent so we must devote a little attention to it. Fighting and slaughter on an unprecedented scale took place during this war. It v·as fought by land, air and sea over an area from north-west Europe to the southern Pacific. It was fought with terrible new weapons of mass destruction and before it finished the atomic bomb, capable of killing and wounding 150,000 people at one blow, had been used. At the end of the war most of the participating countries were shattered and exhausted. It took them years to recover. This applied particularly to the major colonial powers, Britain, France, Belgium and Italy, which had been in the thick of the fighting (Portugal remained neutral throughout the war). The war also brought a change in the international balance of power. Before 1939 the major industrial and colonial nations, Britain, France and Germany had largely dominated world affairs. The U.S.A. was a great commercial power but had held aloof from international politics. Soviet Russia had been too concerned with its own internal problems to be able to play a leading role in the world. After 1945 the U.S.A. and the U.S.S.R. emerged as the world's great 'super powers'. The relations between these two countries and their allies and their frequent clashes in the United Nations Assembly dominated world history for many years.

What is important from our point of view is that they were both opposed to colonialism and brought pressure to bear on the colonial powers to break up their empires. Britain, Portugal and Belgium (the colonial powers involved in southern Africa) resisted this pressure but were not in a very strong position. They needed money to finance their own recovery and had little to spare for colonial development.

African soldiers from the Belgian Congo in the Second World War.

At the same time there was mounting pressure from the colonies themselves. We have already seen how African political movements depended largely on educated leaders and a growing understanding of European ways. More and more Africans gained education and political experience as the years went by. This was probably truer of other parts of Africa than of the area we are studying. It was certainly true that parts of Asia were more politically advanced than African colonies. In 1947 India and Pakistan became the first two European colonies to gain their independence. Once the independence movement had begun it could not help but spread. Everywhere nationalist leaders emerged demanding for their people freedom from European rule. 273

The war had a direct effect on African nationalist aspirations. African soldiers fought in Madagascar, North Africa, Burma, Italy and the Middle East. Many who did not go on active service supported the war effort in the factories and mines of their own land. They endured shortages and lack of development in order to keep their colonial masters provided with vital supplies. They made an important contribution to the ultimate allied victory and they assumed that they would receive rewards in the form of political and social concessions in the post-war years. When these rewards did not materialise resentment stung many Africans into fresh political action. The situation was more crucial for men who had served in the armies and support forces. Throughout the war they had lived in conditions which were better than those at home. They had come into closer contact with Europeans and had come to realise that they were not a master race, born to rule. Many had learned reading, writing and technical skills. After the war they were expected to return to their old living conditions, their old subservience to the white man, their old unskilled jobs. It was expecting too much of human nature to imagine that these men could slip back easily into their former way of life.

The colonial powers gradually realised that independence would have to be granted. In 1947 the British Empire disappeared and was replaced by the Commonwealth, a much looser association of states. Britain hoped that within the framework of the Commonwealth colonies would gain independence but remain in a special relationship with their old 'mother country'. But the big question was 'When?' The governments in London and Brussels did not want to hand over independence until the colonial peoples were 'ready' for it. They wanted time to establish democratic institutions so that the transition of power would be smooth and peaceful. But African nationalist leaders had different ideas about when their people would be 'ready' for independence. They were impatient and believed that the colonial powers were simply holding on to their dependencies as long as possible.

These problems had to be resolved against a world background of political tension and rapid economic development. Throughout the 1950s the world was split into Communist and non-Communist blocs. Each side brought pressure to bear on the leaders of the emerging nations of Asia and Africa (sometimes known as the 'third world' or the 'Afro-Asian bloc'). Offers of arms, technical assistance or money – which were desperately needed – were frequently used as 'bait' by the great powers to win economic or political control. Africa's political leaders needed great wisdom in their relations with other countries. At the same time Africa stood the very real danger of falling further 274 and further behind the world in industrial and commercial development. After the period of post-war recovery the wealthy nations took great strides in technological advance. They built up a complex and sophisticated structure of world trade. African governments wanted to get rid of the white men who had controlled the political and economic life of their countries, but in such a rapidly changing world could they do without the white man's expertise? Could they cope on their own with industrialisation, intensification of farming, improvement of transport facilities? The answer to most of these questions was 'No'; in the short term at least African countries needed outside capital investment and technical assistance. This fact provided a useful excuse for the rulers of South Africa, Rhodesia and the Portuguese colonies to refuse to relinquish control. Zaire, Zambia, Malawi, Botswana, Lesotho and Swaziland took the plunge into independence and their new governments faced up to the immense problems that independence brought with it.

So much by way of introduction. We must now look at individual territories to see how their people coped with the years 1940–65. We start with a chapter on the Congo.

The Congo: economic development

At the beginning of the Second World War Belgium was occupied by German troops. She was no longer able to control Congo affairs and the Congolese government became virtually independent. It organised the economic life of the colony in order to produce as much as possible to help Belgium's allies to fight Germany. Exports of copper, palm oil, rubber, gold, cobalt, tin and tungsten reached their highest level ever. The export of uranium from Katanga also began at this time and America's first atom bombs used Congolese uranium. The temporary severance of close links with Belgium meant that the government in Leopoldville (which had been the capital since 1929) had to look for new export markets. The contacts established during the war were of permanent value to Congolese trade. The enormous expansion of trade can be seen from the export figures. In 1938 the Congo's exports were valued at 1,897,154,000 Belgian francs. In 1948 the figure was 10,817,466,000 Belgian francs.

During the war the Belgian Congo had to learn to be self-sufficient. Factories were opened to manufacture goods which had previously been imported from Belgium. This led to a rise of town populations and also of the number of Africans working in factories. By 1958 twenty-seven per cent of the adult male population worked in the towns. This prosperity continued after the war. By 1953 the Congo produced sixty per cent of the world's cobalt, sixty per cent of the

275

world's diamonds and was second only to Northern Rhodesia in the production of copper. In 1956 exports reached the record figure of 27,105,881,000 Belgian francs. Industrialisation was progressing rapidly and Congolese factories were using almost as much electricity as the industrial centres of South Africa.

Government revenue was correspondingly high and a large proportion of it was spent on providing social services. Hospitals were provided. Urban housing estates were built. Schools were established, although most of the money spent on education was in the form of grants to mission schools. Compared with other African colonies the Belgian Congo had quite a good record as far as education was concerned. In the last years of colonial rule most African boys were attending primary school, though by no means all completed their courses. The picture of advanced education was different. Official figures gave the numbers attending secondary schools in 1959 as over 46,000. This figure represents about three per cent of the total number of children of secondary school age and, in any case, is not representative of the post-war years as a whole, since a considerable boost was given to education immediately before independence. A few thousand Africans were receiving technical training. The first university for African students – Louvainium, a Roman Catholic college – was founded in 1954 and another was opened at Elizabethville two years later. These establishments, of course, produced very few graduates before independence. The educational system was really only geared to the training of Africans for the lower-paid jobs.

Social and political conditions

Materially the peoples of the Belgian Congo were better off than the inhabitants of most African colonies. The Belgians were proud of their colonial record and they thought they could pursue their policy of 'civilising' the Africans until a time was reached (in the distant future) when the two races had achieved a situation of equality and partnership. But, in 1960, independence came to the Congo amidst chaos, bloodshed, racial conflict and inter-tribal strife. Clearly something was wrong in the social and political life of the Belgian Congo between 1945 and 1960. To discover what it was we must look more closely at life in the Congo during those years.

The first point to grasp is that a great difference had developed between African life in the towns and in the rural areas. The industrial areas of the Congo were populated not by migrant workers, as was the case through the rest of South and Central Africa, but by a settled, urban, African population. In the rural areas life was in many ways unchanged. Local government had settled down to a form of indirect rule through approved traditional leaders. Native councils had been established in many areas and some members of these councils were elected. But all important decisions were made by provincial and district commissioners. A major task of the administration in the rural areas was the maintenance of peace. Traditionally hostile peoples were kept apart. But this did not remove hostile feelings. Right up to the imposition of C.F.S. rule the Congo basin had been the scene of massive population movement, conquest, the rise and fall of empires. All this was 'frozen' by the colonial powers. But though inter-tribal warfare was kept to a minimum, hatreds, fears and resentments still existed. Medical attention, missionary endeavours, primary schooling, agricultural advice and technical assistance had improved the lot of most Africans in the rural areas but the colonial rulers had failed in two important respects: they had failed to train African local politicians and administrators and they had failed to encourage people to think of themselves as Congolese rather than Luba, Tetela, Pende, etc.

In the towns the problems were different. There African society was largely detribalised. People lived a way of life that was similar to that lived by Europeans and they were under the direct control of European employers and officials. But they were not allowed to mix freely with the white men. Schools, housing, hotels and bars were segregated and an unofficial colour bar existed in almost every aspect of social life. White men and women were frequently contemptuous of Africans; *singe* (monkey) and *macaque* (ape) were common terms of abuse.

This was resented by most Africans but particularly by the *evolués*. The *evolués* (literally the word means those who have evolved or progressed) formed a growing and important class in urban society. They were men who, because they had received a better education or had accumulated wealth, formed a kind of middle class. They believed that their education and social standing merited better treatment from the Europeans. Instead they, like all Africans, were considered as socially inferior; they were barred from 'white' jobs for which their qualifications fitted them; they were governed by a different set of laws to the whites. The *evolués* grew increasingly resentful of the Belgians who, despite their claim to be 'civilising the natives', were closing the door to further advancement against the more progressive Africans. The situation was made more intolerable by the knowledge that in the neighbouring French Congo the process of racial integration had gone much further. For many years the *evolués* did not consider political action because African political societies were forbidden and the government was known to deal ruthlessly with 'troublemakers'.

There were Belgian politicians and administrators who sympathised with *evolué* demands. In 1948 a commission was set up to study 'the status of the civilised Congo population'. It recommended changes in the law that would have put some *evolués* at least on an equal footing with Europeans. But these recommendations were opposed bitterly by the settlers' representatives in the Council. This clearly demonstrates that white opinion in the settlement areas of the Belgian Congo was virtually the same as opinion in South Africa. 'Africans must be kept at a distance from Europeans except when they are working for them and their social progress beyond a certain point must not be allowed.' This was not official government policy but it was the view that usually prevailed in practice.

The urban situation, then, had potential dangers just as did the rural situation. There were men with social and economic grievances who had no effective, constitutional way of making those grievances known. They were not represented in the central government. They were denied the higher ranks of the civil service and many jobs in commerce which were reserved for whites. A class of men from which politicians and administrators could have been trained was left to frustration and resentment. To crown all, the patronising, even insulting, attitude of the majority of Europeans added unnecessary difficulties.

In 1955 there was no suggestion of independence for the Congo and certainly no preparedness for it on either side. In the space of four and a half years the Congo was rushed into independence. We must now look at the events of those four and a half years.

The path to independence 1956–60

In December 1955 A. A. J. van Bilsen, a Belgian university professor, published *A Thirty Year Plan for the Political Emancipation of Belgian Africa*. It was not an official document but it did express clearly for the first time the thoughts of Belgian moderates and particularly their reaction to the fact that Gold Coast (Ghana) and other colonies were clearly moving towards independence. The paper discarded traditional, vague Belgian ideas such as 'gradual development' and 'civilising the natives' in favour of a definite programme of political and social change which would culminate in self-government and complete racial equality in the Congo at the end of thirty years. The *Plan* provoked fierce opposition from most leaders of European opinion in Belgium and the Congo. But among certain groups of *evolués* it was seen as the first crack in the wall of colonial domination. One such group which met regularly in Leopoldville to discuss social, political and economic

Joseph Kasavubu.

issues responded to the *Plan* with an article in its journal, *Conscience Africaine*. The writers accepted the *Plan* but urged a more rapid racial integration than that envisaged by Bilsen. They urged the formation of a nationwide African political party, the *Mouvement National Populaire*.

A much more extreme reaction came from another source: 'Our patience is already exhausted. Since the hour has come, emancipation should be granted us this very day rather than delayed for another thirty years.' These were the words of Joseph Kasavubu, president of ABAKO. Kasavubu was a Leopoldville *evolué* who had been prevented in 1939 from entering the Roman Catholic priesthood, despite his academic qualifications. After the war his gifts of leadership were turned more and more in a political direction. When he joined ABAKO it was a cultural society of the Kongo (or Bakongo) people, descendants of the rulers of the ancient Kongo kingdom. Under his leadership it became more a political organisation. Kasavubu now urged political action on his followers. Africans should not wait for independence to be bestowed by a paternalistic régime but should work themselves for its speedy accomplishment. However, he had little faith in the idea of a united political party; he believed the struggle should be on a regional basis. Kasavubu knew that only local leaders would have sufficient popular support to be able to fight effectively for independence.

Patrice Lumumba.

It was partly in response to internal and external pressures that the administration made a move towards African representation in urban government. 1956 had seen a major move towards autonomy in the French colonies and the following year Ghana gained its independence. Belgium's first tentative step along the path of African political involvement was the *statut des villes*. It provided for African elected representation on town councils. Elections were held in Leopoldville, Elizabethville and Jadotville in 1957 and Stanleyville, Luluabourg, Bukavu and Conquilhatville in 1958. The *statut* made no provision for the formation of African political parties and it may have been partly for this reason that the parties which now emerged grew out of tribal organisations like ABAKO which were already in existence.

As a result of these elections two men first emerged as important political figures – Kasavubu in Leopoldville and Patrice Lumumba in Stanleyville. Lumumba was the more extreme of the two. He was very bitter about the way Africans were treated by Europeans in their own country. Alone among Congolese leaders he had a truly nationalist vision. He took up the idea expressed in *Conscience Africaine* and founded a nationwide party, the *Mouvement National Congolais* (M.N.C.). In 1958 he attended the All-African Peoples Conference in Accra and was greatly inspired by the activities of nationalist movements in other colonies. He joined the Pan-African Freedom Movement of East and Central Africa (PAFMECA) which had recently been founded by East African political leaders and he returned to tell his supporters, 'The independence that we claim . . . cannot be considered any longer by Belgium as a gift . . . it is a right that the Congolese people have lost.'

Another result of the 1957–8 elections was the creation of a large number of political parties. Most of them were small and almost all of them were tribal or regional in their appeal. As self-government or independence seemed to be drawing nearer old rivalries were revived. Every group feared that when Africans gained control of government it might find itself ruled by its traditional enemies. Rule by Europeans was tolerable; rule by a hostile African people was not. So every community entered the political struggle by forming its own party and the number of political organisations grew alarmingly. By September 1959 there were already 31 parties, yet within eight months this had grown to 120. In some areas inter-tribal hostility went beyond political confrontation. In Kasai province the old Luba–Lulua hatred flared up into acts of violence.

Meanwhile the leading African politicians were preparing their manifestos. Kasavubu favoured a federal constitution for independent

Congo. His party, ABAKO, having its roots in the Kongo cultural heritage, was above all concerned with preserving the customs and language of the Kongo people. Most of the other large parties were in a similar position. Kasavubu sought to ally himself with other like-minded leaders. He became more and more insistent that federalism was the only answer for the Congo.

> Federal conceptions are the most appropriate to permit the development of local autonomous powers linked together at the top by institutions collectively accepted. It is under that form, and that form only, that the unity of the country could be maintained. Powers which are too much centralized and too authoritarian ... will fatally lead to secession.*

This was the view put forward and accepted at a meeting of political parties held at Kisantu in 1959.

Lumumba had less success in his attempt to form a truly national party. The M.N.C. got off to a good start and set before the people a set of radical policies which included immediate independence, the expulsion of the Belgians, the re-distribution of European property, the creation of a socialist state and the introduction of a wide range of social security schemes. But in 1959 the M.N.C. split into two groups, when some of its leaders broke away to form a group which rapidly lost its unitary ideal and eventually joined the federalist camp. But Lumumba still had a following, particularly among small tribal groups who feared their interests might be overlooked by a government dominated by parties such as ABAKO, and a M.N.C. conference at Stanleyville in October 1959 was well attended. Lumumba also had an important advantage over his more numerous rivals: the Belgians refused to contemplate the break-up of the Congo and would not hand over power to a federalist government.

By this time law and order were rapidly disappearing in the Congo. There were racial tensions, tribal conflicts and bitter personal rivalries between politicians and their supporters. There were basic differences of policy between moderates and radicals as there were between those who favoured a united future for the Congo and those who wanted a federal constitution. Anxious Europeans were selling up and leaving the country. Groups of Africans were being stirred up by mob orators who were extremist to the point of irresponsibility. They made the most rash promises of what would happen after independence; European property and money would be redistributed, fine houses would be provided, secondary education would be available to everyone and all families would share in the country's prosperity. Millions

*ABAKO 1950–60 (C.R.I.S.P. Publications), p. 50.

of Congolese were thus led to expect that their way of life would be miraculously transformed by independence and, in order to gain support, politicians had to compete with each other in the making of wild promises which no new government could possibly have fulfilled.

1959 saw disorders in many parts of the country. In January rioting broke out in Leopoldville after the banning of an ABAKO rally. Political agitators were joined by groups of unemployed men and youths. For several days mobs destroyed European property, broke into shops and attacked mission stations. Fifty people were killed and over a hundred seriously injured before the police restored order. Kasavubu, with other leaders, was arrested and detained for some months in Belgium. His detention only served to increase his popularity

Congolese demonstrators in Leopoldville, 1959.

and made the Belgians realise that they would have to negotiate with him. During the year the situation in Kasai deteriorated and a civil war broke out in the Belgium mandated territory of Rwanda-Burundi. In October the MNC conference was followed by riots in Stanleyville and Patrice Lumumba was among those arrested by the police (he was released in January).

The Belgian government was alarmed by the rapidly deteriorating situation. After the January riots it issued a statement describing the next phase of its plan 'to lead the Congolese populations forward to independence in prosperity and peace'. There were to be elections on a universal suffrage to Provincial Councils and, later, to the General Council. This stage of the transfer of power was to last about four or five years. By now the weakness of the colonial régime was obvious to the Congolese political leaders. The Belgians were failing to maintain law and order. Settlers were taking fright and leaving the country. The parliament in Brussels was divided on the independence issue and the Congolese knew they could count on support from Belgian socialists. It was obvious that the colonialists were in no position to resist further demands. So the leading Congolese spokesmen rejected the official proposals, refused to take part in any elections and demanded the immediate granting of independence.

There is only one word to explain the Belgian government's reaction to this aggressive Congolese resistance – 'panic'. It was faced with an appalling choice: to try to organise independence as quickly as possible, or to accept responsibility for the bloodshed which any delay would probably bring about. A colonial war entails heavy financial losses, which a small nation cannot afford. The official policy was, therefore, abandoned and Congolese political leaders were invited to a Round Table Conference in Brussels in January 1960. At this conference no agreement was reached between Kasavubu and Lumumba on the sort of constitution with which the Congo should enter upon independence. What they were agreed upon was that they wanted independence now. They were really forced into this position by the promises they had already made their supporters. African moderates at the conference could see the need for a cautious approach to the enormous constitutional problems facing the country but few were prepared to recommend any delay in the granting of independence for fear of losing popular support. Nor was the Belgian government prepared to insist on a more leisurely approach to the transfer of power. They agreed to hand over control of the Congo on 30 June 1960. The constitutional issue was settled by the support the Belgians gave to Lumumba in the face of opposition from the majority of African delegates. The new state was to be a united republic.

Furious political activity filled the next few months. New parties were formed, others amalgamated. Elections for the new National Assembly were held in May. The results were ominous: several parties were represented in the Assembly, not one of which had a majority. Of the 137 seats contested the M.N.C. won 35; the National Progress Party had 22; the United African Party had 13; ABAKO gained 12;

Moïse Tshombe.

CONAKAT (a party representing a number of Katangan peoples and led by Moïse Tshombe) won 8. The only solution was a coalition government with Lumumba, head of the largest party, as prime minister. Kasavubu was elected President. At midday on 30 June the independent Congolese Republic came into being.*

Political conflict 1960–65

The fragile constitution lasted six days. The first incident in the Congo tragedy which started five years of bloodshed was a mutiny in the Leopoldville garrison of the *Force Publique*. The soldiers had expected that independence would bring promotion of Africans to senior rank in the army just as it had in the government and civil service. But independence day passed and the *Force Publique* still did not have a single Congolese officer. Foreign Communists exploited the situation in order to create a state of chaos from which they hoped to benefit. The mutiny quickly spread to other camps. There was little loss of life but a complete breakdown of authority and a great deal of pillaging. European officers and their families were held as hostages. Panic spread through the – still large – Belgian population in the Congo

---

* It was usually known as Congo Leopoldville to distinguish it from the neighbouring state, Congo Brazzaville. In 1966 the name of the capital was changed, and the country was known as Congo Kinshasa. Later the state was renamed Zaire.

and thousands of white men and women tried to leave the country. It was at this stage that the Belgian government took the fatal decision to send in troops to protect Belgian nationals and avert a 'massacre of

Independence celebrations in the Congo.

Europeans'. Inevitably Belgian and Congolese forces clashed and blood was shed. Lumumba raged against the 'imperialists' who, he said, were trying to take over the country again.

While the mutiny was at its height the province of Katanga seceded from the Congo (11 July). Moïse Tshombe, an ardent federalist, had opposed the independence constitution and now took the opportunity provided by the chaos throughout the country to declare Katanga an independent state. He was supported by the Union Minière, still owned and run by Belgians and by Belgian troops flown in to protect the mines and European property. The loss of the wealthiest part of the country was a greater blow to the government than the mutiny but it was not the only new crisis to develop; Kasai Province now burst into civil war. Within a month two other regions had seceded from the republic. With the situation falling completely out of control Lumumba had to look for help outside the country. He appealed to the United Nations to intervene.

On 14 July the United Nations passed an emergency resolution calling on Belgium to remove its forces from the Congo. The resolu-

tion also empowered the Secretary-General 'to take all necessary steps in consultation with the Congolese Government to provide it with such military assistance as may be necessary'. Immediately U.N. contingents from various countries arrived and gradually the Belgian forces withdrew. But nothing was done about the secessionist areas. Lumumba now turned to the Communist world and asked the U.S.S.R. for aid. With Russian planes and military equipment Lumumba succeeded in subduing Kasai. Government troops now advanced on Katanga. Tshombe mobilised all forces he could find, both Congolese and European, and he hired mercenaries from Belgium. African opinion inside and outside the republic was appalled at the situation which had so rapidly developed. The Congo had become a battleground for Communist and Capitalist forces. A newly independent African state had shown itself incapable of running its own affairs. And the prime minister, Patrice Lumumba, supported by foreign forces, had assumed dictatorial powers.

President Kasavubu now moved to restore some kind of political control to the government. With the support of the army and a number of political leaders, he dismissed Lumumba, who was subsequently arrested and taken to Elizabethville. There he was assassinated by Tshombe's troops (March 1961). Next, the Russians were expelled

The wreckage of Dag Hammarskjöld's aeroplane. One of the many tragedies of the Congolese civil war occurred on 18 September 1961 when Mr Dag Hammarskjöld, the talented and popular Secretary-General of the United Nations, was killed when his plane crashed on its way from Leopoldville to Ndola, where he was going for talks with Tshombe.

from the country. The new Commander-in-Chief of the army was General Mobutu and he now quickly dealt with the remaining Lumumba supporters. A degree of peace was now restored to most of the country. But Antoine Gizanga established himself in Stanleyville as the heir of Lumumba and Moïse Tshombe still controlled Katanga.

There now followed several months of negotiations under U.N. supervision aimed at bringing the various parties together. By August

288   *President Mobutu.*

1961 Gizanga and Kasavubu had been reconciled. A new government was established under the premiership of Cyrille Adoula. Kasavubu remained President and all parties were represented in the administration – except Tshombe's. He refused to take part in the new government or to bring Katanga back into the republic. When all attempts at peacefully reuniting the secessionist state with the Congo had failed, U.N. troops, who until that time had constituted a purely peace-keeping force, invaded Katanga (September 1961). Fighting continued on and off for over a year and it was only at the cost of appalling destruction and bloodshed that Katanga was eventually restored to the Congolese Republic in January 1963.

The Congo's problems were still far from over. Katanga could not be treated as a conquered state. To have done so would have led to an indefinite prolongation of guerilla warfare. It would also have kept the U.N. forces in the country. This was impossible. The enormous expense of the Congo operation was draining U.N. funds and the stories of atrocities committed during the fighting had led to a growing international demand for the withdrawal of the foreign soldiers. After months of negotiations a new government was formed with Tshombe as prime minister (July 1964) and the U.N. forces withdrew.

As well as the political conflicts which had occupied the years 1960–4, tribal clashes and wars had continued. By mid-1964 the country was in a state of utter chaos. Tshombe found the Congolese army inadequate for the task of restoring law and order. Once again he relied on mercenaries. Led by trained and ruthless professional white soldiers the army was more successful but the use of mercenaries made the prime minister very unpopular. After elections held in August 1965 Tshombe was dismissed from office. A brief period of political manoeuvring followed but it soon became clear that most of the leading politicians had, by their juggling for power, forfeited the support of the people. On 25 November General Mobutu headed a military *coup d'état*. He proclaimed himself president and formed a new administration. Then, and only then, was the Congolese Republic able to settle in peace to the task of nation building.

21. Independence
(2) Zambia, Malawi and Rhodesia

From 1940 to 1953 the three British territories in Central Africa continued to develop along separate lines but there was a movement to bring them together in some form of union. In 1953 they were joined together in the Central African Federation. This proved unacceptable to Africans and to many Europeans. African nationalists pressed for majority rule and independence. In 1961 Nyasaland achieved self-government under African rule and two years later Northern Rhodesia was successfully brought to the same position. In 1964 the Federation was broken up. Malawi (the former Nyasaland) and Zambia (the former Northern Rhodesia) achieved full independence. The British government refused to grant independence to Southern Rhodesia (which now called itself Rhodesia) until majority rule had been established there. The white settler régime refused to contemplate handing over power to the African majority and in 1965 made a unilateral declaration of independence.

We must now look at these events more closely. First we shall consider the economic development of this area. Economic and political affairs cannot really be separated but we shall discuss them separately for the sake of clarity.

Economic development

Up to the Second World War economic planning had been geared to the needs of the mining and industrial centres and European farming areas. One modern writer has said about Northern Rhodesia: '. . . the multi-million pound investment in the copper mines tends to crowd out the tribal areas . . . this artificial dualism . . . has been bent to serve the needs of a small alien community seeking political control or political profit; in the long term this geographical imbalance seems to have gravely retarded the tribal areas'.* Most efforts by

* J. A. Hellen, *Rural Economic Development in Zambia 1890–1964* (1968).

African leaders, such as Lewanika, to modernise African agriculture and grow cash crops for home consumption or export were frustrated by inadequate communications systems and lack of government encouragement. Young men were under great economic pressure to leave the land and seek work in mines and factories. As a result areas which in the nineteenth century had been flourishing African farmland became unproductive. After the war, as the possibility of independence grew, this policy was reversed in Northern Rhodesia and Nyasaland but retained in Southern Rhodesia, where the settlers were in control of political affairs.

(1) Northern Rhodesia

Northern Rhodesia's copper industry continued to expand. The war stimulated demand and this demand was maintained as world trade recovered after the war. The value of copper exports more than trebled in the decade 1939–49. In 1951 Rhodesian copper worth £62,000,000 was sold abroad. But much of this money also went out of the country. It went to the shareholders of the mining companies – many of them wealthy Americans and Britons – and to the B.S.A. Co. which still held the mining rights. In 1949, after several years of argument and discussion, the B.S.A. Co. agreed to pay twenty per cent of its royalties to the Northern Rhodesia government for

The tobacco auction floor at Lusaka.

thirty-seven years and to give up all its mineral rights to the government at the end of that period.

Throughout the 1950s the economy was booming. This led to a great increase of white immigration. In 1950 there were less than 50,000 Europeans in the country; ten years later this figure had risen to 77,000. Most of them lived and worked in the steadily growing towns but the number of settler farmers also increased. The main crops were maize and tobacco. In some areas cattle, sheep and goats were reared. The government had long since abandoned its policy of keeping vast areas of land for white settlement. In 1947 the Native Trust Land Order-in-Council took 4,500,000 hectares of Crown Land and redesignated it as Native Trust Land. This left only 5.5 per cent of land in Northern Rhodesia which was available for non-Africans. But European farmers shared in the country's growing prosperity and were responsible for most of the cash crops produced. During the war the need for self-sufficiency had stimulated the farmers to obtain higher yields. The government had encouraged them by guaranteeing minimum prices for wheat and maize. In the 1950s the growth of the towns provided another stimulus because farmers now had a large home market for their produce.

In 1947 the government produced a ten-year plan of economic development. It included provisions for the encouragement of African agriculture, which might have significantly increased living standards and enabled the African farmer to play a larger part in the development of the country. Unfortunately little was achieved under this section of the plan. Although most of the land was now available for the indigenous people, most of it was of comparatively poor quality and none of it lay close to the railway.

This meant that there was little point in Africans producing cash crops because they did not have access to the best markets. There was little attempt by the government to provide training or equipment or to change traditional farming methods. A few African farmers rose above the subsistence level. Some in the Fort Jameson area began to grow Turkish tobacco. As one commentator has said during the period of Federation, 'Though the Government never put it so bluntly, its policy was that Africans would remain subsistence cultivators and migrant labourers for the foreseeable future.'* In the 1960s as the break up of the Federation and the granting of independence drew nearer, the European rulers realised that a healthy,

---

* I. Henderson, *Social and Economic Developments in Zambia in the 20th Century*, a paper presented to the Workshop on the Teaching of Central and East African History, August 1970.

The Kariba Dam under construction.

prosperous African farming community was vital to the future of Zambia. They then introduced schemes to train Africans in cash crop farming and to assist in the marketing of agricultural produce – too little, too late.

The greatest economic achievement during the years of federation was the building of the Kariba Dam. Industrial development and particularly mining in Northern Rhodesia was hampered by an inadequate supply of electric power. Electricity was supplied by thermo-electric power stations fuelled by coal from Wankie. But the Southern Rhodesia field could not provide enough coal and the Copperbelt had to import additional supplies from abroad. When the three countries pooled their resources in 1953 they were able to plan an ambitious scheme to provide them with all the power they needed. The scheme involved a dam across the Kariba Gorge which would hold back the waters of the Zambezi and flood a stretch of the valley 280 kilometres long. Work was begun in 1955 and four years later the first generator began to work, producing 100 MW of electricity. It produced greatly increased power for commercial and domestic purposes – though not, of course, for African townships. The scheme had important side effects. Fishing facilities were improved and irrigation schemes were started. Hotels and lodges on the lake gave a boost to the country's young tourist industry.

293

Social services were improved between 1953 and 1963. There were almost four times as many African children receiving primary education at the time of independence as there had been in 1953. The provision of secondary education, though accelerated, did not keep pace with the needs of the population. In 1962 there were only 4,800 Africans in secondary schools (out of an African population of 3,410,000). Hospitals and health services were improved but most of the facilities provided were in the towns. In 1953 the total amount allocated by the Federation government to African housing, education and rural development was seventeen per cent of the total budget.

(2) Nyasaland

A British government commission had this to say about the economy of Nyasaland as it appeared in 1959:

> ... the Gross Domestic Product of Nyasaland was £19 a head, of Northern Rhodesia £81 and of Southern Rhodesia £89. Without any exploitable mineral resources, with long and expensive communications, a peasant population swollen by continuing immigration from Portuguese enterprise ... and for the employment which such enterprise offers, the economic opportunities open to Africans are few. (Monckton Commission Report)

This summarises clearly the problems facing the country, which was by far the poorest of the three British Central African territories. Overcrowding was a serious problem and many people could not survive on subsistence farming. Many men went to work in the industrial areas of South Africa and the Rhodesias. At any one time up to a third of the adult male population was away from home. There was little that could be done to make more land available. In 1946 the government bought back over 1,200 hectares of alienated land in the Shiré Highlands and redesignated it as African Trust Land.

More Africans were joining the ranks of the cash crops farmers and Nyasaland steadily exported more and more of its farm produce. Tobacco and tea remained the most important crops but African farmers in the north began to grow coffee in the 1940s. Other cash crops were cotton, groundnuts, rice and beans. The government encouraged experiments. For a while in the 1940s European farmers did well out of tung oil (used in the manufacture of paint). The government also sponsored systematic afforestation and organised fisheries research. The Federation government approved a large scheme for the drainage of the lower Shiré marshland for the purpose of growing rice, sugar and cotton. During the period of Federation old roads were improved and new roads built. But Nyasaland remained the Cinderella of the Federation and continued to lag far behind economically.

> Federation has meant to Nyasaland nothing more than a paltry subsidy – less than £4 million a year – from the Federal Government. Is it for that that the proud people of Nyasaland have been asked to give up their hopes of natiónal independence and told to throw in their lot with a handful of white rulers living hundreds of miles away?*

(3) Southern Rhodesia

It was Southern Rhodesia which experienced the most complete economic transformation during this period. In 1940 it was a land of white commercial farmers and black subsistence farmers. There was little industry. One effect of the Second World War was to stimulate

Tea picking on a plantation at the foot of Mulanje Mountain, Malawi.

agriculture and industry in Southern Rhodesia. The young iron and steel industry expanded and, though many men were away from home, agricultural production increased. Minor industries were founded to meet the needs of a wealthy white community denied European exports. Light engineering, textiles, sugar refining and a host of other new industries made their appearance. Minor industrial

* T. Franck, *Race and Nationalism* (New York, 1960), p. 324.

production, which was worth £5,000,000 in 1939, had risen in value to £31,000,000 ten years later.

Development was even more rapid during the ten years of the Federation. Southern Rhodesia derived far greater benefit from federation than her partners. It was pressure from the Salisbury government which resulted in the joint hydro-electric scheme being sited on the Zambezi instead of on the Kafue, as had earlier been decided. Power from this new source boosted the development of Rhodesia's industries. Asbestos and chrome mining boomed. Deposits of iron, copper, tin and nickel were discovered and exploited. Production of beryllium and lithium reached a high level during the 1950s. Chemical plants, canning factories, motor car assembly plants and building material factories were just a few of the many new ventures begun in the boom years when Southern Rhodesia was 'milking' Federation funds to the utmost in order to create a white man's paradise.

The government did its utmost to encourage the boom. They negotiated finance with other countries. They encouraged large international companies to set up factories and depots in Southern Rhodesia. They devised an overall economic plan. They resurfaced the main roads. They built bridges. They constructed a new railway line from Bulawayo to Lourenço Marques. They negotiated a trade agreement with South Africa in 1955. Manufacturers also benefited greatly from the free trade arrangements within the Federation.

The growth of industry brought a great increase in European immigration. In 1941 there were about 69,000 white people in Southern Rhodesia. By 1946 there were 82,000. By 1951 there were 135,000. By 1961 the total had risen to 221,000. African urban population also increased enormously. The labour pattern for Africans was changing. The new industries demanded a permanent work force, so the old migrant labour gradually died out. More and more African men lived with their families in townships on the edge of the industrial centres.

But agriculture remained the mainstay of the country's economy. In 1941 the National Resources Board was set up to plan major schemes such as irrigation projects, crop research, and education in modern techniques. By damming rivers, building irrigation schemes, planting windbreaks, encouraging ridging, terracing and the use of fertilisers more land was brought under the plough and intensively farmed areas were protected from becoming sterile or eroded. The backbone of the economy was European farming. Government sponsored marketing boards helped the farmers to distribute their maize, wheat, meat and vegetables to the growing

296

centres of population. Tobacco continued to be the principal export. Production rose rapidly, particularly when large trade agreements were made with Britain and Australia in 1948 and 1949 respectively.

Federation funds made possible new irrigation schemes in the 1950s. Projects were set in motion for the damming of the Sabi and other rivers in the south-east. This made profitable farming on the low veldt possible for the first time. Not only were European plantations such as the Triangle Sugar Estates established in this area; thousands of Africans were also able to make a living from the soil.

Government activities and the enterprise of chiefs and farmers led to a growing prosperity in the reserves. Subsistence farmers consolidated their holdings, drained and ridged their land and discovered that they had a surplus for sale. Compulsory measures such as the dipping of cattle, destocking and the consolidation of holdings (introduced in the Native Land Husbandry Act, 1951) caused some resentment but resulted in better farming. Educational facilities for Africans were improved. By 1963 most African children had some primary education and there were nearly 7,000 in secondary schools. Urban overcrowding forced the authorities to provide better housing for Africans but dwellings in European areas (as the towns were) were only available for workers; men who were out of work or too old to work had to return to the reserves. Wages improved over the years. In 1954 the average African wage was £67 a year. By 1963 this had risen to £120. Africans who could accept the social and economic changes imposed by the government certainly improved their standard of living in the years following the Second World War.

Settlers certainly developed any African country in which they established themselves. In Rhodesia their achievements were outstanding. And whether they intended it or not, the advances they pioneered also spilled over to Africans. What is harder to judge or to weigh is the personal humiliation, the sense of inferiority that many Africans suffered at the hands of Europeans. The Africans were made to feel inferior, the laws treated them as inferior and enforced their subordination. Person-to-person relationships, colour bars, segregation, all were indignities which the African had to bear. To be called 'boy', to have to stand in queues and let any white person go ahead, signs 'for whites only', these things scarred and angered Africans, especially the educated ones. For these reasons settlers have to be judged not only by their economic achievements but also by their moral and human values.*

* P. Duignan and L. H. Gann (eds.), *Colonialism in Africa*, Vol. 2 (C.U.P., 1970), p. 135.

Political development 1940–53

Now we must turn our attention to political affairs. There are two important themes running through the history of British Central Africa in these years. One is the growth of African nationalism and its challenge to white domination. The other is the movement of the three territories towards closer union. After 1953 these two themes merged completely but it is possible for us to consider them separately in the years leading up to federation.

(1) Northern Rhodesia

At the beginning of the Second World War white settlers were well entrenched in the Northern Rhodesian legislature. The Legislative Council consisted of nine official members and nine settler-elected unofficials. They fought hard against any policies which, they felt, might weaken white supremacy or control. But often they were up against British governments and their representatives who believed that African interests should be paramount. The objective of the settlers was self-government or 'responsible government' as they called it and gradually they seemed to be moving towards this goal. In 1945 they achieved an elected majority on the Legislative Council. In 1947 the Governor ceased to preside over the Council, his place being taken by a Speaker. In 1948 three unofficials joined the Executive Council and in 1953 they were given ministerial posts. A settler-controlled autonomy seemed just around the corner.

But African representation in the legislature was also taking place. In 1948 the first two Africans took their seats in the Legislative Council and, in addition, two unofficials were appointed to represent African interests. By 1953 the number of African members had risen to four. But the white minority had nothing to fear. Very few Africans had the vote, which was restricted to adult British subjects (almost all Africans were classed as 'Protected Persons') with an income of over £200 a year. Most Europeans were more than content to keep things that way as was indicated by the fate of Mr S. Gore-Browne. He was a settler of long standing, had been a member of the Legislative Council since 1935 and had been the leader of the unofficials most of that time. But he lost popularity when he began to argue for faster African advancement. He was ousted from leadership by Mr R. Welensky who made no secret of his attitude towards ninety-nine per cent of Northern Rhodesia's population:

We believe that the African should be given more say in the running of his country, as and when he shows his ability to contribute more to the general good, but we must make it clear that even when that day comes, in a hundred or two hundred years' time, he can never hope to dominate the partnership.*

At local-government level some Africans were gaining experience of administration and politics. The powers of the Native Authorities and Urban Advisory Councils were gradually increased. In 1947 all African Town Management Boards were set up to administer local government in the Copperbelt townships. Urban courts were established for the trial of minor offenders in accordance with African customary law. But there was very little opportunity for radical African opinion to make itself felt through any of these bodies.

As time went by it became obvious to the white minority that Britain would be unlikely to grant self-government under European rule. The break-up of the empire began in 1947 and it was known that Britain wanted to divest herself of colonial burdens – but only on terms of handing over power to democratically elected majority governments. In 1957 Gold Coast became the first African colony to gain self-government – under black leadership. The future looked bleak for Northern Rhodesia's white population. Already tensions were growing on the Copperbelt as educated Africans demanded access to skilled and semi-skilled jobs. Welensky seized upon the idea of union with Southern Rhodesia as a means of creating a strong white front. This was by no means a new idea, as we shall see. The British government was not deceived by Welensky's insistence on the economic advantages of amalgamating the two Rhodesias. He therefore shifted his ground and began to press, not for amalgamation, but for a federation, which would include Nyasaland as well. This idea was put forward at a settler conference at Victoria Falls in 1949. Welensky argued that a federal constitution would seem to contain greater safeguards for Africans and might, therefore, prove more acceptable to the British government.

It was the movement towards federation which provoked a response from educated Africans leading to effective political activity. The roots of nationalism are to be found in the welfare societies which were set up by workers in various parts of the Copperbelt from about 1942. They were associations for the discussion of local grievances and for negotiation with mine owners and local authorities. Because they were successful they grew in number and in scope. In 1946 representatives of many groups met in Lusaka to form the Federation

*Quoted by B. S. Khrishnamurthy in an article entitled *Central African Federation and African Nationalism in Zambia* (presented at the Workshop on the Teaching of Central and East African History, Lusaka, 1970).

299

of Welfare Societies. The Federation immediately interested itself in a wide range of subjects and two years later reconstituted itself as the Northern Rhodesia Congress, an openly political organisation. From the beginning it opposed ideas of amalgamation and federation.

Like political groups we have considered in other African countries the N.R.C. had a basic weakness – it represented the small class of urban and educated Africans and had little contact with the mass of the people. Nevertheless the movement of which the N.R.C. was a part was sufficiently active and successful to provoke a response from the government. They created African Provincial Councils. On these councils sat Native Authorities, representatives of Urban Advisory Councils and of the welfare societies. In 1946 an African

Harry Nkumbula.

Representative Council was established to co-ordinate the views of regional councils. This purely advisory body was sponsored by government as a moderate, 'respectable' African organisation which would, hopefully, satisfy the people's need for political expression. Gradually the N.R.C. became more radical, more active and more widely based. In 1950 a group of young men in Ndola formed themselves into an Anti-Federation Committee. They published broadsheets and a pamphlet, *A Cast Against Federation*. They were brought within the N.R.C. movement. In the following year the leadership of the Congress was taken over by a well-known, fiery opponent of Federation, Harry Nkumbula. An ex-teacher who had studied at Makerere College (Uganda) and in Britain, Nkumbula had already

Simon Kapwepwe.

301

Kenneth Kaunda.

fallen foul of the government because of his outspoken views. In 1949 he had signed with Hastings Banda a memorandum condemming the Victoria Falls Conference proposals. In 1951 the N.R.C. changed its name to the Northern Rhodesia African National Congress. It forged strong links with other bodies representative of African opinion, such as the trade union movement and the African Representative Council. It won support in the rural areas, partly through migrant labourers who were constantly passing to and fro between the towns and the Trust Lands and partly as a result of enthusiastic local organisers. Such organisers were Simon Kapwepwe and Kenneth Kaunda. The latter returned to his home area in Chinsali to become organising secretary for the Northern Province. He travelled hundreds of miles on his bicycle addressing meetings and whipping up support.

As British Central Africa moved closer to Federation despite
mounting opposition from the majority of the people involved the

activities of Congress became more fervent. At an emergency meeting in 1952 a Supreme Action Council was set up with wide powers to organise African protest. Protest meetings were held throughout Northern Rhodesia and a delegation was sent to London. For the first time African leaders were heard calling for self-government and majority rule. Prominent members of Congress were arrested. In 1953, shortly before the federal constitution came into effect, Nkumbula made an eleventh hour bid to halt the proceedings. He publicly burned the British White Paper on Federation, called for a national strike and two days of national prayer and petitioned the queen. It all came to nothing, but the immense energy which had been roused by the Federation scheme was now channelled into the movement which was to result in independence and democracy.

The trade union movement began in Northern Rhodesia in these years. In a country so dependent on industrial production from a few major centres the workers were in a strong position. We have already seen the appalling results of the strikes of 1935 and 1940. The workers were not crushed by the suppression of those outbreaks but they realised the need for proper organisation. In 1947 they obtained help from the Labour Party in Britain. The result was several unions of which the most powerful was the Northern Rhodesia African Mineworkers' Union. Their strength was tested in 1952 when a three-week Copperbelt strike was successful in gaining substantial wage increases.

(2) Nyasaland

The political situation in Nyasaland was much simpler. There was no powerful settler group and as a result there was little change in the governmental structure for many years. All members of the Legislative Council were nominated and, until 1948, all were Europeans (one member, always a missionary, was appointed to look after African intersts). In 1948 two African members were admitted to the council, which was now composed of nine officials and nine unofficials. Another African joined the council in 1953 but the political life of the protectorate continued to be dominated by civil servants. The aims of the settlers were the same as the aims of the white community in Northern Rhodesia. As their leader had said some years before, 'The introduction of indirect rule in this country might prove a bar or stumbling block to any union with the Rhodesias. Now that Union ... is what many of us in this country are working to procure. We would like to see one strong British territory stretching as far through Central Africa as possible. The feeling is that the   303 interest of Nyasaland is really more akin to the Rhodesias than to Tanganyika Territory.'*

But the settlers were a very small minority and the situation in Nyasaland was always different from the situation in the Rhodesias. The protectorate was regarded by most Africans as a haven of security in a white man's world. Migrant labourers knew that Nyasaland was economically backward but they also knew that there was less racial discrimination there. Educated Africans and Africans with any experience of conditions in other white-dominated territories were determined not to let their land go the way of the Rhodesias.

Africans played an increasingly important part in local government. In 1944 Provincial Councils were set up and two years later a Protectorate Council came into being to co-ordinate the work of the Provincial Councils. Africans served on these bodies and more and more were also taken into the civil service at various levels. In 1950 Urban Advisory Committees came into existence to help with the work of local government in the towns.

The system of incorporating traditional rulers and a missionary trained élite in a European-style government had its critics. This is what one African had to say about the system of native courts:

> It functions according to European principles of justice and not in accordance with African ideas ... Every litigant has to pay the cost of summons to have his case heard. Fines are imposed in practically every case. This leaves people to say openly that these courts are instruments of the European government instituted to extract yet more money from the African. These courts have become increasingly jealous of their sole right to hear cases and settle disputes, removing these functions from the village headman which form the basis of his prestige and privilege.†

It was this sort of feeling which led to the foundation of the Nyasaland African Congress in 1944 which sought to work on a protectorate-wide basis, uniting the efforts of all those working for improved conditions. For many years Congress confined itself to working for such objectives as better educational facilities and more African representation on the Legislative Council.

It was the threat of federation which gave the Congress movement a new cause and a new urgency. In 1951 Congress made its position quite clear:

> We oppose Federation not only because of the oppressive racialistic policies of Southern Rhodesia ... We oppose Federation because we are a *Protectorate*. Our country is not a colony for European settlement as

---

* Quoted in A. J. Wills, *op.cit.*, p. 282.

† Manser Bartlett in a report to the Legislative Council, 1960. Quoted by B. S. Khrishnamurthy, *Colonial Administration in Malawi*, p. 12.

Southern Rhodesia is. That is why we cannot accept the partnership of Europeans. Our political goal and the political goal of Europeans are poles apart. Our is African self-government (that is, government by ourselves) and the establishment of a sovereign state when we have passed through our tutelage. To obtain that self-government and sovereignty we must develop without let or hindrance. Our destiny is like that of our fellow Africans in the Gold Coast, Nigeria and the Sudan. The goal of the European settlers is the establishment of a Central African Dominion, like South Africa, Australia, New Zealand and Canada, in which they will have an imperium over the African people, doing with them as they please, and denying them equal political and economic rights.*

(3) Southern Rhodesia

By 1939 the white minority in Southern Rhodesia had gained almost complete self-government and had already moved far along the path of separate racial development. It was unlikely that they would want or welcome further political change and, indeed, there was very little in the years before Federation. Huggins and the United Party grew in strength, particularly as a result of a new wave of immigration after the war. The Rhodesia Party disappeared but a challenge was presented in the 1940s by the Labour Party and by a newly formed Liberal Party, which attracted the support of the Afrikaner community and wanted to push the country into closer association with South Africa. In 1948 the United Party won a major election success by a policy of loyalty to the Crown, retaining English as the only official language and closer relationships with the other British Central African territories. Dislike of Northern Rhodesia's liberal racial policies was overwhelmed by fear of being swallowed up by South Africa.

African political activity was expressed in different ways. Among the Ndebele there was still a group working for the creation of an independent Ndebele state. In Shonaland there was an ever growing number of breakaway churches. The Southern Rhodesia African National Congress catered for the minority of educated Africans. The I.C.U. represented some of the African industrial workers. There was no means of uniting the activities of these various groups, all of which were striving for different aims. There were no local government councils which could have given Africans a forum for airing their views and a means of gaining experience in administration.

But new pressures in the post-war years led to new expressions of discontent. White immigration led to an increase in the size of towns.

*Congress Paper, *Why we Oppose Federation*, quoted by A. J. Wills, *op.cit.*, p. 285.

Areas where African townships stood were required for European housing. So the Africans were forced back to the reserves, many of which were already becoming over-populated. Immense hardship resulted in both urban and rural areas. In 1945 the railway workers at Bulawayo went on strike and succeeded in obtaining improved pay and conditions. Three years later there was a more widespread strike of workers in Salisbury and Bulawayo. Behind these outbreaks were organisations like the Reformed Industrial and Commercial Workers' Union of Charles Mzingeli, Congress and the African Voice Association of Benjamin Burumbo. These groups also protested against the Land Husbandry Act of 1951 which stopped the communal ownership of land and thus took away the means of livelihood from many Africans. Such successes as African movements gained were, however, small. Before Federation there was little sign of an effective nationalist movement in Southern Rhodesia.

The Central African Federation 1953–63

The idea of amalgamating British territory in Central Africa was not a new one in the 1950s. It had been suggested in the early 1930s. As far as the ruling groups in the three territories were concerned federation had both economic and political advantages. The economic resources of the Rhodesias and Nyasaland were in many ways complementary; Northern Rhodesia had industry, Southern Rhodesia had agricultural produce to offer and Nyasaland was a supplier of manpower. Politically the white minorities saw in Federation a means of combining their strength against the African masses, of achieving more independence from London, and of establishing a strong British state as a counterbalance to Afrikaner-dominated South Africa. Federation was an attractive proposition to the British government, particularly after the Second World War when Britain was trying to disentangle herself from the empire. It seemed to be one way of creating an economically stable Central African state in which all inhabitants could enjoy a reasonable standard of living. But from the beginning there was African opposition to the federal idea. A British government commission in 1938 recommended that the three territories should be drawn closer together but not until the people could be persuaded to accept closer union.

During the Second World War the governments of the three territories had to work closely together on a number of issues and after 1945 this co-operation was continued with the setting up of the Central African Council, an advisory body for co-ordinating economic policy. Godfrey Huggins in Southern Rhodesia and Roy

Welensky in Northern Rhodesia were both in favour of closer union and the latter suggested at the Victoria Falls Conference (1949) that the British Labour government, which was doubtful about complete amalgamation of the territories, might agree to a federal constitution. This scheme was supported by some powerful international businessmen who saw the opportunity of making a great deal of money out of Central Africa. The Labour government was unconvinced but in 1951 the Conservative party came to power in Britain and the official attitude changed completely. A conference of officials from the territories was held in London almost immediately. This was followed by the Second Victoria Falls Conference (September 1951). The British Colonial Secretary invited to this conference representatives of all bodies interested in the future of British Central Africa but the meeting was boycotted by the leaders of African opinion in the two protectorates. These leaders, as we have seen, made their own protests, rejecting the whole idea of federation. They were ignored. The Second Victoria Falls Conference worked out a constitution which, with minor changes, was put to the electorates of the territories in 1953. The Legislative Councils of Northern Rhodesia and Nyasaland passed the necessary legislation despite African opposition. In Southern Rhodesia the overwhelmingly white electorate approved Federation in a referendum. The new constitution came into force in October 1953.

The avowed object of the Federation's constitution was the establishment of multi-racial society. Liberals saw it as an experiment in racial partnership which would permit full 'development' of the African peoples while at the same time preserving the position of the white man. The Federal Parliament consisted of thirty-five members, six of whom (two from each territory) had to be African and three of whom were Europeans appointed specifically to safeguard African interests. The representation by territory was: Southern Rhodesia 17; Northern Rhodesia 11; Nyasaland 7. Clearly the dominant views were those of the Rhodesian whites. The Federal Executive was a committee appointed by the prime minister from among the members of parliament. The important subject of the franchise was not fully considered by the framers of the constitution. Elections to the first Federal Parliament were based on the existing franchises of the three territories. No provision was made for extending voting rights to more Africans. The Federal Parliament had authority over most matters which affected the Federation as a whole, such as economic development, communications, defence, customs and health. The territorial administrations retained control of the police, local government, housing, mines and 'African Affairs'. As a safeguard against racial discrimination an African Affairs Board was set up as a permanent committee of the Federal Parliament.

Before the Federation had been in existence very long two facts became obvious. The first was that 'partnership' meant the indefinite domination of black by white. The colour bar remained in existence. African school enrolment was not significantly increased. Few better jobs were made available. Only after a great deal of pressure from the few Africans in the Federal Parliament was more technical education made available for Africans. Meanwhile Federation had given a fresh boost to European immigration and it seemed to many Africans that their country had become even more of a white man's land. The second fact was that Southern Rhodesia was gaining more from Federation than its partners. Salisbury was chosen as the site for the Federal Parliament. Many foreign companies which came to begin operations in Central Africa also made their headquarters in Salisbury. We have already seen how Federation funds were used to establish many new industries in Southern Rhodesia and how pressure from south of the Zambezi led to the resiting of the proposed dam and hydro-electric scheme at Kariba. Since most of the Federation's income was earned on the Copperbelt there was increasing discontent in Northern Rhodesia at the unfair distribution of funds. It was estimated that between 1953 and 1959 membership of the Central African Federation cost Northern Rhodesia £50,000,000.

African political activity suffered a setback with the failure of the Congress movement in the two protectorates to prevent Federation. Only as frustration at continuing discrimination rose did African political groups recover their strength. In 1954 the Northern Rhodesian legislature approved the Moffat Resolutions, one of which stated that 'every lawful inhabitant of Northern Rhodesia has the right to progress according to his character, qualifications, training, ability and industry without distinction of race, colour or creed'. The resolution was not acted on. The following year the Congress had to organise urban demonstrations to gain a partial cancellation of the colour bar in shops and post offices. Race Conciliation Advisory Boards were set up to investigate cases of racial discrimination.

Small changes in central government representation did little to satisfy African political leaders. In 1957 the number of African members in the Federal Parliament was raised to fifteen but the size of the assembly was also raised to sixty, so that Africans still only held a quarter of the seats. African-nominated membership of the territorial parliaments was also increased slightly. In 1956 Welensky became Federal prime minister, pledged to the ideal of independence for the Federation. Welensky's racial views were well known and the fear of perpetual white domination was now very real. In 1957 Britain handed over more powers to the Federal Parliament. The prospect of independence introduced a new urgency into the political life of British Central Africa. Racialism took over. Moderate compromises proved unacceptable to either side. Plans in Southern Rhodesia for the establishment of a multi-racial university college and the opening of certain clubs and hotels to educated Africans aroused immense, though unsuccessful, opposition in the Salisbury legislature. Further moderate changes in the Northern Rhodesia Legislative Council (1958) were regarded as inadequate by Congress and Harry Nkumbula publicly burned the British government's White Paper outlining the new proposals. When Nkumbula nevertheless agreed to participate in the 1956 elections the Congress movement was split between moderates who supported him and radicals who formed the Zambia African National Congress (26 October 1958). Kenneth Kaunda was the President of Z.A.N.C. and Simon Kapwepwe its first Treasurer.

Vigorous nationalism was also emerging in the other territories. African political activity had declined for a few years in Southern Rhodesia as African leaders attempted to make the multi-racial experiment work. The new prime minister, Garfield Todd, was a moderate who wanted to extend the rights of Africans and to gain the co-operation of their leaders. Africans were even welcomed to join the United Rhodesia Party. Todd counted on African support because his policies angered many of the whites. But African grievances, especially over the Land Husbandry Act, were growing more serious and radical political leaders who began to appear in the late 1950s found willing supporters among those who had been deprived of their land rights. In 1957 these radicals revived the Congress movement in Southern Rhodesia and elected Joshua Nkomo as their leader. The A.N.C. quickly gained the support of many sections of African opinion. Many moderates joined the movement after the downfall of Garfield Todd who, in 1957–8, was deserted by his government colleagues. Todd resigned and was replaced by Sir Edgar Whitehead, leader of the newly formed United Federal Party. Shortly after coming to power Whitehead declared a state of emergency in Southern Rhodesia, banned the A.N.C. and detained several of its leaders.

This was the official Southern Rhodesian response to a general worsening of the situation and, in particular, to events in Nyasaland. Here too, the coming of Federation had been followed in nationalist circles by a period of stunned inactivity. In 1953 there were riots in Cholo district provoked by agrarian grievances but these were officially condemned by Congress leaders. By 1955, however, more radical elements were gaining control of the Congress movement. 309

Henry Chipembere and Kanyama Chiume were the leading spokesmen in a new demand for self-government and universal suffrage. The new radicals campaigned throughout the country calling on people to honour the memory of earlier African champions such as John Chilembwe. The strength of the Congress grew rapidly. In July 1958 it gained the experienced leadership of an older man: Dr Hastings Banda returned to Nyasaland after an absence of forty years. He immediately began to make extreme demands – universal suffrage and an African majority on the Legislative Council. In December 1958 he attended the first Pan-African Congress at Accra. As well as being inspired and encouraged by his contact there with other African leaders, he made an agreement with Kaunda and other Central African delegates that he would help to break up the Federation. During his absence irresponsible elements within the Nyasaland African National Congress turned to wild demonstrations and violence. In March 1959 the government declared a state of emergency, banned Congress and imprisoned Banda and other nationalist leaders. At about the same time a similar sequence of events in Northern Rhodesia led to the banning of Z.A.N.C. and the detention of Kaunda and his colleagues.

Imprisonment and persecution only strengthened the nationalist movement. New parties were formed to replace the ones which had been banned – the Malawi Congress in Nyasaland, the National Democratic Party in Southern Rhodesia and the United National Independence Party in Northern Rhodesia. In the two protectorates the aims of the nationalist movements were identical – majority rule and an end to Federation. Across the Zambezi the N.D.P. concentrated more on local problems and opposition to the new Southern Rhodesian constitution.

In Northern Rhodesia Kaunda was released in January 1960 and took over the leadership of U.N.I.P. The party was well organised throughout the territory and was pledged by its president to the achievement of its objectives by non-violent means. However, passions were now roused and there were frequent clashes between U.N.I.P. members and government forces. Kaunda continually pressed the government to introduce constitutional reforms in Northern Rhodesia which would lead to majority rule and thus to secession from the Federation. In 1961 the Colonial Office proposed a new constitution which would lead quickly to African control. Welensky and the federalists were furious. They brought such pressure to bear on the British government that that government went back on its word. New proposals were put forward more favourable to the Europeans. Now it was the turn of U.N.I.P. to react. Despite the moderating

Independence comes to Zambia, October 1964.

efforts of the leadership violent clashes and bloodshed occurred. The British government realised that the Northern Rhodesian majority could not be pressed into supporting continued white rule. An acceptable compromise was worked out and elections were held in October 1962. The indecisive result showed that the new arrangement was a failure and the work of constitution-drafting had to begin all over again. It was another year before a workable constitution was devised. Elections were held in January 1964 and U.N.I.P. won fifty-five out of the seventy-five seats. Kaunda became prime minister of Northern Rhodesia's first African-controlled government. In October of the same year Northern Rhodesia became fully independent as the Republic of Zambia.

But Nyasaland was the first British Central African territory to gain independence. It became obvious to the colonial government in 1960 that no peace or progress could be achieved as long as they refused to negotiate with Banda. In April he was released and shortly afterwards he led a delegation to London for talks with the colonial secretary. The result was a constitution providing for the election of all the twenty-eight unofficial members of the Legislative Council. The franchise was changed so that most of the members would be African. Elections held under this constitution in August 1961 led to a sweeping victory for the Malawi Congress Party. The new assembly settled responsibly to its work and, though Banda remained unmoved in his opposition to Federation, Britain was soon planning with him the next steps towards internal self-government. In January 1963 Dr Banda became prime minister and over the next eighteen months more and more authority was handed over to him. On 6 July 1964 Nyasaland became the independent Republic of Malawi.

Self-determination in the two protectorates inevitably involved the break-up of the Federation. Let us see just how this came about. In 1960 the Federation constitution was due for review. To prepare for this a royal commission headed by Lord Monckton was sent to

312   *Malawi independence.*

Central Africa in February. It gathered opinions from all interested parties and made the following recommendations: (a) the Federation should stay in being because of the economic advantage it brought to member countries; (b) the Federation could only continue if African hostility towards it was overcome; (c) this would mean major constitutional changes in favour of African representation; (d) it would also mean a cancellation of Southern Rhodesia's racial policies; (e) the new constitution should place more authority in the hands of territorial governments; (f) member countries should be allowed to secede from Federation after an agreed period of time. The commission thought it necessary to make the last of these recommendations because of the strong anti-Federation feelings of nationalists north of the Zambezi. It was hoped that its inclusion might induce Banda and Kaunda to give a reformed Federation a fair trial.

The Federal Review Conference met in December 1960. It could not reach agreement. The views of the various groups concerned were irreconcilable. It was decided to postpone the conference until after the two northern territories had gained self-government. This left the initiative with Kaunda, Banda and their supporters. Banda made it abundantly clear that he would ask to secede from the Federation as soon as his country achieved self-government. In December 1962 the British government agreed to allow Nyasaland to secede. U.N.I.P. was also committed to secession and the majority of Southern Rhodesian whites did not favour continued association with states ruled by black men. Reluctantly, therefore, the British government agreed to put an end to the federal experiment and, after 31 December 1963, the Central African Federation ceased to exist.

It remains only to see what was happening in Southern Rhodesia in these years. Whitehead's United Federal Party was pledged to the continuance of Federation and could not afford to continue black–white confrontation. In 1960 most of the nationalist detainees were released and the government began to introduce legislation designed to deal with some of the Africans' grievances. A large programme of African education was set in motion. Some aspects of the colour bar vanished. Schemes for improved African urban housing were introduced. Restrictions on African trading were reduced. It was even suggested that the Land Apportionment Act (see above, p. 224) might be repealed. These policies failed in two ways: they did not win the approval of African nationalists, and they alarmed a large section of the white population who feared that the 'disintegration of civilisation' which they thought they could see occurring in other parts of the continent as the colonial tide receded was about to occur in Southern Rhodesia. 313

In 1961 a new constitution was discussed at a conference in London and subsequently put to the people of the colony. It provided for a complex system of voting on two rolls which would, while ensuring white control of the legislature, considerably increase black representation. The proposals were rejected by the N.D.P. which organised vigorous anti-constitution demonstrations. Whitehead responded by banning the party. In 1962 the party re-formed under the name of the Zimbabwe African People's Union (Z.A.P.U.) and continued to oppose the new constitution. The administration refused to regard the new party as anything other than a potentially dangerous band of politically immature troublemakers. This lack of understanding provoked incidents, many of which were violent. In 1962 Z.A.P.U. was banned. In the following year a split occurred in the Nationalist ranks which led to the formation of the Zimbabwe African National Union (Z.A.N.U.), led by Sithole.

Meanwhile elections under the new constitution had occurred in December 1962. The white electorate rejected Whitehead and his concessions to Africans. Instead it pinned its hopes on the right-wing Rhodesia Front, led by W. Field. The nationalists boycotted the

Mr Wilson, the British prime minister, and Mr Smith on board H.M.S.
Fearless for talks aimed at breaking the constitutional deadlock in Rhodesia.

elections, so all the African members elected were moderates prepared to co-operate fully with their white masters. The new government wanted independence, like the other ex-members of the Federation – independence under minority rule. This the British government would not tolerate. But the mood of Rhodesia's whites grew more determined. In 1964 the new prime minister, I. Smith, organised a referendum which came down heavily in favour of independence. He tried to use this evidence of support to persuade the British government into giving him what he wanted. But, after several meetings and attempts at negotiation Britain's leaders stood firm on the principle of 'no independence before majority rule'. In November 1965 Rhodesia, having failed to get Britain to grant independence, simply took it in a unilateral declaration of independence (U.D.I.). With the support of the white population, the control of the police and armed forces and with all 'militant' nationalists in exile or behind bars, Smith's government was in a strong position. Britain certainly could not risk a prolonged and bloody conflict. Rhodesia was not recognised as a nation by any other state. It has no accredited diplomatic representatives in any foreign capital. It is banned from many international sporting and cultural activities. It was repeatedly condemned in the United Nations. International trade sanctions were imposed on it. But it was supported by the Republic of South Africa and many nations avoided sanctions. It was the determination and armed resistance of the African people that paved the way for the independence of Zimbabwe in 1979.

22. The white-dominated South

While the other states of southern and Central Africa were achieving independence the rulers of Angola, Mozambique and South Africa were bracing themselves against the mounting tide of African nationalism. In this last chapter we shall see how these alien régimes kept themselves in power. First we shall consider the Portuguese territories and then South Africa. Finally we shall see how the High Commission territories achieved independence

Portuguese Africa

(1) Economic development

President Salazar's government maintained a policy of regarding its African territories as provinces of Portugal. In economic terms this began to pay off in the 1940s and 1950s. Portugal was one of the few European countries which remained neutral during the Second World War. Though still a poor nation it did not suffer the same economic hardships as its neighbours in the immediate post-war years. Portugal was thus able to begin moving towards its goal of complete integration with its colonies. The economic recovery of those colonies was based on four foundations: protective tariff barriers, European immigration, development projects, and minimum expenditure on social services.

All imported goods not made in Portugal or Portuguese colonies were subject to very heavy duties. Similarly goods passing through on the Beira and Benguela railways were heavily charged. For many years the governments' principal income came from import and export duties. The policy also had the advantage of assuring a ready market in the colonies for Portuguese goods. Foreign companies operating in Angola and Mozambique were heavily taxed and Salazar followed for many years a policy of discouraging foreign investment. One reason for this was his fear of his isolationist and repressive policies being weakened by the presence of more liberal elements in the colonies. The tariff barriers helped to make Angola and Mozambique financially stable but only at the cost of considerable hardship to black and white communites alike. As one visitor to Angola complained: 'The cost of living is the greatest absurdity I encountered on my Angolan trip ... being, without exaggeration, 100 per cent higher than in the metropolis.'*

After the war the Portuguese government was at last able to interest large numbers of its people in settling in Africa. The rise in immigration was quite astonishing as the following table shows.

European Population of Portuguese Africa

	1930	1940	1950	1960
Angola	30,000	44,000	78,000	170,000
Mozambique	18,000	27,500	48,000	85,000

Most of the newcomers were poor, unskilled peasants who had little to lose by leaving Portugal. Many of them went to the towns but others were set up by the government in *colonatos*, farming settlements where each man had his own house, land and stock but shared other facilities with his neighbours. Importing uneducated Portuguese peasants obviously created clashes with the unskilled African workforce but the government saw it as a vital part of their plan to 'people Africa with Europeans who can assure the stability of sovereignty and promote the "Portuguesation" of the native population .

The colonial rulers were now able to devote money to projects they had not been able to afford before. The Portuguese National Development Plan was announced in 1953. The colonies' development was to be based on a series of six-year plans and hundreds of millions of pounds were to be spent on communications, improvements and agricultural schemes. In Mozambique a dam was built across the Limpopo at Caniçado which provided water to irrigate over 50,000 hectares of land, as well as carrying a new railway running from Rhodesia to Lourenço Marques. Other dams were built to provide hydro-electric power for Lourenço Marques and Beira. Agricultural settlements were established in a number of places. Southern Angola was the scene of considerable activity. Moçamedes harbour was improved and its railway link extended further inland. An irrigation

---

* Quoted by J. Duffy in *Portuguese Africa*, p. 333.

Cabora Bassa dam.

and hydro-electric project was begun at Matala. These and other irrigation and communications developments were designed to serve new *colonatos* in southern Angola.

While money was being spent on projects likely to show financial return expenditure on social services was kept to a minimum. In 1957, for instance, the government of Angola had a total budget for the province of £30,000,000 from which it budgeted a mere £56,000 for African housing. Government, like private companies, paid extremely low wages to African workers. The average industrial wage for Africans throughout the period was about £5 a month, nor was it increased to keep pace with rising prices. Educational facilities were meagre. This had two advantages for the régime: it saved money and it prevented the emergence of a politically conscious African élite. State schools were only set up in cities and towns and were almost exclusively for Portuguese and *assimilado* children. Some mission schools existed in the rural areas to provide a very elementary education. Secondary education was only provided for Africans in mission boarding schools where the fees were higher than Africans could afford. In 1959 only forty-one Africans entered secondary schools in Mozambique. It is no surprise to learn that approximately ninety-three per cent of the population could not read or write. Health services also were grossly inadequate. The small band of trained medical staff only served the European population. In the 1950s some clinics were set up in rural areas and a rudimentary inoculation service was started to prevent epidemics of serious diseases. By the mid-1960s the African population and even the bulk of the European population was poor and lacked many of the amenities of modern civilised life. Thousands of Africans managed to improve their standard of living by taking better paid seasonal jobs in South Africa and the Rhodesias. Portuguese authorities tried to restrict emigration but by 1950 there were as many as 1,500,000 Africans from Portuguese colonies who were seeking employment elsewhere.

(2) Political development

Throughout the period the dictatorial government of Dr Salazar continued to regard Portugal's African territories as extensions of the 'motherland', rather than colonies. The government was determined to resist African nationalism, United Nations' pressure, world opinion and any force that seemed intent on turning Portugal out of Africa.

> We are in Africa and it is our duty to stay there, for ourselves, for the West to which we belong, for the peoples which have been entrusted to us and which have mingled with us in the same moral unity.*

Assimilation was a vital part of the theory of 'greater Portugal'. There was to be no colour bar. All races were to mix freely. As the native became 'civilised' he would become a freely participating member in a multi-racial society. But theory and practice were poles apart. There were two main reasons for this. First of all the African was regarded (as he always had been) as a provider of labour. Secondly the influx of immigrants created a large settler community which kept itself separate and aloof from the *indigena*.

Every African adult male was obliged to work for six months in every year, either for himself or for someone else. In addition to this legal requirement was the need to earn money to pay taxes. Slavery and forced labour had, in theory, disappeared from Portuguese colonies and all free labour was contract labour which a man entered by his own choice and on negotiated terms. In fact the pass system invol-

---

* D. Salazar (1960) quoted by J. Duffy in *Colonialism in Africa 1870–1960*, ed. P. Duignan and L. H. Gann, Vol. 2. (C.U.P., 1970), p. 190.

ved virtual slavery. Every adult African male had to carry a pass which showed, among other things, how much work he had done. If it was not enough he could be made to work. Under these conditions employers were not under any pressure to offer fair wages. The Portuguese even managed to persuade themselves that this system was for the good of the *indigena*.

> It is necessary to inspire in the black the idea of work and of abandoning his laziness and depravity if we want to exercise a colonizing action and protect him. . . . If we want to civilize the native we must make him adopt as an elementary moral precept the notion that he has no right to live without working. A productive society is based on painful hard work. . . .
> It is to be an unenlightened Negrophile not to infuse the African with the absolute necessity for work.*

In addition to this so-called 'free' labour there was forced labour frequently imposed by the courts on those found guilty of criminal offences. There were different laws for black and white. The Europeans and the *assimilados* were governed by Portuguese law. The rest of the population was controlled by the *regime do indigenato*. This was merely a debased code of Portuguese law and bore no relationship whatsoever to African traditional law.

Perhaps the situation would not have been quite so bad for the Africans if the labour laws had been adhered to but after centuries of corruption and oppression it was impossible to force estate owners and minor officials to treat their employees properly. Chiefs were illegally forced to supply labourers. False charges were brought against Africans so that they could be found guilty and forced to work. Children were made to work. Contracts were illegally extended. Pay was withheld. Workers were beaten and ill-treated. Accommodation and work conditions were sub-standard. It is difficult to draw a distinction between this kind of life and slavery.

Many of the earlier administrators and settlers had not believed in a colour bar. There had, indeed, been a large number of mixed marriages. What the government had insisted on was not white racial superiority but white cultural superiority. To become an *assimilado* (and thus a full citizen) an African had to virtually renounce his traditional background and beliefs. He had to be able to speak, read and write Portuguese. He had to have a good job, educational qualifications and a good financial standing. It is not surprising that out of an approximate African population of 10,000,000 in the two colonies there were only about 35,000 *assimilados* in 1960.

*Quoted by J. Duffy in Duignan and Gann, *op. cit.*, Vol. 2, p. 183.

With the growth of immigration the attitude of the majority of Europeans towards Africans changed. The colour bar was applied in shops, restaurants, cinemas, clubs and hospitals. White and black residential areas were divided in towns. Farmers on the *colonatos* were forbidden to employ African labour. In the 1950s the government began to establish separate black *colonatos*, where 'approved' Africans and their families were provided with housing and land to be worked on a community basis. The men were exempted from the labour draft. The most successful of these settlements was at Caconda in south-western Angola where 700 families were settled on 1,200,000 hectares of land. Desirable as this tendency might have been from an economic point of view, it marked another stage in the movement towards separate development.

During the 1950s and 1960s criticism of the régime grew. Educated Africans, world opinion, the Afro-Asian bloc at the U.N. and liberals in Portugal condemned the racialist colonialism of the governments of Angola and Mozambique. There were two sides to the official reaction. On the one hand security was tightened to guard against rebellion. On the other hand reforms were carried out in the hope of disarming criticism. The secret police were introduced from Portugal in the late 1950s. 'Loyal' Africans were used as spies and informers to pry into the activities of suspected 'troublemakers'. Those reported on by the informers were arrested without trial, beaten, tortured, murdered, imprisoned or exiled. All this took place, of course, in secret as far as possible. Not so the 'liberal' measures introduced to impress outsiders rather than to set official policy moving in a new direction. In 1955 the Organic Law introduced a new local government system for rural areas in which approved Africans had some share. Local officials were urged to do all in their power to encourage racial harmony. Portuguese leaders took pains to establish close relations with the white rulers of South Africa and Rhodesia. As other colonies gained their independence Portugal prepared itself to seek out African nationalists and their supporters. As Salazar told the United Nations Assembly in 1960:

The Portuguese people are not going to suppose that the fate of millions of men, the order and peace of their way of life, the fruit of their work, the principles of civilization they have adopted, can be handed over to the emptiness of speeches at meetings and the anarchy of the so-called movements of liberation . . .

It would now be most unwise for us to innovate with practices, feelings, and concepts different from those which have been the secret of the work we have achieved and which are still the best safeguard for the future.

I do not see that we can rest in our labours nor can we have any other care than to hold with one hand our plough and with the other our sword . . . Great sacrifice will be called for, as well as the most absolute devotion, and if necessary, also the blood from our veins.*

(3) African nationalism: Angola

Blood was to be shed in Angola sooner than Dr Salazar expected. There were several groups of discontented Africans in the colony and despite Portuguese attempts at repression these groups grew until they were able to give violent expression to their grievances in 1961. There were three main areas where discontent was strongly felt. In the north disaffection was centred on the old Kongo kingdom. Strong traditionalist sentiments had not been destroyed by over three centuries of Portuguese control. The Kongolese were supported by their brothers across the border in the Belgian Congo. The real crisis began in 1955 when the government, as usual, installed its own nominee, Dom Antonio III, as the new king. The appointment was opposed by a Protestant group of Kongolese leaders which eventually set up a political party, the *União do Populacões de Angola* (U.P.A.). From this party there emerged a group which regarded itself as the true government and which operated from Congo Leopoldville. In northern Angola others were fanning the flames of resistance. Simão Toco was a religious separatist who preached the establishment of an African church and prophesied that God would overthrow the Portuguese régime. Toco's preaching was received favourably not only by Kongolese nationalists but by workers on the Portuguese-owned coffee estates. In 1960 world coffee prices slumped and many Angolan estate owners came close to ruin. The first economy to occur to most of them was not to pay their workers. This, of course, resulted in massive resentment among the African labourers. By the end of the year the situation was very tense.

The second nationalist group was to be found among the small class of *assimilados* and semi-educated Africans of Luanda and the surrounding region. Some had been educated in Portugal where, far from losing their cultural identity and becoming 'black Portuguese' they had met together in cultural or secret political groups. They were also in contact with radical political groups in Europe and Africa. In the 1950s secret groups were formed in and around Luanda and pamphlets were produced urging people to obtain education so that they would be better equipped for the coming struggle. In 1956 these groups united to form the Movimento de Libertacão de Angola (M.P.L.A.). Under the leadership of ardent, educated nationalists

* Quoted by J. Duffy in Duignan and Gann, *op. cit.*, p. 192.

*Armed Angolan rebels. They are examining the casing of a napalm bomb
dropped in a raid by the Portuguese.*

such as Amilcar Cabral and Agostinho Neto the M.P.L.A. developed a
programme and a rudimentary organisation. But the secret police
began to act against the movement in the late 1950s. In 1960 Neto
was arrested and deported, being held without trial first in the Cape
Verde Islands and later in Lisbon. When a sympathetic crowd
gathered at his parents' home the police opened fire, killing about
thirty people.

The third branch of the nationalist movement was not as well
defined. It consisted of small groups of educated and semi-educated
men in towns, schools and seminaries throughout southern and eastern Angola. The Ovimbundu were particularly active, many of them
being resentful of enforced cotton planting. One of the more extreme
of these groups was the Associacão Africana do Sul de Angola,
founded at Nova Lisboa in 1954. From the very beginning its leaders
were pledged to violent revolution. In 1957 surprise police raids on
Bailundo villages revealed a horde of arms and ammunition.

In 1960 most British, French and Belgian colonies in West Africa
and the Congo basin gained independence. At the same time there was
considerable international pressure on the Portuguese to relinquish
their overseas possessions. These facts, coupled with internal problems, led to a rash of nationalist outbursts in the early months of 1961. 323

Guerilla training in Tanzania.

First there was a strike among the Ovimbundu cotton workers, who were protesting against non-payment of wages. The employers called for government support in suppressing the demonstration. Troops were sent and weeks of violence and bloodshed – known as Maria's War – ensued. Thousands of Africans were killed and many more fled to Congo Leopoldville. While government forces were still occupied in the interior trouble broke out in Luanda. Early in February the M.P.L.A. organised a raid on a police post to free some prisoners. This alarmed the white population and racial warfare broke out in the streets. The situation in Luanda had scarcely cooled down before the worst conflict of all had broken out in the north. Beginning on 15 March with trouble on the coffee estates, fighting rapidly spread throughout the whole Kongo area. Many European settlers were murdered as undisciplined mobs gave vent to the pent-up fury of years. The movement had neither united leadership nor clear aims. After the initial shock the authorities were able to counter with massive land and air forces. In a campaign which far excelled in violence and brutality anything that the nationalists had done, the Portuguese used bombs and bullets to devastate large areas, killing an estimated 20,000 men, women and children in three months.

   If the Portuguese thought that such extreme measures would wipe out all trace of nationalist activity they seriously miscalculated. M.P.L.A. leaders fled to Leopoldville. Then, after clashing with the

324

U.P.A., they moved on to Brazzaville. In 1962 Neto escaped from Portugal and took up the leadership of the exiled M.P.L.A. In the Congo the Angolan nationalists trained guerilla groups and sent them into Angola to harass their enemies. The Portuguese found themselves with a continuing war on their hands.

African nationalism: Mozambique

The nationalist movement in Mozambique had many similarities with the movement in Angola. There were two early political groups, the União Democratico Nacional de Mozambique (UDENAMO) and the Makonde African National Union (M.A.N.U.).

Uria Simango was the founder of UDENAMO. He received an education at the hands of Protestant missionaries and became an ordained missionary himself in 1956. Before this he had already been in trouble with the authorities. In 1953 he and his father had been gaoled for a short time for criticising local administrators and refusing to pay taxes. Simango was a marked man. In 1959, finding constant police supervision intolerable, he moved to Rhodesia. In Salisbury he began missionary work among migrant labourers from his own country. It was there that he founded the secret UDENAMO, a group of fellow countrymen as dissatisfied as he was himself with the state of affairs in Mozambique. But Rhodesia was scarcely a safer place for African nationalists than Mozambique. In 1961 the threat of imminent arrest forced Simango to move to Tanganyika (Tanzania)* where he continued to organise UDENAMO from Dar es Salaam.

M.A.N.U. was a Makonde cultural and political organisation formed by 'Mzee' Lazaro Nkavandame in the late 1950s. It aimed to restore the political and cultural unity of the Makonde who lived on both sides of the Mozambique–Tanganyika border. For a while Nkavandamo's organisation worked in north-eastern Mozambique under the guise of a farming co-operative. But eventually the police began to probe too deeply into the organisation's activities. In 1960 M.A.N.U. leaders fled across the border and established a new headquarters in Dar es Salaam.

There were other small groups of nationalists throughout Mozambique but due to lack of organisation, inadequate educated membership and continual bullying and spying by the police they did not

---

*The name was unchanged until 1964 when Tanganyika merged with Zanzibar to form the Republic of Tanzania.

form a significant part of the nationalist movement. In Dar es Salaam the leaders of M.A.N.U. and UDENAMO were constantly in conflict and the nationalist movement was in danger of fizzling out in a welter of personal animosities. In 1962, thanks largely to pressure from President Nyerere of Tanganyika, a conference of Mozambique nationalists was held in Dar es Salaam. The result was a coalition of existing groups called the Frente de Libertacão de Mozambique (FRELIMO), under the presidency of Eduardo Mondlane. Mondlane was an educated Mozambican who had studied in the U.S.A. and worked for some years in the United Nations secretariat. He thus had considerable knowledge of world affairs as well as a good education and gifts of leadership.

The immediate aims of FRELIMO were threefold. First, the organisation recruited, trained and equipped guerillas to go into Mozambique and wage continuous war against the white rulers. Secondly, the leaders sought to inspire and educate Africans throughout the country. These secret nationalists would be able to help guerilla activities and would be the vital support of a future nationalist régime. Thirdly, there was the preparation of individuals for leadership in a future African administration. Individuals were selected for higher education, often overseas. Guerilla warfare began in 1964 and in the same year important secret bases for the training of freedom fighters were established on the island of Zanzibar. Arms and technical assistance came from Communist countries. FRELIMO made considerable progress in many areas and in 1968 it was able to hold its second congress within Niassa Province.

The movement had its setbacks. Many guerillas were killed or captured in combat. Some captives were tortured into revealing FRELIMO secrets. The Portuguese secret police were able to infiltrate the Fronte's organisation even in Dar es Salaam. Personal rivalries within the leadership continued and in 1968 Nkavandame defected to the Portuguese; in the following year Mondlane was assassinated. But the struggle continued. After the death of the Portuguese dictator Salazar a new official attitude was adopted towards the overseas territories. Troops and officials were hastily withdrawn. Guinea Bissau became independent in 1974. Mozambique and Angola followed a year later. But the lack of proper preparation for self-government led to a period of civil war in Angola. Stable government was established in 1976.

South Africa

(1) The Second World War and its effects

During the Second World War South African troops fought in Ethiopia and North Africa. Some units crossed to Italy and saw service in the European campaigns. The effect at home was to divide the Boers and the British more than ever. Some Afrikaner nationalists committed acts of sabotage and the Afrikaners as a whole gave their allegiance to extreme politicians. Hertzog was forced to resign and D. F. Malan became the leader of a new Afrikaner party, the Nasionale Party (N.P.). Afrikaner extremism flourished in the post-war atmosphere. There was a flood of new British immigrants. Throughout the British Empire subject peoples were beginning to demand freedom. Afrikaners feared that South Africa might move towards complete independence under some constitution which gave the coloured peoples political rights. That would be the end of the Afrikaner's 'cultural purity'. In 1948 racialist opinion rallied behind Malan and the N.P. won the parliamentary elections of that year with a small majority.

(2) Apartheid and the growth of Nationalist power.

The Nationalists now had two aims – to increase their parliamentary majority and to carry out their policy of *apartheid*. They pursued these aims ruthlessly and unscrupulously. *Apartheid*, though never closely defined, meant racial separation. The Nationalists planned to increase the process of forcing Africans into tribal areas. But there was always a basic difficulty about this policy: mine owners and industrialists relied on a supply of cheap African labour and their wives had grown accustomed to having African servants.

To strengthen their political position the H.N.P. put an immediate stop to British immigration. Furthermore, under the terms of the Citizenship Act (1949) new immigrants were barred from voting for five years instead of two years as had been the case previously. In predominantly Afrikaner areas children of the two white races were prevented from mixing in schools so that pure Afrikaner culture should not be diluted by British liberalism. Having increased its support among young people the H.N.P. reduced the voting age to 18 in 1958. In the same year South West Africa was incorporated in the Union (see below, p. 335). The immediate reason for this move was that it added six new members to the House of Assembly and four to the Senate. All of them were H.N.P. members. In 1953 South Africa took a further step away from Britain by restricting the use of 327

Father Trevor Huddleston.

the British national anthem and flag and by making constitutional changes which weakened the position of the British queen in South Africa.

The implementation of *apartheid* also began immediately. Below you will see a list of the major *apartheid* legislation introduced during the first decade of Nationalist rule.

1949	Prohibition of Mixed Marriages act
1950	Immorality Amendment Act
1950	Population Registration Act
1950	Group Areas Act
1951	Bantu Authorities Act
1951	Separate Representation of Voters Act
1953	Bantu Education Act

1956	South Africa Act Amendment Act
1959	Extension of University Education Act
1958	Promotion of Bantu Self-Government Act

The first two Acts in this list were designed to keep racial distinctions quite clear. Sexual relationships between people of different colour became illegal. The Population Registration Act was also designed to distinguish between the races. Everyone had to register and have his racial category established for the record. The Group Areas Act began the progressive separation of people into different residential areas by law. African, Indian and Cape Coloured people were forcibly moved into less attractive areas where housing was more expensive. This led to considerable suffering. Family businesses were forced to close and many people could not afford to buy houses in their allotted group areas. In 1955 thousands of Africans were moved, with great brutality, out of Sophiatown. An Anglican missionary, Trevor Huddleston, shocked the world with his account of this event in a book entitled *Naught For Your Comfort*.

It was in their attempts to deprive the Cape Coloured people of their political rights that the determination of the government was shown most clearly. In 1951 they pushed through Parliament the Separate Representation of Voters Act which removed the Cape Coloureds from the common voters' roll and allowed them to be represented by four Europeans. Some of the voters protested that the Act was a breach of the constitution and went to court to have it overruled. In March 1952 the Act was declared invalid. The government countered by making a new law, the High Court of Parliament Act, which declared that the two houses of parliament could form themselves into a court of appeal to pass final judgement on any case. In other words, the government, if it had a majority in both houses, could overrule any court decision. It immediately did so in the case of the Separate Representation of Voters Act. But the courts now challenged the High Court of Parliament Act. In 1953 and 1954 the government tried to get new representation acts on the statute book but failed to obtain a majority. In 1955 two new Acts were passed; one increased the number of Appellate Division judges needed to consider constitutional cases and the other almost doubled the membership of the Senate. These Acts had the effect of increasing Nationalist control of the parliament and the courts. Now the scene was set for the disenfranchisement of the non-white voters. The South Africa Act Amendment Act of 1956 removed the Cape Coloureds from the common roll.

In the field of education the Nationalists had two aims, the control of the minds of all young South Africans and the provision of different syllabuses for Africans so that they would always only be fitted for inferior positions. The Bantu Education act brought all African schools under state control. The missionaries, who ran most of the schools, were faced with a choice of submitting to government control or closing their schools down. By the Extension of University Education Act non-whites were excluded from European universities and special colleges were set up for non-whites. All teachers were now brought under close government control.

Because of the economic difficulties involved (the need for black labour in white areas and the cost of providing land for African settlement) full *apartheid* remained a mere dream. Some moves were however made towards the expansion of African reserves into semi-autonomous Bantu homelands. The Bantu Authorities Act set up government-approved chiefs as governors of the reserves. The Tomlinson Commission was set up to examine the best way of achieving full *apartheid*. It reported (in 1955) that the expansion of the existing reserves would be costly and would only accommodate about half of the African population. The Promotion of Bantu Self-Government Act four years later did two things: it abolished all African representation in parliament and it provided for the creation of Bantustans. These were to be semi-autonomous tribal areas with nominated

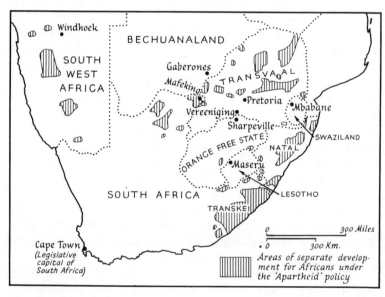

The Bantustans.

governments. Besides these tentative, positive measures there was an enormous amount of negative legislation extending the colour bar to every sphere of life.

With the disappearance of an independent judiciary and with the tight control of education the South African government had taken a large step away from democracy and towards totalitarianism. It became increasingly oppressive not only towards the non-white population but towards any who sympathised with or encouraged African aspirations. Behind the H.N.P. lay the *Broederbond*, a secret, fanatical Afrikaner organisation which worked by all possible means for the full implementation of Boer racialism. The secret police and paid informers were active everywhere and the Nationalists created new laws to undergird their power. The Suppression of Communism Act (1950) was a notorious measure which enabled the Minister of Justice to ban any organisation, censor any publication, dismiss or bar from office any person he declared to have connections with Communism. The Act was, of course, simply used to silence critics of the Nationalist régime. The Criminal Law Amendment Act (1953) provided severe penalties for anyone inciting another to break a law and the Public Safety Act of the same year empowered the government to proclaim a state of emergency and govern by decree whenever it considered it necessary.

(3) Opposition to the Nationalist government

The policies and actions of the Nationalists provoked considerable opposition from all sections of the non-white majority and from white liberals. There was also mounting criticism of the régime from newly independent African nations, from Europe, Asia, America – in fact from almost every other country. South Africa's racialist policies were frequently attacked in the U.N. Assembly. International sporting bodies such as the International Olympic Committee refused to accept from South Africa teams selected on the basis of *apartheid*. In 1961 the Union broke its last ties with Britain. Tanganyika was approaching independence and refused to join the Commonwealth if South Africa remained a member. It was obvious that other British colonies would follow Tanganyika's lead as they gained independence. The H.N.P. leaders took this opportunity to hold a referendum of the white electorate on the subject of maintaining the link with the British crown. By a narrow majority the voters decided to proclaim South Africa a Republic. The leaders of the new republic did not apply for admission to the Commonwealth.

All this was of little comfort to the majority population of South

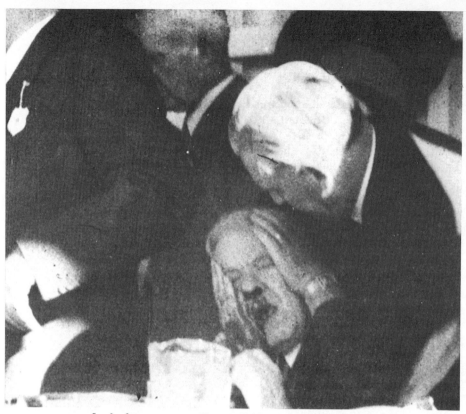

In the first attempt on Verwoerd's life, 1960, he was shot twice at close range at a Union Exposition.

Africa. In striving for civil rights and greater freedom they were hampered by two things – the efficient and ruthless suppression of all political activity by the government, and divisions within their own ranks. Indians, Cape Coloureds, various Bantu groups, industrial workers – all were struggling on their own behalf and were rarely able to unite. Some anti-government organisations were infiltrated or taken over by Communists. White liberals were divided also: some were moderates who believed in white supremacy but wanted repressive legislation repealed; others, particularly church leaders, university staff and students, wanted to see an end to all racial discrimination. The closing of all constitutional channels of protest led some to acts of violence. In 1960 a white man made an assassination attempt on the prime minister, Dr Verwoerd. A similar attempt on 6 September 1966 was successful.

Concerted action by non-whites began in 1952. Up to that time riots and disturbances had grown steadily more frequent. They achieved little and only gave the authorities 'proof' of the necessity of harsh measures to keep the 'blacks' in order. So the African National Congress organised a campaign of passive disobedience. Thousands of Africans and some white sympathisers took part in mass defiance of pass laws and colour bar laws and refused to co-operate with civil officials. The government rode out the storm and filled the prisons. The Africans realised that the only weapon left to them was their numerical strength and that they needed to work together. By this means they achieved some successes, such as a pegging of Johannesburg bus fares by a mass boycott in 1956. But violent protest continued also and there were frequent cases of arson, rioting and murder.

Albert Luthuli.

In 1955 the leading non-white organisations met at Kliptown, near Johannesburg, to plan concerted action. There were representatives of the A.N.C., the South African Coloured People's Organisation, the South African Indian Congress, the South African Congress of Trade Unions and the Congress of Democrats (a white, socialist organisation). They formed themselves into the Congress of the People and drew up a Freedom Charter which demanded a multi-racial constitution and universal suffrage. Six months later the police arrested 156 of the people most closely connected with the Kliptown meeting in a series of night-time raids. They were tried for high treason – and acquitted. That did not, however, mean that they could all enjoy their liberty. Many were later re-arrested and detained without trial. Active African nationalists were growing disillusioned with the idea of peaceful protest, though the A.N.C. leader, Chief Albert Luthuli, in fact won the Nobel Peace Prize in 1961 for his attempts to win African political rights without recourse to violence.

In 1958 Robert Subukwe formed the Pan-Africanist Congress as a more active breakaway from the A.N.C. The Congress aimed to force the government's hand by launching co-ordinated mass demonstrations. The first day of nationwide protest was to be 21 March 1960. Africans stayed away from work. Demonstrations were held in many towns and cities. Fifty-thousand protestors marched into the centre of Cape Town. But it was a smaller demonstration at Sharpeville, near Johannesburg, which made history. There, police opened fire on the

Dead and wounded outside the Sharpeville police station.

unarmed demonstrators, killing 69 and wounding 180. Subukwe and others were arrested, tried and sent to the prison on Robben Island. Nelson Mandela was another A.N.C. member who tired of the quiet ineffectiveness of Congress. He organised armed groups of guerillas and saboteurs. The secret police eventually tracked Mandela down and he was sent to Robben Island in 1964, in the same year that the A.N.C. was banned.

Despite growing unrest, world criticism, the filling of goals with political prisoners and the deportation of whites who sympathised with African nationalism, the government pursued its apartheid policy. In 1963 the first Bantustan was established. This was the Transkei, a Xhosa homeland. Theoretically it enjoyed a considerable degree of autonomy and the right to elect members of its legislature. In fact it was under the strict control of the government. That government did not hesitate to set aside the popularly chosen Chief Minister and install in his place a 'safe' man, Chief Kaizer Natanzima. Only in the 1970s did internal and external pressure lead to a slight modification of Apartheid.

(4) South West Africa

During the post-war years South West Africa was fully incorporated into the Union despite U.N. protests. In 1946 Smuts tried to persuade the international body to endorse incorporation. It refused, demanding instead that the territory be placed under trusteeship and administered by South Africa. This demand was ignored. In 1949 a major step towards incorporation was taken in the South West Africa Affairs Amendment Act. This gave settlers in the territory the right of representation in the South African parliament. In 1956 the U.N., after repeated attempts to make South Africa behave with responsibility and humanity towards the people of South West Africa, appointed a committee to supervise the affairs of the territory. South Africa withdrew its delegation from the Assembly. From then on the Nationalists went their own way. In 1963 they published a report indicating their intention of creating homelands in South West Africa similar to those planned for the rest of the Republic. In other words apartheid was to be applied fully in South West Africa. The U.N. made repeated attempts, supported by judgements of the International Court, to assert its right of supervision of South West African affairs. When all else had failed the U.N. Assembly adopted a resolution in 1966 which terminated South Africa's mandate. As in all other matters, the Nationalists ignored world opinion on this issue and the U.N. was powerless to enforce its decision.

(5) The High Commission Territories

Despite many attempts by the Cape Town government to bring the High Commission Territories under its control, Swaziland, Bechuanaland and Basutoland remained under British authority and eventually achieved complete independence. All of the territories were closely bound to South Africa by economic ties. Many of their menfolk worked in the Rand mines and there were white settlers within their borders. The South Africa Act of 1910 had made provision for the possible transfer of the territories to the Union. In 1921 white settlers in Swaziland succeeded in getting an elective Advisory Council formed. In 1933 the Bechuanaland ruler, Tshekedi Khama, was deposed and it seemed that Britain might impose direct rule as a prelude to a hand-over to South Africa. It was the emergence of Hertzog and the Nationalists which prompted Britain to resist any such move.

After the Second World War the South African government renewed its claim to the Territories. This posed a problem for Britain. The three protectorates were small and poor. They would probably find it difficult to exist as independent nations and would always be partly dependent on the Union. On the other hand Britain did not want to administer them indefinitely and knew that they would never consent to being handed over to the Afrikaners. The British government delayed making a decision but seriously undertook the economic development of the territories.

As time went by and the Nationalist government of South Africa became more and more reactionary it became obvious that complete independence was the only answer for the territories. Constitutional changes were planned. In 1959 Basutoland received a National Council which was partially elective. The following year provision was made for elected regional councils. In 1961 Bechuanaland received a Legislative Council with an elected, unofficial majority. In 1964 Swaziland followed suit. Complete internal self-government swiftly followed. In 1966 Basutoland and Bechuanaland became independent under the names of Lesotho and Botswana respectively. In 1968 Swaziland became the last British colony to obtain its freedom.

Index